CW01582545

GALLOPING HORSES

Artist Xu Beihong and His Family in Mao's China

Xu Fangfang

Beihong Arts Publishing, LLC | Saint Louis, MO

Copyright © 2016 by Xu Fangfang

All rights reserved.
Published by Beihong Arts Publishing, LLC, St. Louis, Missouri, USA

Galloping Horses: Artist Xu Beihong and His Family in Mao's China

No part of this book may be used or reproduced in any manner whatsoever, or stored in a retrieval system, or transmitted in any form or by any means including electronic, mechanical, photocopying, recording, scanning, or otherwise without written permission of the Publisher.

Printed in the United States of America

Library of Congress Control Number 2015960638
Xu, Fangfang, 1947-

ISBN 978-0-9970574-1-6 (paperback)
ISBN 978-0-9970574-2-3 (e-book)
ISBN 978-0-9970574-3-0 (Chinese-language e-book)

First Edition: 2016

Photograph of Xu Fangfang © Xu Fangfang

Interior photographs: Xu Beihong family collection

For information, visit Publisher's website at www.BeihongChinaArts.com.

Frontispiece. *Portrait of Xu Fangfang*, drawn by her father Xu Beihong (1895-1953), 1950, 35 x 25 cm, pencil on paper, collection of the artist's family

To my father Xu Beihong and my mother Liao Jingwen,
who dedicated her life to her late husband's artistic legacy

CONTENTS

ILLUSTRATIONS

GALLOPING HORSES

Artist Xu Beihong and His Family in Mao's China

CHAPTER 1

Raid on the Museum

One sunny afternoon in June 1966, I came home from school, the Preparatory Music High School in Beijing. A piano performance major, I had long fingers and nails trimmed to the quick. At eighteen, I was tall and athletic, with long legs. Two thick pigtails bounced on my shoulders, yet my expression was serious and determined. I wore a plain short-sleeved blouse with my red Communist Youth League badge pinned on its left, and loose-fitting cotton pants. As I entered the Xu Beihong Memorial Museum, adjacent to my home, I froze: Posters with big Chinese characters in thick black strokes covered the front porch of the museum's Forbidden-City-style exhibition gallery. The posters attacked my mother, Liao Jingwen, the museum's non-Communist-Party-member director and the widow of Xu Beihong, a major Chinese artist. They accused her of being an anti-Party person—a target of the Cultural Revolution. Instantly I knew that my mother and the museum were both in danger. Xu Beihong, my father, would have felt the same pain and disappointment had he lived to see this.

My parents had married in Chongqing in 1946. At the time he was fifty years old, a well-established painter, and she was a twenty-two-year-old who left college for him. After he died in 1953, she held on to her love for him and devoted her life to his artistic causes. Her continued dedication had made the Xu Beihong Memorial Museum possible.

In the spring of 1966, my mother had a small staff working at the Xu Beihong Memorial Museum, at 16 East Shoulu Street, Beijing. Wang Shuxiao, the only Party member on the staff, was responsible for personnel affairs and political study. She monitored the museum employees' personal files to make sure these employees were utilized according to the Party's guidelines. The other staffers included Huang, an accountant; doorman Lao Zhang; and Lao Bai (Old Bai), who did chores. Lao Ma (Old Ma), the museum's former messenger, had been recently transferred to the Beijing radio station, and because his new employer could not provide housing, Lao Ma and his family still lived in the museum's staff living quarters. The Xu Beihong Memorial Museum was special: It had on-site living quarters for five staff members and their families.

Painter Guo Weiqu,[1] the only professional staff member, for a few years in the late 1950s arranged the display and rotation of paintings, archived the collection, and photographed museum events. At the museum he studied Chinese paintings in Xu Beihong's extensive personal collection. This helped Guo develop his own innovative freehand-style bird-and-flower painting, a specialty in Chinese ink brush painting. When he held his own exhibition, Mom bought a painting for sixty *yuan*, half of her monthly salary. Guo became well known and with my mother's support and permission was transferred to the Central Academy of Fine Arts (CAFA) to teach.

Mom and her staff had generally good relationships. While Lao Zhang was recovering from a minor electrical shock, Mom brought food to him each day. Lao Ma's two-year-old son played in our living room. My blond-haired doll was the same height as the boy; he was afraid of her. Mom gave Lao Ma's wife a jacket I had outgrown. Lao Bai always showed respect to Mom. When she walked by, he stood and called her "Good Mrs.," as in the old days.

Party member Wang Shuxiao was the exception. An aggressive woman in her forties, Wang, formerly a worker in the Beijing Rug Factory, had requested a transfer from the factory to the museum job, left vacant by a Party leader's recent retirement. My mother, a non-Party director, had no say in this. With only a primary-school education, Wang had little understanding of the arts but pretended that she did. She once made a fool of herself by saying, "Look, Zhao Shuli's cartoon pictures are so very good." But Zhao Shuli was a well-known writer, not a painter.

Wang Shuxiao's coarse language and mannerisms were my first impressions of her. In winter she wore a blue padded cotton jacket, her arms stuffed into the tight-fitting sleeves, and padded yellow pants. Sometimes she decorated herself with a thin white silk scarf. In her much-tanned yellow face was a pair of small eyes and a squarish mouth. Occasionally her gaze turned vicious, and that always shocked me.

Wang's husband, Yang, had been an officer in the People's Liberation Army (PLA), where he was caught raping a soldier. In the 1950s, while head of a sports stadium in Beijing, he raped a janitress working there. This time he was jailed and sent away to serve his sentence. Wang complained loudly and long about the prison's poor living conditions. After Yang was released from jail, Wang asked Mom to find him a job in Beijing. Transfers to Beijing were difficult for anyone, and impossible for a convict. Without a job he had to stay working in the jail. One day in 1965, about a year before the Cultural Revolution, Wang was all smiles when she said to Mom, "You know Guo Lao (Guo the Elder) so well. Why don't you ask him to find a job for my Lao Yang (Old Yang)?" Guo Moruo, a famous poet, had been my parents' friend. After 1949, he became the first president of the Chinese Academy of Sciences.

Mom felt imposed upon. Any association with a jailed person brought severe political consequences.

She said, "I am afraid that I will not be able to ask Guo Lao to fulfill your request because your husband is an ex-convict."

Wang Shuxiao persisted, her head tilted to one side, eyes lit up with some hope: "How about talking to your brother, Liao Ping? Can he find a worker's job for Yang in his factory? Even a temporary worker's job will do." My third uncle, Liao Ping, was then the acting Party secretary of Beijing No. 1 Machine Tool Plant. Mom felt awkward replying, "Liao Ping takes his position at the factory very seriously and will not grant favors based on personal connections. He is also a very stubborn man. I can try to talk to him. But I am not sure whether I could persuade him."

In China, business deals had been frequently done through *guanxi*: personal connections. But Liao Ping's principles did not allow him to use his position for personal gains. During the famine in 1961, his factory helped farmers in the countryside repair their tractors. The farmers sent a wagonload of cabbages to the factory as their thanks. Although every Beijing resident's daily ration of cabbage was limited to only one ounce, Liao Ping returned the cabbages, saying, "Repairing tractors for the farmers is our obligation. We should not expect anything in return." Mom did ask him about a job for Wang Shuxiao's husband, and Liao Ping said, "I've never hired anyone because of my personal connections."

Wang Shuxiao had begrudged my mother ever since.

As soon as the Cultural Revolution broke out, Wang Shuxiao wrote and hung big-character posters denouncing my mother as the loudest advocate for Xu Beihong, "the worst reactionary bourgeois authority." She also branded my mother "a bourgeois reactionary authority" and "a rightist who had escaped through the net." Most importantly, Wang accused Mom of having said that Madame Mao (Jiang Qing) and a man named Huang Jing, then a college student and an underground Party member, had lived together in Dengshikou, Beijing. According to Mom, she had said only that Jiang Qing and Huang Jing shared communal facilities in a common courtyard. Having read the big-character posters, I understood Mom's worries. One weekend that June, Mom and I had a talk in our living room. She wore a full-length sleeveless summer dress, worn while dancing barefoot on our large green carpet, imitating a ballerina. With the start of the Cultural Revolution, she stopped dancing. On that weekend, her pretty eyes closed and her thin eyebrows knotted as if she were about to cry.

She said, "Wang Shuxiao led other staff members to attack me. What should I do? Am I in real trouble?"

I was surprised and a little proud that Mom shared her thoughts with me as a grownup. I said, "Mom, please tell me. Are any of the things Wang Shuxiao wrote in the posters true?"

"No."

I had learned about my father's lifelong friend, now Premier Zhou Enlai, protecting her in the Anti-Rightist campaign nine years before. I did not think that Mom could be considered a "bourgeois reactionary academic authority," a target of the Cultural Revolution, because she was not a famous artist or professor—all professors were attacked.

"I don't think you've done anything wrong. You should have faith in Chairman Mao and the Party," I said. "My only concern is Wang's accusation about your supposed remark regarding Jiang Qing and Huang Jing. If Wang could make such a lie believable, then you would face trouble. Please be very careful about that issue."

Mom seemed to feel better after our talk. But in the museum office, Wang Shuxiao led criticism sessions in which she spoke against Mom while everyone else kept silent. One day Mom explained a detail about Xu Beihong, calling him "Beihong," her usual way of referring to her late husband.

Wang Shuxiao stood up, yelling, "Shut up about Beihong. Xu Beihong already stinks."

My mother said, "Xu Beihong does not stink, but your husband does!"

Then Wang jumped on my mother, held her arms down with both hands, and spat in her face.

Shortly after that, on August 26,[2] ten male Red Guards from Beijing No. 8 and No. 4 High Schools broke into our house. The first thing they demanded from my mother was four letters Chairman Mao had written to my parents in the early 1950s. She did not hand them over. The Red Guards searched every corner of our house, upstairs and downstairs, tearing up all the paintings and prints they found. So much torn paper was piled in our hallways and bedrooms that one could hardly take a step. They ruined original drawings and ink brush paintings by Father. Torn to pieces and lying in the debris were Qingping's albums of French Impressionist and Russian paintings. Mom had kept on file hundreds of national flag-design proposals for the new China established in 1949, designs evaluated by Father. These too were destroyed.

In my bedroom, the Red Guards smashed a sculptured nude which Dad had brought from France. They tore in half a photo of me and broke my framed portrait of Mussorgsky. All my dolls had their heads pulled off. Broken phonograph records from my collection littered the floor. The Red Guards forced Mom to smash her own classical music records. Among them was her favorite record of a string ensemble, exchanged for two bags of wheat flour during the Chinese Civil War in the late 1940s.

On the museum's gate were written in thick sloppy brush strokes: "DOWN WITH REACTIONARY AUTHORITY XU BEIHONG!" and "DOG NEST," and "BIG BLACK NEST." In the museum's east yard, where Father had planted many fruit trees, were more scrawls: "SMASH YOUR DOG HEAD, LIAO JINGWEN," "BEWARE, CHILDREN OF DOGS," and "XU QINGPING, XU FANGFANG, IF YOU WANT TO DO REVOLUTION, YOU MUST REBEL AGAINST YOUR REACTIONARY FATHER." In that east yard, my sanctuary, I had reminisced about Father and dreamed about my future. My heart ached seeing my treasured space defaced.

The Red Guards had scrawled those same words on the backs of some original scroll paintings by my father. These and other artworks by Father belonged to Mom, who had collected them after my father's death in 1953. The Red Guard campaign to wipe out the "four olds" forced owners and collectors to hand over paintings by famous ancient and contemporary artists. These were then piled up and burned. Anyone caught hiding these paintings risked losing his or her life or political future.

The Red Guards finally found Mao's four letters among Mom's personal belongings. But they did not find anything to use against her. They dragged her and Second Uncle, her second brother, who lived with us, out to the museum's newer courtyard for interrogation. Disabled by polio in childhood and unable to work, Second Uncle had lived mostly in his home village with his landowner father. When their father passed away in 1958, Mom brought him to our home in Beijing. Second Uncle had been categorized as a landowner in 1950 while living on a landowner's income as an adult. The Red Guards in August 1966 forced him to wear a sign in public saying "landowner" around his neck.

The Red Guards yelled, "Hey, landowner. Did you think you could hide your crimes here in the city?"

Second Uncle said, "Please don't beat me. I'm disabled. I will go back to my home village."

Second Uncle Liao Xueru spent most of his time quietly in his bedroom. He was tall, like my mother's other brothers and sisters, but polio had withered his right arm and he walked only slowly, dragging his right leg. In his thirties his hair was almost gone. He sometimes had epileptic fits. I once heard him saying to Mom in their Hunan dialect, "Look at our third brother, Liao Ping. He is doing so well. How nice if I had been able to finish school and get a good job like him!" Instead, Second Uncle tried to make himself useful around the house. He learned to take buses and run errands. While I was busy studying piano in music school, he waited in line for me to get concert tickets for performances by foreign pianists.

The Red Guards forced Second Uncle to his knees, pulled his shirt off, and with their leather belts whipped his head and bare back.

Mom had overheard Wang Shuxiao saying, "Xu Beihong's paintings are worth a lot of money overseas." It dawned on her that Wang Shuxiao and the Red Guards might steal the paintings.

The Red Guards dragged from the museum an oil painting depicting three Guangxi Nationalist leaders[3] who had fought the Japanese invaders in the late 1930s. Xu Beihong had painted this in support of them. One of the Red Guards yelled at Mom, "Do you know about these three people Xu Beihong painted?"

Mom suspected Wang Shuxiao had told the Red Guards about this particular painting in order to fabricate a political affiliation between Xu Beihong and the Nationalists (Kuomintang), enemies of the Communists. The Red Guard continued, "Xu Beihong was a spy. He was so poor. How could he afford to go to France to study painting? He must have been a spy." Then he turned on

Mom: "Why did you marry Xu Beihong? You were so young. Why did you marry such an old man? You must also be a spy!"

The ten male Red Guards then circled her and took turns whipping her head and body wildly with their belts. When a belt buckle hit her eye, Mom tried to cover her eyes with her hands.

"Spy! Where are your guns and ammunition?"

"I have no guns and ammunition."

"Confess your crimes, you spy."

"I am not a spy!"

The Red Guards whipped her until she passed out. Then they poured cold water over her. After she came to, they whipped her again. She passed out three times. The last time they were not able to revive her. Fearing that she might die, the Red Guards called the neighborhood first-aid clinic. The nurse gave Mom artificial respiration and a shot to revive her.

That night the Red Guards locked Mom into one of the smaller rooms in the museum. Second Uncle brought meals to Mom in her detention. Wounds covered his face. She said to me later, "I could endure the beating by the Red Guards. But I was really sad to see your second uncle being beaten. Poor thing. He is disabled."

For the next few days, one of the Red Guards, Li, tried to force Mom to write a confession about her and Xu Beihong's supposed crimes. Li came to the room repeatedly, punching her in the chest or kicking her. But Mom wrote nothing. She said firmly, "I am not a spy. I did not do anything against the Party."

Feeling she could not endure the humiliation and torture, Mom contemplated suicide. There was a live, bare electric wire in the room. All she had to do was touch it. Struggling to choose whether to die or live, she remembered one of the Red Guards saying, "Xu Beihong's paintings are all bourgeois. Why not burn them all?" She could not let that happen to Beihong's life's work.

On a night of heavy rain, in the dim light of the small room, Mom saw in her mind's eye her two children, Beihong's and her children, Qingping and Fangfang. She heard them calling: "Mama! Mama!" When she looked around, her children were not there. Yet the sounds of their voices stayed with her. Qingping and Fangfang had lost their father. They should not lose their mother now.

Beihong, on his deathbed, had worried about his two young children. Mom told herself, "I must live for Beihong and take care of the growing children for him." She had vowed to Beihong more than twenty years before, in Panxi near the Jialing River, "I have gradually overcome the barrier of age difference between us and have come bravely before you. I would like to devote my whole life to you and your work."[4]

The night the Red Guards allowed my mother out, despite her wounds and bruises she wrote a letter to Premier Zhou Enlai, a supporter of the Xu Beihong Memorial Museum. She asked Premier Zhou to protect the museum's Xu Beihong works and those in Xu Beihong's personal collection. That was her only hope. She marked the envelope "urgent."

The next day my older brother, Qingping, a nineteen-year-old college student, took the letter to the west gate of Zhongnanhai ("Central South Sea"), the CCP headquarters on Fuyou Street. He told the guard he had a letter for Premier Zhou from his mother, Xu Beihong's widow, and asked for Premier Zhou's secretary to come to the gate and take the letter.

At that time, many people must have been appealing to Premier Zhou for help. Qingping did not know what to expect. But Zhao Maofeng, Premier Zhou's secretary, dressed in a blue cotton uniform, came to the gate. Without a word, but in a friendly manner, he took the letter, leaving Qingping reassured.

While Mom waited for Premier Zhou's response, the Red Guards kept harassing her. But within three days a group of government workers, accompanied by officers from the Beijing Military Control Commission, came to the Xu Beihong Memorial Museum with Premier Zhou's instructions. The Red Guards could not challenge the Military Control Commission. The government workers packed and removed from the museum all the works, including those by Xu Beihong and those in his collection, all in one day without saying where they would be stored.

The paintings were now safe, but my mother was not. My own situation was precarious. I wanted to protect my mother, but I knew any attempt to obstruct the Red Guards' revolutionary actions met with violence. I had seen a Central Conservatory of Music (CCOM) teacher's son fight the Red Guards invading his house. The Red Guards dragged him onto the stage of the CCOM auditorium and beat him in front of a mass rally.

For self-protection, I went to talk with Jiang, one of the Red Guards from Beijing No. 8 High School, who said, "Your mother is a spy. Did you know she had a close relationship with a Yugoslavian student at Peking University?"

Yugoslavia as a socialist country was friendly with China in the early 1950s. Mom had indeed known a Yugoslavian student at Peking University in 1954, but only for a short while before he returned to his country. Now China considered Yugoslavia a revisionist regime which had betrayed Marxism-Leninism.

I said, "I am not aware of that association of hers. I am a Communist Youth League member. You can trust that I will clearly draw a line between my mother and myself if she has ever done anything against the Party."

Jiang sneered at my Youth League badge and said, "Nowadays we don't wear this badge anymore." The Communist Youth League of China (CYL), recently accused of revisionism, stopped functioning during the Cultural Revolution, and I had not known that.

After the Red Guards' actions in August, Qingping and I came home from our schools whenever we could. Almost immediately after Mom was beaten, her second husband and my stepfather, Uncle Huang, moved out and lived for the next year in his office at the China Film Workers Association. He had given Mom his monthly salary of 70 *yuan* for her to manage while she earned 120 *yuan* a month. In 1966 Wang Shuxiao, following rebel groups' initiatives, cut Mom's salary to 60 *yuan*, more in line with a low-level professional's salary, and Huang stopped sharing his money. The care of their three-year-old son, Maomao, was left to our grandaunt, Shenpo, paid solely by Mom.

My mother lost all emotional connection with Uncle Huang after he moved out. Perhaps their relationship had not been built on a solid foundation. I was a little disappointed by Uncle Huang. We had kept up what I thought was a good rapport during my teenage years, and I hoped I could count on his help. When Mom was locked up, I visited him in his office. He offered no sympathy or emotional support.

I never went to see him again. In the horrible months of 1966, the only family member I could rely on was Qingping. He and I helped each other survive the red terror.

CHAPTER 2

Learning from Nature[5]

Sixteen years before the last Chinese emperor's deposition, in 1895, artist Xu Beihong was born in Jitingqiao (Jiting Bridge), a small riverside town in Yixing County near Lake Tai. Two hundred miles west of Shanghai, south of the Yangtze River, this area around Lake Tai was renowned for its natural beauty and artistic and literary heritage. Generations of painters, poets, and scholars had lived and gathered there. Known as the pottery capital of China, Yixing since ancient times had produced fine pottery made from its special clay.

Xu Beihong's parents named him Shoukang (longevity and health). Chinese parents embed good fortune, a dream, or a prayer in their children's names. His parents wanted him to enjoy a long healthy life. But later, while a struggling young artist, my father changed his name to Beihong (a sad wild goose).

His grandfather was Xu Yangeng (working with ink slab), suggesting that he made his living with pen and ink. In the late 1850s, Xu Yangeng fled his hometown, Jitingqiao, because of the Taiping Rebellion. Upon returning, he found his house burned to the ground.

Xu Beihong recalled, "My grandfather, the revered Yangeng. . .after ten years of hard work was able to build himself a small cottage by the river bridge as shelter from the weather. My father was born in that cottage which was simple and crude. But he felt fortunate that nature lavished boundless beauty on all of us with South Mountain like a painted screen in the background and the Tang River like a flowing path. . . ."[6]

Xu Beihong's father, Xu Dazhang, a self-taught artist, was known locally for his landscape, figure, and flower paintings. Xu Dazhang taught Xu Beihong to observe nature, and expressed a wish that his son would become a better artist than himself.

During the final decade of the Qing dynasty, foreign powers penetrated and claimed control over Chinese foreign trade, markets, and territory, and China was practically "carved up like a melon." The countryside around Lake Tai became impoverished when peasants, small traders, and craftsmen went bankrupt.

Unable to continue making a living selling his calligraphy and paintings, Xu Beihong's father relied on the income from a small watermelon plot. Xu Beihong helped his father with the work. To plow the field, they borrowed the neighbor's water buffalo. In exchange, Xu Beihong took care of the buffalo. While it grazed on hillsides and along streams, Xu Beihong searched for wildflowers.

At age six, when his family was unable to afford formal schooling for him, Xu Beihong took Chinese classics lessons from his father. By age nine he had finished studying the *Four Books* and other Confucian classics, required reading for scholars of the time. Then his father taught him the basic skills of traditional Chinese painting[7] while encouraging him to draw from life. Traditional Chinese painters developed specialized techniques to portray different elements in nature such as rocks and trees. With few toys to play with, Xu Beihong acquired an interest in the animals and birds around him, developing keen observational skills. The water buffalo, horses, geese, and cats were later brought to life in his Chinese ink brush paintings.

When Xu Beihong was thirteen, his hometown was flooded. To support the family, Xu Dazhang and Xu Beihong traveled around southern Jiangsu, earning a living painting portraits and landscapes, writing poetic couplets, and custom-carving the seals to be stamped on letters, artworks, or documents as a personal signature or symbol of legitimacy. Because photography was available only in big cities, painted portraits were still in demand. Xu Beihong's love for painting images of people continued throughout his career. The hard life of an itinerant artist also brought him into closer contact with laboring people. He sympathized with their hardships.

During his years as an itinerant artist, Xu Beihong saw reproductions of Western paintings and was impressed. He dreamed of studying painting in Europe. However, the wandering life took a toll on his father, who fell seriously ill, and they returned to their hometown.

When his father died, nineteen-year-old Xu Beihong went to Shanghai to seek employment and opportunities to further his painting studies. He was rejected by several potential employers, including a university and a publisher's illustration department. Pained and disappointed, he briefly contemplated ending his life. But he thought to himself: ". . .if a person at the end of his resources can still press on, then he is not a coward. . . ."[8]

Left with no other means, Xu Beihong sent one of his horse paintings to Gao Jianfu. He and his brother Gao Qifeng were famous painters of the Lingnan school, among the first to explore a possible synthesis of East and West in traditional Chinese painting. Gao Jianfu wrote to Xu Beihong praising his painting, saying, "Even the ancient Han Gan [a famous Tang-dynasty horse painter] could not have done better than this." The Gao brothers had a bookstore and press called Shenmei Shuguan (Aesthetic Bookstore), which published Xu Beihong's horse as a print.

Gao Qifeng asked Xu Beihong to paint four traditional Chinese paintings of beautiful ladies for the store. Xu Beihong knew it would take a week to complete the four paintings. He had only twenty cents, enough to buy one glutinous rice ball a day for four days. He believed that the small glutinous rice ball could stave off his hunger longer than other foods. On the fifth day, he continued to paint without eating. Amid heavy snow, he took the four completed paintings to Shenmei Shuguan, but Gao Qifeng was not there. Xu Beihong left the paintings with the doorman.

Xu Beihong did not give up. He took the entrance examination for Aurora University in Shanghai and was accepted. A friend from Yixing lent him money for tuition, allowing him to attend a university for the first time. He had taken French-language lessons before entering the university, hoping to realize his dream of studying painting in France. At the university he studied French while continuing to paint.

He saw a newspaper ad soliciting a painter for a portrait of the legendary inventor of Chinese characters, Cangjie. In response to the ad, placed by the Hardoon Garden, Xu Beihong submitted a large watercolor of Cangjie, painted according to descriptions from ancient Chinese literature. Xu Beihong's version depicts a hairy-faced giant with two pairs of penetrating eyes. Hardoon Garden authorities were so impressed that they offered him a position as a painter and lecturer at Hardoon Garden's affiliate, Mingzhi University.

With the fees earned for his Cangjie portraits, Xu Beihong traveled to Japan in May 1917. He and Jiang Biwei, a young lady from a scholarly family in Yixing, had fallen in love. Jiang was eighteen; he was twenty-two. Jiang Biwei's parents had arranged for her to marry a son of the Cha family. Tradition did not allow her to break that engagement. Having no other choice, she eloped with Xu Beihong to Japan.

During his half-year stay in Japan, Xu Beihong saw certain Japanese painters who had freed themselves from convention and developed individual styles through careful observation of nature. These alternative approaches broadened his perspective.

In 1918, Xu Beihong was hired by Cai Yuanpei, Chancellor of Peking University, to teach at the Painting Methods Research Society of Peking University. Beijing was then the center for new ideas. After the Xinhai Revolution overthrew the Qing dynasty, Chinese artists, writers, and intellectuals re-evaluated the legacy of China's traditional culture. They called for the creation of a new Chinese culture based on global and Western standards, especially democracy and science. This New Culture Movement, as it was known, was active from the mid-1910s into the 1920s. Its *New Youth* journal offered a forum for debating the causes of China's weakness, blaming Confucian culture. On May 4, 1919, students in Beijing protested the Paris Peace Conference, which gave Germany's rights over the territory of Shandong to Imperial Japan, turning this cultural movement into an anti-imperialist and anti-feudal movement. It then became known as the May Fourth Movement, which started the era of new democratic revolution in China.

Xu Beihong formulated a direction for painting in the New Culture Movement. He expressed the opinion that Chinese painting had declined steadily during the previous three hundred years, beginning in the late Ming dynasty. Lifeless stereotypes based on formalities had gradually come to dominate traditional Chinese painting. By the early Republican Era, few artists could paint figures effectively. He attributed the decline to conservatism, believing that it stifled creativity and the tradition of "learning from nature."

In his 1918 article, "Improvement Methods for Chinese Painting," Xu Beihong wrote, "Retain the good ancient methods, revive the moribund, correct the bad, strengthen the inadequate, and integrate those elements from Western painting that can be used."[9]

This outline laid the foundation for Xu Beihong's future efforts to develop Chinese painting through his own creative work and his teaching. Later in his career, he demonstrated two fundamental ways to improve Chinese painting:

"focusing on human activities" and rejuvenating the tradition of "learning from nature."

Xu Beihong finally got to France in 1919 and spent eight years in Europe studying art, and developed into an influential painter. Later, integrating the strengths of Chinese art traditions and Western painting techniques, Xu Beihong trained several generations of Chinese artists. Many became accomplished artists and leading art educators in twentieth-century China.

• • •

My parents moved to Beiping, present-day Beijing, in 1946, and shortly after their arrival my brother Qingping was born.[10] In the following year, they bought their first house at 16 East Shoulu Street in the eastern part of Beiping with proceeds from my father's painting sales. In winter 1947, I came into my parents' lives.

Our house was a variation on the quadrangle-style house common in Beijing's *hutong* (alleys). The property was enclosed by brick walls. One entered through the main doorway and passed the spacious west and east yards, separated by an inner wall with a moon gate. At the north end of the east yard, one arrived at the entrance to a courtyard with modest rooms, our living quarters, on three sides. The yards had been neglected and the two mimosa trees in the east yard were dying when my parents first moved in. But they really liked two other large trees: in the west yard, a huge locust tree about one hundred years old with exuberant foliage, and a forty-foot tree of heaven in the courtyard, providing comfortable shade in summer.

My parents planted grapevines, and persimmon, peach, date, and walnut trees. Part of the west yard became a vegetable garden with tomatoes, cucumbers, reddish-purple amaranth, and perilla. My parents nurtured the vegetable garden and fruit trees with water and fertilizer. In his spare time my father pruned the fruit trees and revived the dying mimosa trees. Their numerous flowers, each a burst of pale magenta, nodded their heads in the gentle breeze as if smiling at their new owners.

On lovely summer evenings I sat with my family in the shade of the large tree of heaven, eating my favorite treat, watermelon. My father sat in his usual cane chair with its comfortable curved seat. He threw ping-pong balls for our cats to play with and observed them running, jumping, and climbing the trees.

His sketches of the cats caught their liveliness. He selected one with black-and-white-blotched fur as his subject for a painting because those colors were best suited to Chinese ink brush painting.

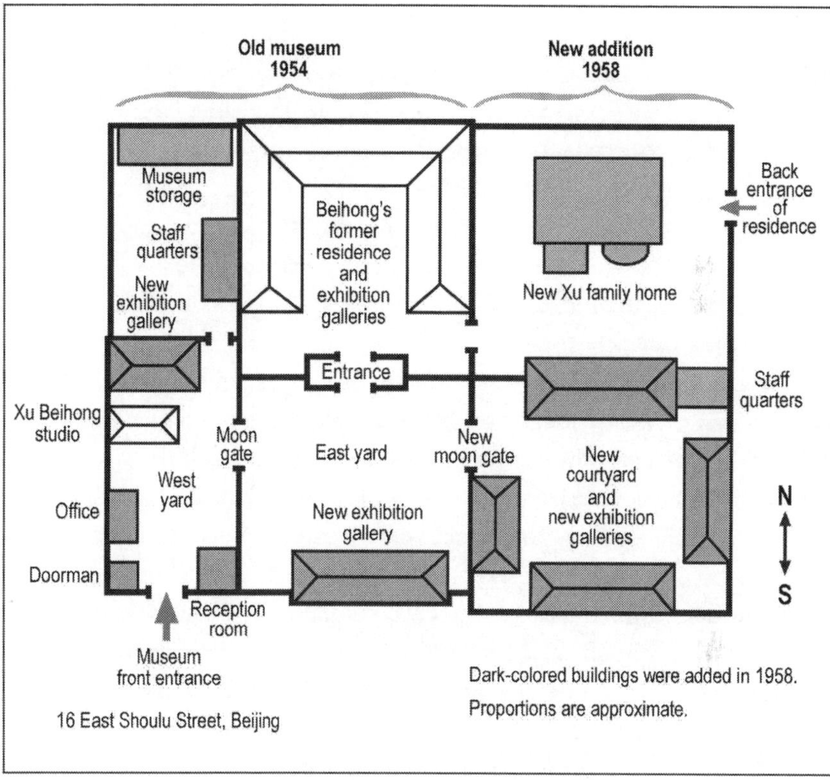

Figure 1. Xu Beihong Memorial Museum diagram (1954 and 1958)

On summer mornings my parents picked tomatoes from our garden to make fresh, sweet-tasting salads. Mom liked food spiced with hot chili peppers, a typical Hunan flavor. I enjoyed her homemade *larou* (cured smoked meat, usually made in winter) and *labadou* (fermented soybeans, made in winter), both Hunan delicacies. Having grown up near Lake Tai, Father loved eating fish and crabs. Very often after eating small fish with many thin bones, he arranged the fish bones to display the entire skeleton. His favorite dish was river crabs from Yangcheng Lake near his hometown. Because river crabs were hard to come by in Beijing, when they were available Mom cooked them mainly for Father to enjoy. Qingping and I were told that they were bugs, and as small kids we certainly did not know how to eat them.

My happiest days were Sundays spent with my parents, because I did not see my father much during the week when he worked at CAFA. Sometimes on Sundays our parents took Qingping and me to Zhongshan Park, formally an imperial garden, where we saw art exhibitions in a large hall. We enjoyed walking in the park with the blooming peonies and butterfly flowers. I felt warmth, holding Father's big, gentle hand.

Often we went to Wangfujing, a busy shopping district in downtown Beijing. Our parents visited art galleries while Father's driver, Lao Cao (Old Cao), took Qingping and me to eat dinner in the arcade-style Dong'an courtyard of shops nearby.

As president of CAFA, my father had access to a car and a dedicated driver, Lao Cao, formerly employed by the National Beiping Arts College. In the early 1950s, riding in a car was a rarity in Beijing. As the proud little daughter of a famous artist, I enjoyed riding to art shows in Dad's old black big-nosed Ford. I loved seeing the car bringing Father home in the evenings, and usually cried when the car drove away in the mornings. To my brother and me, Lao Cao, a well-built man with tanned skin and crew-cut hair, was a hero. Qingping used to walk closely behind Lao Cao with hands crossed behind his back, mimicking his stride and posture. One day some of my parents' friends asked me what I would like to be when I grew up. I answered that I wanted to become a driver.

My favorite uncle was my mother's younger brother, Liao Ping, whom we called Third Uncle because he was the number-three boy in his family. As a college economics student in Beiping, he had joined the underground Chinese Communist Party (CCP) before Beiping was liberated in January 1949. During China's drive to build its heavy industries in the late 1950s, he became assistant director of Beijing No. 1 Machine Tool Plant, an important factory with about six thousand workers.

Third Uncle Liao Ping was tall, handsome, and unmarried, so he often visited our family and played with me. He was the only adult male family member I got to know well after Father died. I liked his joyfully talkative manner, and sitting on his lap listening to his jokes and stories. He told me about a turtle and eel trying to get into a grand party at the dragon king's palace. The entrance requirement was that every guest had to weigh at least eight ounces. Neither the turtle nor the eel could get into the palace because the turtle weighed six ounces and the eel weighed two ounces. But they played a trick: The eel coiled around the turtle's neck, disguised as his scarf. Together they weighed eight ounces, and off they went into the palace. A good dancer, Third Uncle also took me to dance floors and taught me ballroom dancing. Although a very short dance partner, I fully enjoyed twirling around the dance floor with him.

When I was five, relatives from the south visited us for about a month: my father's uncle Lu Shunchuan, his younger sister Xu Ai'e, and his younger brother Xu Shou'an. This was my first time with our extended family, and the last time my father would see relatives from his home region. My father's uncle was his mother's younger brother. I thought he looked like a Peking opera character with his long white beard and traditional Chinese robe. Dad told me that this uncle was his favorite. He ran a teahouse out of his house in Dacheng, a small town near Jitingqiao, Father's hometown. When my father was a child, this uncle took him to see Peking opera, a performing art my father had enjoyed ever since. My aunt Xu Ai'e made me a beautiful silk blouse using the material from one of my mother's old traditional Chinese robes.

Father took our relatives to see the local sights. He arranged for friends to take them to more distant sites. At the end of their visit, when asked how he felt about his stay, my father's uncle said that only two things disappointed him: the formal requirement of using serving chopsticks at meals, and not meeting Chairman Mao.

Father seldom had cash at hand since he regularly spent much of his income purchasing paintings of high artistic merit for his collection. When he was too busy to visit the art shops he frequented, the art dealers from Liulichang, the art shop district, brought to our house Chinese ink brush paintings wrapped in blue cloth covers. Father also loved Chinese arts and crafts such as lifelike clay figures. One day he invited into our house an itinerant craftsman whom we watched model an exquisitely detailed foot-high heavenly lady dressed in a long gown with flowing sleeves and trailing ribbons. It took him a whole day to finish the figure, made from wheat-flour dough, some of it richly colored. I remember the very lifelike gesture of the lady, her delicate hands, and fine facial features. Father displayed the figure in an enclosed glass case in our living room alongside his own paintings.

Father's ex-wife had not supported his art collecting, but my mother did, because she shared his joy in discovering works of high artistic merit. To save money for his collecting, Father wore second-hand clothes and leather shoes bought from a junk shop. He used street barbers, who charged less than barbershops. Mom managed our household frugally. Our staple food was rice and millet cooked together, cheaper than rice alone. When tuition was due for six-year-old Qingping to attend Beijing Huiwen No. 1 Primary School, a good private primary school nearby, Mom pawned her clothes to get the cash.

I remember Mom as young, beautiful, and sometimes stern-looking when she disciplined us. When I was about three years old, she marked the heights of Qingping and me on our bathroom wall. Unwilling to accept that Qingping was taller, I secretly moved my mark above his. After discovering that, she told me in a serious voice, "Xiao Mei (Little Sister, my nickname), you should never cheat and lie. You should always tell the truth."

Father's painting studio was one of my favorite places. I remember a large unfinished canvas for his planned oil painting *Lu Xun and Qu Qiubai*, with these two figures, both important Chinese writers, sketched in charcoal. When Father was not there, Qingping and I sneaked in and hid under the table used for mounting Chinese ink brush paintings. We secretly played cards made from inch-high wheat-straw paper. Mom did not allow this, fearing we would develop gambling habits. I hid the cards under an art magazine until Mom discovered them. Then for punishment I was locked inside the large studio, forced to hear the echoes of my own yelling and crying. I was scared, alone and facing Father's large white canvas with two sketched men staring directly at me.

I was four when my father fell ill. He looked older and a little worn down. Mom, Qingping, and I slept in the west-side rooms so that our cries at night would not disturb Father, who slept alone in a bedroom on the north side. I remember Father in his fifties, dressed in a thin white linen shirt and pants, his back slightly bent, tending the fruit trees in the garden. When he smiled, the fine lines around the corners of his eyes looked like rays of the sun. He often rested after lunch on his reclining chair in the living room. Coming home from kindergarten in the afternoon, I greeted him there, kissing both his cheeks, my lips often touching the greyed bristles on his pointed chin. However, at times he became upset with me. Once, I played in the rain puddles around our yard. Seeing my wet shoes, he became impatient, showing serious eyes and hardened lines around his mouth.

I can imagine, now, his concern for his small children and awareness that his life would most likely end before we reached adulthood. He expressed his love in his sketches of Qingping, me, and his two children from his previous marriage. One day as Qingping was opening the living-room screen door, Father asked him to hold the pose. A sketch of five-year-old Qingping with bright eyes and soft facial lines was finished in a few minutes. He also drew portraits of me, with short hair and fringes covering my forehead. It was a feat to catch me sitting still: I was a very active, although chubby, toddler. My father, the visual artist, teased me about my elephant legs. But I outgrew that, and by age five I had become a pretty girl. Although the youngest of Father's four children, I look the most like him, having his dense hair, dark bushy eyebrows, facial structure, small mouth, and pointed chin. One day when Mom, Qingping, and I came to his bedroom to say good night, he said to me affectionately, "Xiao Mei, you will grow up to be a beautiful lady, wearing a fur coat and high heels." These warm words stayed with me as I grew up.

One morning in September 1953, Qingping and I had just got up when people poured into our house, several struggling to keep my mother on her feet. Our quiet living room suddenly filled with noise and commotion. Mom, who seemed always to have strict control of our daily lives, collapsed on the floor, her face buried in her hands, sobbing heavily. Father was not with her. Other people around her were weeping while trying their best to comfort her. Qingping and I were told that our father had died early that morning.

Three days before, on September 23, 1953, my father had presided over the Second National Congress of Literary and Arts Workers as the executive chairman. He attended the all-day session and in the evening, at a banquet honoring a Polish delegation, suffered a cerebral hemorrhage. My mother was at his hospital bedside for two days and three nights until he passed away on September 26.

Later that day, Mom dressed Qingping and me in black mourning clothes and we went with her to Beijing Hospital to pay our respects. Father lay motionless under a white sheet, head raised high on a pillow. My heart sank when I saw his still-open eyes retaining his usual expression of warmth, as if he had been quietly expecting us. Mom told us that when she rushed to see him immediately after his stroke, he said, "Why didn't the children come?" Those were his last words. I caressed his cold hands. How I wished that he could hear me say, "Dad, I am here. I love you and really miss you!" Mom found in his pocket his thirty-year-old pocket watch and three hard candies he had saved from the banquet that night for my mother, Qingping, and me.

That day we met Premier Zhou Enlai, who also came to the hospital to pay his last respects. Wearing a black band on his arm, he said very sadly, "Xu Beihong is irreplaceable. His death is a great loss to us. Why was he allowed to attend that meeting from morning until night with sickness? From now on, we should not let this kind of thing happen again!"[11] He expressed condolences to my mother. That day a sculptor's assistant made a plaster mold of my father's face.

Chairman Mao Zedong wrote the following personal letter of condolence to my mother:

> Comrade Jingwen:
>
> I received your letter of October and the galloping horse by Mr. Xu a while ago. I am very grateful. I am concerned about you and am sending Comrade Tian Jiaying to inquire about your situation. If you have any difficulties, please let me know.
>
> Respectfully,
>
> Mao Zedong
> December 13, 1953

Mom kept Mao's letter to her, and also those Mao had written to her husband, as personal treasures. She also received condolence messages from people both in China and abroad.

At the request of the teachers and students of CAFA, Father's remains lay in state for three days in the academy's auditorium. There, teachers, students, workers, and staff members took turns keeping vigil beside his coffin.

Mom, Qingping, and I went to CAFA several times during those three days to see Father. In the auditorium, a large photo of Father, with black silk strips draped around the frame, hung above his remains. Several teachers and students stood by, watching him in silence or murmuring. Qingping and I knelt beside his coffin. Father lay quietly in his grey cotton Sun Yat-sen-style jacket. Around his gracefully lined lips lingered a faint smile, a familiar expression, intimate and comforting, and it lodged in my heart.

On the funeral day, Mom, Qingping, and I knelt by my father's coffin to see his face for the last time before the coffin was sealed and painted black. Teachers and students from CAFA together with our family escorted his coffin to the Babaoshan Revolutionary Cemetery in the western suburbs of Beijing. Leaders of the CCP, generals from the People's Liberation Army, and other important contributors to the country were buried there. Representatives of artists and writers from all over China attended the funeral.

In December that year, a memorial exhibition of Xu Beihong's works in Beijing attracted thousands including artists, art lovers, and ordinary people who admired his artworks. Premier Zhou Enlai came to the exhibition. He appreciated Xu Beihong's syntheses of some foreign, Chinese, ancient, and present-day techniques in his works.

My father once told my mother, "One ought to leave behind for the coming generation something noble and valuable."[12] My mother, although heartbroken, managed to pull herself together to carry forward her late husband's legacy. She was determined to support his goals for Chinese art and art education. She also took the responsibility of bringing up their two children by herself.

My father's wish was to establish for his people a public museum of Chinese artistic heritage, and to honor this wish my mother donated more than 1200 of Xu Beihong's original sketches, drawings, oil paintings, and Chinese ink brush paintings. She also donated his entire personally selected collection including more than 1000 artworks. His collection encompassed calligraphy and paintings by accomplished artists of the Tang, Song, Yuan, Ming, and Qing dynasties, and of contemporary times, along with masterworks by Western artists. Also in his collection were valuable art books, printed pictures, and stone rubbings, totaling more than ten thousand. To establish this museum soon after his death in 1953, my mother also donated our house.

My father had dedicated to my mother the paintings he considered his best, inscribing them as gifts to her. Donating all my father's works including those inscribed to her was her way of expressing continuing love for him. Her decision ensured that this collection would be the best and largest in the world, and displayed permanently.

With Premier Zhou Enlai's recommendation, the Xu Beihong Memorial Museum was established in our house in 1954. The first art museum in China dedicated to a single artist and funded by the government, it displayed works by Xu Beihong and those from his collection.

At a banquet hosted by Premier Zhou Enlai for an Indian cultural delegation, Mom asked Premier Zhou to write in calligraphy "Beihong's Former Residence" for the Xu Beihong Memorial Museum. He agreed on the spot. Later he sent her two versions of his calligraphy to choose from. When he asked her whether he should put his signature on the calligraphy, Mom said no. She felt that her request for Premier Zhou's calligraphy came from her respect for him and for his friendship with Xu Beihong, not a desire to show off the premier's signature. Premier Zhou Enlai's words, "Beihong's Former Residence," were inscribed on a horizontal wooden tablet. His calligraphy showed boldness and vigor.

• • •

After Mom was allowed out of the detention room, the Red Guards from Beijing No. 8 High School kept her under heavy surveillance, staying in the museum's reception room, sometimes hiding above our ceiling to eavesdrop.

One night there was a light knock on the door. The museum's former messenger, Lao Ma, had climbed over an inner wall and jumped into our yard. I led him to our living room quietly. He whispered to Mom, "How are you? I was very worried about you." Creases of concern surrounded his eyes. "Let me know if I can help you with anything. But I have to keep this a secret from the Red Guards." Mom and I were both very touched by Ma's offer, made in spite of considerable risks. He stayed for only about ten minutes, then climbed back over the wall, and disappeared into the darkness.

During the chaos in August 1966, I was surprised to find the horizontal wooden tablet with Premier Zhou's inscription, "Beihong's Former Residence," still hanging at the entrance to our old home. I heard that the Red Guards had attempted to take it down to be smashed. But Lao Ma stopped them. He said, "These words were written by Premier Zhou. You should not destroy the tablet." I admired Lao Ma's courage to speak up.

Meanwhile, Second Uncle was packing to go back to his home village in Hunan, because during the Cultural Revolution all landowners were being sent back to their home villages. One night when the Red Guards were not around, Mom said to Second Uncle, "Why don't you go to the train station quickly now?" She asked him to remove from around his neck the cardboard sign the Red Guards had forced him to wear: LANDOWNER with a large X drawn over it.

I had heard of Red Guard questioning and brutality at the train station. Mom hoped Second Uncle could leave without being identified as a landowner. She gave him two hundred *yuan* from her small savings for the trip. He left from our private entrance on West Kusi, carrying his baggage with his good hand.

The next day our neighbors talked about a tall, bald man they had seen beaten to death at the train station. The description matched that of Second Uncle. We traced his baggage. It had arrived at his home village, but Second Uncle never made it there. We suspected that the Red Guards staying in the museum caught him at the train station and beat him to death. I still remember Second Uncle's worried face on that dark night when he left our house. That was the last time we saw him.

In September, severe beatings from the Red Guards let up for a while. But Mom, living in constant fear, found day-to-day life difficult. She slept on the couch downstairs because the bedroom floor upstairs was covered with the torn-up paper that she intentionally left untouched to discourage further home raids. Once she tried to walk to Zhongnanhai to ask Chairman Mao for an answer to her situation. But the Red Guards caught her halfway there, on Chang'an Avenue, and forced her to return home. The most Mom dared to hope for at the time was a peaceful if impoverished life in a remote village away from harassment and violent intrusion.

Mom said that a few of my classical music records including Beethoven's *Piano Concerto No. 5 in E-flat Major* survived the Red Guards' raids because Qingping had hidden them beneath the piano. During these painful days, Mom's only comfort was listening to the concerto and the other classical music records secretly, late at night when the Red Guards were not around.

The Red Guards lived in the Xu Beihong Memorial Museum for about a month, digging in the yards around the museum and our house, and even through the pile of coal in our boiler room. We wondered what they were digging for. But they found nothing to use against Mom. They tried forcing her to incriminate herself, but their attempts came to nothing. In order to survive, children sometimes reported their parents' supposed reactionary behaviors to the rebel groups in control. Qingping and I did not write anything against Mom.

Having found nothing, the Red Guards from Beijing No. 8 High School left our house in late September. Then two female Red Guards from my music school searched our house when I was not there. They lied about which school they came from, but Mom recognized the school badges they wore. Violin students sent by the "August Eighteenth Red Guard" group in CCOM, the girls spent half a day searching our already messy house. One cursed at the contents of my bookcase, saying, "Look at these poisonous weeds that Xu Fangfang was reading!" They interrogated Mom and whipped her with their belts, but got no confession from her.

One Red Guard from Beijing No. 8 High School, named Li, reappeared in October. He pulled Mom to the museum yard and yelled, "Admit that you are a spy. You are a bourgeois reactionary authority!" When Mom refused to yield, he punched her in the chest so hard that she fell on the ground. When she stood up, he repeated his demand and punched her again, eight or nine times. Once she fell onto the low fence surrounding the museum's lawn, breaking its wooden boards.

I suspected that somebody, possibly the Party member Wang Shuxiao, for some political reason had fabricated accusations so the Red Guards would persecute Mom. I also suspected that Wang Shuxiao had called over Red Guard Li, the most violent of all the Red Guards from Beijing No. 8 High School, to force a confession from my mother. Red Guard violence could come at any time.

CHAPTER 3

Xu Beihong's Journey[13]

My mother had just completed her studies at Peking University when in 1957 she was appointed director of the Xu Beihong Memorial Museum by the Ministry of Culture. Wu Zuoren, vice president of CAFA, had directed the Xu Beihong Memorial Museum until then.

Our family not only lived in the Xu Beihong Memorial Museum, but in Xu Beihong's spiritual world. Mom devoted herself to showing the museum to visitors. She frequently received student groups from universities, middle schools, and primary schools. She impressed many visitors with her personal narrations about Xu Beihong's life and his paintings. In the visitors' notebook they wrote of their admiration for Xu Beihong's artworks and for his example of patriotism, particularly during China's War of Resistance against Japan (1937-1945). The Xu Beihong Memorial Museum also served as a studio for art-college students assigned to copy Xu Beihong's paintings and drawings as part of their curriculum.

While Mom spoke to visitors, I followed her and listened. Gradually I came to appreciate Father's paintings, his artistic attainments, and his powerful will that achieved his career goals. By the time I was nine, I understood that my parents expected me to set and achieve high artistic goals, and thereby become a worthy daughter of such an accomplished artist.

Xu Beihong had been among the first Chinese students to study Western art in Europe. With the support of Cai Yuanpei and Fu Zengxiang, minister of education, Xu Beihong finally earned a government scholarship to study in France. On May 10, 1919, he set foot in Paris on his mission to study the advanced methods, techniques, and other useful elements of Western painting in order to improve and develop Chinese painting.

In the first few months, Xu Beihong spent all his time visiting major art museums, studying some available examples of Western art from previous centuries, before enrolling in the Académie Julian to study drawing.

Later he entered the École Nationale Supérieure des Beaux Arts after passing its entrance examination. Xu Beihong[14] studied under François Flameng, president of the school, a historical painter distinguished for his natural fluid style and mastery of portrait painting. Xu Beihong also studied privately with Pascal-Adolphe-Jean Dagnan-Bouveret, a leading French artist, whose guidance played an important role in Xu Beihong's progress. He wrote that aside from his loving father, no one else had guided him as had Dagnan-Bouveret.[15] As a former student of Camille Corot, Dagnan-Bouveret related this advice of Corot to Xu Beihong: ". . .an artist should have conscience and confidence. One should not give up creativity in order to follow other people."[16] Dagnan-Bouveret also said to Xu Beihong, "The matter of art is most difficult. One should not follow fashions nor be satisfied with small accomplishments."[17]

During his first two years in France, Xu Beihong, suffering from poverty and stress, developed intestinal spasms. He continued painting, sometimes in nearly unbearable pain. To make things worse, in 1921 the Chinese government suspended scholarships for Chinese students abroad. To continue studying, he had to work part-time, sometimes living only on bread and water so he could pay for oil-painting materials.

He decided to go to Berlin where the devalued German mark made his French francs last longer. There he met Arthur Kampf, president of the Hochschule für Bildende Künste in Berlin, and saw works by Kampf, Adolf von Menzel, and Giovanni Segantini.

Xu Beihong loved painting to the marrow of his bones.[18] While in Germany, he painted almost ten hours every day. During his eight years in Europe, he studied the concepts and methods of Western painting in art museums in France, Germany, Belgium, Switzerland, and Italy. Artists he liked included Titian, Jusepe de Ribera, Gustave Courbet, Jean-François Millet, Eugène Delacroix, Antoine-Louis Barye, Claude Monet, Pierre Puvis de Chavannes, and French Symbolist artist Eugène Anatole Carrière. He disliked paintings by Paul Cézanne and Henri Matisse because he thought they lacked content. He copied masterpieces by Pierre-Paul Prud'hon, Delacroix, Diego Velázquez, Jacob Jordaens, and Rembrandt van Rijn, his favorite. In a German museum, he carefully copied Rembrandt's work, often without stopping to take food or water. He worked particularly hard on copying the portrait of Rembrandt's second wife, Hendrickje, and felt rewarded by his efforts.

In Rome he discovered a new standard for quality, scale, and dynamics in the human figures done by Renaissance artists. He could not tear himself away from the superb sculptures in St. Peter's Basilica or Michelangelo's frescoes in the Sistine Chapel. Michelangelo expressed strong emotions through his handling of the human body. Michelangelo's works reassured Xu Beihong that his own art should express human emotions with so much sincerity that it would appeal to divine powers.

During the 1920s, he created several important oil works, including *Sound of the Flute* (Fig. 5), *Old Woman, Hearing from Afar, Honeymoon, Woman Caressing a Cat*, and *Violin Lesson.* In 1927, nine of his works were selected for exhibition at the Salon of the Société Nationale des Beaux-Arts. Few Chinese artists of the time had attained his level of achievement in Europe. *Sound of the Flute*, painted in 1926, became one of his representative works. It combines classical form, romantic atmosphere, and Impressionist coloring with a Chinese subject, expressing a woman's feelings as she reminisces about her homeland, China.

After eight years, in 1927 Xu Beihong was ready to return to China and dedicate himself to improving and developing Chinese painting through the realism movement in art, through extensive teaching, and through his own creative works. Soon after his return to China, he co-founded the Nanguo Academy of Arts in Shanghai with Tian Han and Ouyang Yuqian, playwrights for the new culture. Xu Beihong served as head of the painting department, volunteering his energy and teaching.

Xu Beihong strongly believed that artists had social and moral responsibilities. Seeing China and the Chinese being bullied and humiliated by foreign powers, Xu Beihong demonstrated concern for his country in several historical paintings. Around 1928, he started work on a large oil painting, *Tian Heng and His Five Hundred Warriors.* Tian Heng was from a third-century BCE noble family of the State of Qi. He chose suicide rather than submission to the overwhelming forces of the Han emperor. Upon hearing of Tian Heng's death, his five hundred followers also committed suicide. Xu Beihong portrayed their uncompromising moral integrity, a quality his country needed when confronted with national crisis.

In the same year, Xu Beihong accepted the professorship of fine art at National Central University in Nanjing. As an influential professor, he insisted on rigorous training in sketching for all art students, encouraging them to emphasize carefully selected details while maintaining a sense of the whole. In the late 1940s, he also stressed memory drawing to sharpen students' observational skills. Students were trained to recreate from memory a drawing they themselves had done from life, a methodology he developed.[19]

The Japanese occupied China's northeastern provinces by force in 1931. Deeply concerned, in the early 1930s Xu Beihong worked on a large oil painting, *Awaiting the Deliverer*, based on a theme from the ancient *Book of History*. Set in the sixteenth century BCE, this story expresses the people's hope for a leader able to liberate them from brutal oppressors.

Xu Beihong created a large Chinese brush painting, *Jiufang Gao, Horse Judge* (Fig. 4), in 1931. According to the Chinese classic *Liezi*, Jiufang Gao, a common laborer in the Spring and Autumn period, possessed a superb ability to identify good horses. The black stallion central to the painting is exuberant upon meeting Jiufang Gao, who recognizes at once the strengths of this "thousand-*li* horse" (a horse capable of a thousand *li*- or 186-mile run in one day). This painting implies Xu Beihong's frustration with talents stifled in old China, and his desire to develop potentially talented artists.

Among his efforts to promote Chinese painting abroad, Xu Beihong organized and held an exhibition of several hundred Chinese ink brush paintings in several major European cities during 1933 and 1934. Most were contemporary works by more than seventy accomplished Chinese artists including himself. This was the first influential exhibition of contemporary Chinese paintings in Europe. Xu Beihong's goal was promoting international recognition of China's artistic and cultural heritage, particularly then, while China's northeast was occupied by the Japanese. Such an endeavor was not easy because China had little public support for art exhibitions and few established art museums had modern management infrastructure.

With great success, the exhibition toured seven European cities in France, Belgium, Germany, Italy, and the Soviet Union. The Musée du Jeu de Paume in Paris bought twelve paintings from the exhibition, including *Old Cypress* by Xu Beihong, to be exhibited permanently in a new gallery of contemporary Chinese painting. Interest in the exhibition resulted in major European museums and universities devoting another three galleries to contemporary Chinese art. Xu Beihong wrote, "This is the first time permanently dedicated galleries in world-class museums have been set up for displaying contemporary Chinese paintings."[20]

Because of Xu Beihong's expanding reputation at home and abroad, some Kuomintang government officials tried to persuade him to paint a portrait of Chiang Kai-shek. He refused and expressed discontentment with Chiang Kai-shek's government, especially its failure to resist the Japanese invasion. Xu Beihong's stand on this issue brought him threats and open attacks organized by Kuomintang secret agents. His unyielding character is expressed in a couplet he composed: "Alone, I maintain my biased viewpoint. Alone, I go my own way." He hung the couplet in his studio.

When harassment and threats from the Kuomintang secret agents became too severe, Xu Beihong left Nanjing temporarily for Guilin. In 1937 in Guilin he painted his famous Chinese ink brush painting, *Spring Rain on the Lijiang* (*Li River*) (Fig. 7). A large splashed-ink painting with an Impressionistic result, it portrays the beautiful mountainous landscape along the Li River dissolved in the spring rain and mist. This groundbreaking painting integrates reflected light and shadow with traditional Chinese landscape painting.

During this period Xu Beihong and his wife Jiang Biwei broke up over their differences in politics and life goals. Xu Beihong dedicated his life to art, but Jiang Biwei did not share that dedication. They had a son, Boyang, and a daughter, Lili. In 1936, Xu Beihong moved out of their house in Nanjing.

The Japanese invaders plundered and destroyed countless Chinese art treasures. In the late 1930s, Xu Beihong acquired what he considered to be a Tang-dynasty masterpiece, a figure-painting scroll titled *Eighty-seven Immortals*, purchased during the war from a German lady in Hong Kong. The graceful shapes and lively gestures of the eighty-seven figures walking in procession were accomplished entirely by line drawing, without colors. To this painting, Xu Beihong affixed a seal, bearing the words "I, Beihong, hold this painting as dear as my own life." The broad spectrum of his collection included artworks by Tang-, Song-, Yuan-, Ming-, and Qing-dynasty masters as well as contemporary Chinese and Western artists. In the interest of the Chinese people's aesthetic education, he hoped to establish a public art museum of best ancient and present-day Chinese paintings representing Chinese artistic heritage.

Soon after the Sino-Japanese War began in 1937, Xu Beihong returned to his professorship at Central University, which had moved from Nanjing to Chongqing. During this period he painted *Poor Sichuan Woman* and *Water Carriers of Sichuan*, portraying the hardships suffered by the people.

At the invitation of the Indian poet Rabindranath Tagore, Xu Beihong went to India at the end of 1939, holding an exhibition at Visva-Bharati and another in Calcutta in the following year. Xu Beihong was deeply concerned for his motherland, then in the most difficult stage of the War of Resistance. In India he created a large Chinese brush painting, *The Foolish Old Man Who Removed the Mountains* (Fig. 3). A popular Chinese fable recorded in the Chinese classic *Liezi* tells of a man called Foolish Old Man who was determined to remove two mountains blocking the view from his doorway. He believed that the task could be accomplished by generations of his descendants. In this painting, Xu Beihong depicted the invincible spirit of the Chinese people whom he believed would win the War of Resistance if they persevered, as had the supposedly foolish old man and his descendants. This painting broke new ground in the history of Chinese brush painting, with its large-scale nude figures dominating the composition. The portrayal of these figures incorporates Western sketching techniques. Influenced by Michelangelo's effective use of foreshortening, Xu Beihong applied it to create dynamic figures.

In India Xu Beihong rode horses on the plains near Darjeeling where he occasionally enjoyed a fast gallop. He traveled a long distance to Kashmir on horseback. The horses in India struck Xu Beihong as special: graceful, sturdy, with long necks, long steely-hooved legs, pointed ears, broad noses, strong chest muscles, and fine coats with a silken sheen. Intoxicated by the presence of these animals he had loved since childhood, he came to better understand their admirable temperament. After his experiences in India with this type of horse, the horses he painted exhibit noticeably greater vigor. Ancient Chinese paintings usually show tamed, plump, and groomed horses painted in fine detail. Xu Beihong used a big Chinese brush to portray lean, anatomically strong, galloping horses, filled with fire and spirit, based on accurate Western sketching principles.

As in his other animal paintings, Xu Beihong expressed his sorrow and joy as well as his hopes for a bright future for his country through his horses and the inscriptions he chose for his horse paintings. On his galloping horse painted in

1941 in Penang, Malaysia, he inscribed, "I am very worried about the Second Battle of Changsha." (Fig. 2)

During the War of Resistance Xu Beihong once rode in a horse-drawn cart near Chengdu. The cart driver told him that the horse was not only his source of income but also his most loyal friend. Sometimes he starved, but he never let his horse starve. When the horse looked unhappy, the driver carried the load himself. Xu Beihong was so touched by this thoughtfulness that he gave the cart driver one of his ink brush horse paintings. The driver was informed that the painting had some value and that he should not give it away lightly.

In order to help China's War of Resistance against Japan, in 1939 and 1941 Xu Beihong held benefit exhibitions of his paintings in Singapore and Malaysia. According to the estimate of *United Evening Paper*, a Singapore Chinese-language newspaper, Xu Beihong left more than 1000 paintings behind in Singapore and Malaysia, including those sold at the exhibitions, given to friends, and prepared for a U.S. exhibition.[21] The exhibitions drew visitors in record numbers. All paintings offered for sale were sold, the majority purchased by overseas Chinese. Xu Beihong donated the entire proceeds from the exhibitions to help alleviate the suffering of refugees driven from their homes in Japanese-occupied areas of China. While in Singapore in 1941 he was preparing to mount a U.S. exhibition of his own works, sponsored by the American Aid to China Federation. He yearned to promote international recognition of China's artistic and cultural heritage and gain U.S. public support for China's War of Resistance against Japan, still in its most difficult phase, which would last another year. The show was halted by the shocking news of the Japanese attack on Pearl Harbor.

Xu Beihong returned to Chongqing in 1942. While still teaching at Central University, he began establishing the China Academy of Fine Arts, a research-oriented art institute. Conditions were difficult for him. Living in Panxi on the northern bank of the Jialing River, each day he crossed the river to lecture at Central University, and at night painted by kerosene lamplight. He lived on mildewed rice and water from rice paddies. The hard life and overwork caused him hypertension and chronic nephritis. Nevertheless, during the period between the 1930s and mid-1940s, despite the wartime hardships, Xu Beihong created some of his best paintings. Many featured energetic horses, docile water buffalo, drowsy cats, and arrogant eagles. In his Chinese ink brush paintings, he expressed his own feelings through lively characterizations of animals and birds. His Chinese brush painting

Unconcerned portrays two cats at leisure. It was painted in 1934 after the Japanese occupied northeastern China. Xu Beihong inscribed the painting, "Indifference is their best approach. To be muddleheaded is natural. They have been used to playing around since they were young. Extreme danger will not shock them." It is a satire on those indifferent to the national crisis in China.

During the War of Resistance, Xu Beihong's personal life changed dramatically when he met my mother, Liao Jingwen. She came from a scholarly family in Liuyang, Hunan Province, in southern China, where her family owned a small amount of land. Both her parents were well-educated in classical Chinese literature. Her mother started her on classical Chinese and calligraphy lessons, but died when Liao Jingwen was only eleven.

Her father, Liao Kangfu, found it difficult to raise four sons and three daughters all by himself. So early on in her life, my mother learned to be independent. She said that sometimes she wore broken shoes because her father could not afford new ones for her. But valuing education for his sons and daughters, Liao Kangfu managed to send all of them to school and later to college. His salary as a general administrator at a factory in Changsha was not enough to pay their tuitions, so he sometimes borrowed money.

Inquisitive and willing to work hard at school, Liao Jingwen was good at math and science, but she also had learned many Chinese poems during childhood, and, like her parents, was well-versed in classical Chinese literature. She spent six years in the Zhounan Women's High School in Changsha, the best private high school in Hunan Province, alma mater of several female leaders such as Xiang Jingyu and Cai Chang. Her Chinese literature teacher, Zhou Shizhao, who had been Mao Zedong's classmate at the First Normal School of Hunan, appreciated her essays. Zhou Shizhao impressed Liao Jingwen with his knowledge of Chinese poetry, lecturing always without notes, quoting ancient poems from memory.

Liao Jingwen was on the school volleyball team and other athletic teams. An elected leader of Zhounan's student organization, she organized student performances including well-known dramas such as *Thunderstorm* and *Sunrise* by Cao Yu.

Influenced by Yang Zhang, the underground CCP leader at Zhounan and also the niece of Mao Zedong's late wife Yang Kaihui, at age fourteen Liao Jingwen joined the National Liberation Pioneers, a CCP youth organization.

One of its missions was to fight the Japanese invasion. She organized a singing group to sing at shelters for injured Chinese solders. She and fellow members helped feed the injured solders and write letters home for them.

The underground CCP organized and held secret activities such as reading sessions. Liao Jingwen attended, reading *Twenty-five-thousand-li Long March* and *The Youth of Mao Zedong*. These activities inspired her to join the CCP under the name of Liao Xin (New Liao) at age fifteen. As a new member she delivered undercover CCP documents to the Eighth Route Army Representative Office in Changsha. Liao Jingwen and some patriotic comrades secretly planned to go to Yan'an in northwestern China, the Communist base central to the fight against the Japanese invaders. Many idealistic youths hoped to go there. On the day of her departure, Liao Jingwen was intercepted by her concerned father. He told Xu Teli, head of the Eighth Route Army Representative Office in Changsha, "My daughter is too young to leave home. She needs to finish high school."

Later when the Japanese bombed Changsha, Liao Jingwen moved with the Zhounan Women's High School to Lantian, a small town in Hunan away from the air raids. In Lantian, she worked in her high school's nighttime program for poor local peasants' children, who attended at no cost. However, after the move she lost touch with the CCP. Studying with limited resources, she graduated in 1941.

Liao Jingwen left her village in Hunan Province the following year. Surviving air raids and other challenges, she arrived in Guilin hoping to go to college or find a job there. Fortunately she found employment as a singer for a performance troupe in Guilin, performing concerts to raise morale for the War of Resistance. Liao Jingwen met Xu Beihong when, at the end of 1942, she answered an ad in the newspaper for a librarian in the preparatory office of the China Academy of Fine Arts. Xu Beihong had stored his collections of valuable art books and paintings in the Qixingyan Cave (Seven-Star Cave) in Guilin to protect them from bombings. He planned to have a librarian help him sort out some of the books to take to Chongqing. Ranking first in the written examination for job applicants, Liao Jingwen was interviewed by Xu Beihong, the examiner for the academy. Impressed with her good writing skills, her knowledge of Chinese poetry and literature, and most importantly her interest in art, he offered her the librarian's job.

By that time Xu Beihong was already an established artist with a national reputation while Liao Jingwen was only nineteen, twenty-eight years younger

Liao Jingwen, mid-1940s.

than he. While helping Xu Beihong sort the art books and paintings in his collection, she marveled at the masterpieces and his knowledge of and dedication to art. She also respected his empathy with common people and his personal integrity.

Xu Beihong had been separated from his wife, Jiang Biwei, for about seven years. Although a very accomplished artist, his personal life was lonely. Liao Jingwen, a beautiful and sincere young lady with bright eyes, shared his love of art. They went on a boat trip together to Yangshuo along with one of Liao Jingwen's female friends. Surrounded by the beautiful mountainous landscape along the Li River, the romance between Xu Beihong and Liao Jingwen began. On the boat, Liao Jingwen and her girlfriend hummed Schumann's *Träumerei*, taking him to an imaginary world.

Love did not develop easily. Liao Jingwen struggled with anxiety, hesitation, and pain over the age difference and her desire to finish college. Also Jiang Biwei tried to sabotage Xu Beihong's relationship with Liao Jingwen even though Jiang had decided never to reunite with Xu Beihong. In fact Jiang Biwei had continued a long love affair with Zhang Daofan, a high official of the

Kuomintang government. She wrote to Liao's father and sister, accusing Liao Jingwen of destroying her family. Faced with the opposition from her father and sister, Liao Jingwen applied to college to quell their anxiety. Admitted to Ginling Women's College, a Christian missionary college in Chengdu, she majored there in chemistry, hoping to become a scientist as accomplished as Madame Curie. Yet the love between Liao Jingwen and Xu Beihong deepened. Finally she gave up her studies and her dream of becoming a scientist to return to Chongqing and marry Xu Beihong.

However, in 1944 Xu Beihong, overworked and with high blood pressure, suddenly fell seriously ill. The hospital's doctor said his condition was life-threatening. Some of Liao Jingwen's friends advised her to think twice about marrying Xu Beihong, considering his chronic high blood pressure and the ever-present threat of losing him. But Liao Jingwen was willing to sacrifice anything, including her life, for him. Even if their lives together might be short at best, Liao would not regret her commitment, born first from her respect for Xu Beihong's contributions to art in China. Willing to give him the love and care he needed during his illness and afterward, she was also determined to support his goal of improving and developing Chinese painting. At the moment, she enjoyed true love she would cherish for decades after Xu Beihong passed away. Little could she imagine the frustrations and persecution she would undergo because of her love and commitment.

After nine years of separation, in 1945 Xu Beihong formally ended his unhappy marriage. According to Liao Jingwen, in response to Jiang Biwei's initial terms, Xu Beihong had given Jiang two hundred thousand *yuan*, forty ancient Chinese paintings, and fifty of his own paintings. The final divorce settlement to Jiang Biwei included Xu Beihong's additional payment of one million *yuan*, an additional one hundred Chinese ink brush paintings by Xu Beihong, and twenty thousand *yuan* per month for each of their two children. This was a generous settlement. Receiving long-awaited proceeds in 1945 from his painting sales in Yunnan enabled him to pay for his divorce settlement that year.

Having gradually recovered from his illness under Liao Jingwen's care, Xu Beihong and Liao Jingwen held their wedding ceremony in January 1946 at the Sino-Soviet Cultural Association in Chongqing. They were both very happy after the anxiety and emotional pain before and during his illness. He finally had a real home, although a humble one. He said to his new wife, "I have found my real sweetheart! Nobody except you can love me with such true, unwavering, pure, and selfless love. . . ."[22]

After the end of the War of Resistance against Japan, Xu Beihong left Chongqing to go to Beiping via Shanghai to take the position of president of the National Beiping Arts College. Many people had advised him not to move to Beiping because the peace negotiations between the Communist Party and the Kuomintang were about to break down and the north seemed unstable. In Shanghai Xu Beihong encountered Zhou Enlai, whom he had known during his student years in France. Zhou Enlai had become his lifelong friend. Despite Kuomintang threats in 1945, Xu Beihong firmly supported the democratic movement backed by Zhou Enlai. In Shanghai in 1946, Zhou Enlai encouraged him to go to Beiping, saying, "I hope that you will manage the college well and train many capable artists for the people."[23]

The National Beiping Arts College then offered visual arts only, including Chinese painting, oil painting, sculpture, ceramics, and decorative pattern design. Xu Beihong added a music department, hiring Zhao Meibo as the director. Zhao, a well-known Belgian-trained vocalist, was also an outstanding music educator and choral conductor. During the next few years, the college developed many artistic and musical talents.[24]

Xu Beihong strengthened the National Beiping Arts College by recruiting accomplished artists and capable art teachers in all disciplines, including those who demonstrated creativity in traditional Chinese painting specialties such as landscape, bird-and-flower, and figure painting.[25] At the college, Xu Beihong implemented his new teaching system on a large scale. According to my mother, he chose to forego a comfortable life in order to pioneer innovation in art education and develop Chinese painting.

Xu Beihong stipulated that sketching be a two-year course required of all students in the departments of Chinese painting, oil painting, sculpture, and decorative pattern design. The course's main objective was to teach art students basic skills in drawing from life. The remaining three years of the Chinese painting program were devoted to developing students' traditional Chinese painting skills for animals, flowers, trees, and the many things that could be observed from nature. In addition, the sketching course helped the Chinese ink-brush-painting students learn to paint human figures. Students were encouraged to paint creatively according to their own observations. Against strong opposition from some traditional Chinese painters in Beiping,

Xu Beihong persisted in his beliefs. In 1947 he published an article, "Steps to Establish New Chinese Painting," issued to the press as a personal manifesto. In this article he advocated learning directly from nature and encouraged traditional Chinese painters to portray people's lives.

As president of the college, Xu Beihong protected his teachers and students who had participated in "anti-starvation, anti-civil war" demonstrations. His progressive viewpoint towards the democratic movement and his educational innovations brought open attacks from the Kuomintang authorities and their agents in traditional Chinese art circles. In the fall of 1947 an "Anti-Xu Beihong" campaign organized by Kuomintang agents issued the declaration, "Xu Beihong Is Destroying Chinese Painting," and their newspapers jointly attacked him. Xu Beihong did not bend or bow to their pressure. He and the majority of his teachers continued to teach as planned.

Inspired by the victory of the People's Liberation Army under the CCP in northeastern China in 1948, and by the upcoming campaign to liberate Beiping, Xu Beihong resisted all attempts by the Kuomintang government to move the National Beiping Arts College to the south. Encouraged by messages from Mao Zedong and Zhou Enlai brought to him by his playwright friend Tian Han, he was determined to do his best in Beiping to prepare for its liberation.

Although surrounded by the People's Liberation Army, Beiping was still controlled by Kuomintang troops. As concern about the impending battle intensified, the Kuomintang commander organized a discussion session with prominent scholars and educators to hear their opinions. Xu Beihong expressed the hope that the city would be liberated peacefully, a view supported by all attendees.

After the peaceful liberation of Beiping, Zhou Enlai sent a delegation, including Xu Beihong and accomplished writers, to represent the new China at the World Peace Congress held in Prague in 1949. At a particular moment at the conference, the delegates from other countries enthusiastically cheered Nanjing's liberation. Deeply moved by this response, upon his return to China, Xu Beihong painted a large Chinese brush painting depicting the enthusiasm of the World Peace Congress delegates. This painting includes specific portraits of many Chinese delegates at the conference.

On October 1, 1949, Xu Beihong surely felt proud to share with many Communist Party and government leaders the honor of being present on the Tiananmen rostrum. Together they witnessed Mao Zedong announcing to the world the founding of the People's Republic of China (PRC). Xu Beihong shared the optimism with most of the Chinese people as China finally became a respected unified nation, independent of foreign powers and their humiliations and control.

In new China, Xu Beihong was appointed president of the Central Academy of Fine Arts. The academy, initially named National Academy of Fine Arts, combined the National Beiping Arts College with the North China United University art department run by the Communists in the 1940s. He was also elected chairman of the All-China Art Workers Association, forerunner of the Chinese Artists Association. This was the only national visual-art organization, authorized by the government to organize national art events including national art exhibitions and art publications.

As a non-Communist-Party person, Xu Beihong held the highest honorary position in visual arts in China. Although he had no administrative power to determine the teaching program's content at CAFA, as a senior teacher he could influence the many faculty members who were his former students. The Communist administrators in the academy made staffing, financial, and other decisions.

The CCP led the "three-anti" and "five-anti" campaigns from 1951 to 1952. The former was against the "three evils" in government agencies, schools, organizations, armed forces, and political parties: corruption, waste, and bureaucracy. The latter was against the "five evils," targeting private business owners in industry and commerce. The "five evils" were bribery, tax evasion, theft of state property, doing shoddy work with inferior materials, and stealing government economic information.

During these campaigns, CAFA's Party leader detained a few of Xu Beihong's former students. Xu Beihong had hired them in the late 1940s as administrative personnel with financial responsibilities for the National Beiping Arts College. According to my mother and several CAFA teachers, the Party leader attempted to implicate Xu Beihong by forcing these administrative people to confess to alleged embezzlement, but they refused to admit to crimes they did not commit. At the end of the "three-anti" and "five-anti" campaigns, the Party leader announced at a school-wide meeting that these administrative people, incarcerated at CAFA for about a year, had been cleared of the alleged charges. Even so, they chose to leave their administrative duties and return to teaching.

Xu Beihong wrote to Mao Zedong in 1949, asking him to write the school name, National Academy of Fine Arts, in calligraphy to be permanently inscribed as the school sign. Mao honored Xu Beihong's request by writing the school name in ink brush. He also wrote the following letter in his ink brush handwriting to Xu Beihong:

> Mr. Beihong:
>
> I received your letter. I wrote a piece and wonder if it can be used.
> Wish you the best with your teaching.
>
> Mao Zedong
> November 29, 1949

After the establishment of the PRC, the Communist Party controlled CAFA and all other art institutions. The Party urged artists to serve the people, especially workers, peasants, and soldiers, and to make their artworks serve the Party's policies. Many traditional Chinese painters, especially bird-and-flower and landscape painters, who could not paint human figures, were uncertain about how to survive under the new policy. Some were forced from their jobs. Xu Beihong wrote in 1949, "Although I advocated realism for more than twenty years, I was never able to get close to laboring people. In fact I had no way to get to know them. In an unjust society, the vast laboring population and art are completely detached."[26] He was eager to adjust his thoughts to make his creative works serve the masses in the new China. He praised the expressiveness of peasant characters in some artworks by painters from Communist-controlled liberated areas. He requested that his teachers and students be allowed to participate in the land reform, where they would experience life among the peasants and draw from life.[27]

His major oil during this period was a large painting, *Chairman Mao among the People*, painted in 1949 and 1950. Xu Beihong told his wife, Liao Jingwen, that he wanted to depict intellectuals' support of Chairman Mao. CAFA oil painting teacher Dai Ze said, "Xu Beihong invited two CAFA art teachers from liberated areas to look at the painting when it was almost completed. I was there when they said, 'Chairman Mao should be portrayed among workers, peasants, and soldiers. But the people in the painting look bourgeois.'"[28] According to Dai, Xu Beihong responded, "I want to show the people of the entire country, and not just workers, peasants, and soldiers, supporting Chairman Mao."[29] As a result of its content, this painting was never exhibited.

Despite his disappointment, Xu Beihong continued to paint enthusiastically for the new China. His works include portraits of Mao Zedong and of many model workers and soldiers. He made studies for his oil painting titled *Lu Xun and Qu Qiubai* in 1950 and 1951. In spite of CAFA Party leaders' rejection of painting lacking human content, Xu Beihong continued to paint ink brush paintings of birds and horses, including the galloping horses he did at the request of the Chinese People's Volunteer Army soldiers during the Korean War.

Meanwhile, people in Shandong Province were cutting through Yishan (Yi Mountain) to conduct the Shu River's floodwaters to the sea. Excited about this first major attempt made by new China to change nature, in summer 1951, despite feeling ill from his high blood pressure, Xu Beihong traveled to the construction site in Shandong Province. At the site, living with the people working on the project, he made many studies of the workers, preparing to create a large oil painting reflecting China's reconstruction. While working on this painting after his return, he suffered a stroke and was half paralyzed. "If only I had been born ten years later!" he said.

In CAFA's early years, the Communist leaders eliminated traditional Chinese bird-and-flower painting, landscape painting, seal carving, and calligraphy from Xu Beihong's traditional Chinese painting curriculum, considering them unsuitable for serving new socialist China's needs. Communist administrators and Xu Beihong differed as to how to adjust the teaching program's content for the Party's new direction. Nevertheless, CAFA retained almost all of Xu Beihong's faculty and some of his major teaching principles, including drawing from life.

Although not fully recovered from his illness in 1953, Xu Beihong returned to teaching at CAFA. Some Chinese teachers and students had visited the Soviet Union and brought back one type of drawing by some Russian art-middle-school students. Under this Soviet influence in CAFA in the early 1950s, some students were polishing for weeks every detail of their fine-pencil drawings. Xu Beihong opposed this practice, believing that the students might lose the ability to capture the essence of the subject. He required students to emphasize selected details to quickly capture the essence, a skill acquired through drawing many short but finished poses, each completed in a few hours. During his lifetime, this was the only glimpse of the Soviet influence just beginning to appear.

Eager to share his knowledge of art, Xu Beihong gave a series of lectures to the 1953 graduating class and also to a group of teachers taking a refresher course in sketching and oil. In these lectures he used as examples and references his own oil paintings and many reproductions of diverse-style Western European artworks from his own collection.

Xu Beihong had a passion for helping young artists. The hardship he had suffered early in his career helped him empathize. He went out of his way to secure educational opportunities for promising Chinese artists. Quite a few famous twentieth-century Chinese painters, such as Qi Baishi, Fu Baoshi, and Wu Zuoren, benefited from his help.

Xu Beihong in the late 1940s had been delighted to receive a letter from a primary-school student in Nanchang in southern China, who had sent his own horse paintings, modeled after Xu Beihong's ink brush horses. In his reply letter, Xu Beihong told him not to model his paintings after Xu Beihong's but to observe and learn from real horses. He gave the young artist some basic instructions about drawing from life and even painted horse leg joints in ink to show him examples. The young artist recalled that Xu Beihong's letters were warm and sincere, as if he were talking to a friend. Xu Beihong encouraged him to set a goal of becoming a world-class artist and not be satisfied with small improvements. He also told this young artist to work diligently at all the sciences and liberal arts subjects, knowledge that Xu Beihong considered necessary to become a good artist. He advised him to apply to the National Beiping Arts College after graduating from middle school. If he was admitted, Xu Beihong said he would be very willing to teach him personally. Following Xu Beihong's suggestions, this young artist did enter the National Beiping Arts College and studied with Xu Beihong. Seeing that he looked frail and needed nutritious food, Xu Beihong invited him to his home on Sundays to eat with his family and to critique the young artist's drawings and paintings. Later this young artist became a good Chinese ink brush painter.

Xu Beihong's role as a leading art educator helped him achieve his goal of developing Chinese painting. He was the first Chinese artist to introduce the high-standard Western practice of sketching from life, and established sketching as the foundation for all art students in China's major art institutions. He advocated realism and held that art ought to explore what is important in people's lives. He was the first Chinese artist to establish oil-painting programs in China's major art institutions, which produced accomplished Chinese oil painters. He was also the first to achieve significant skill with oil painting and apply it with creative intuition to his own major oil works.

Xu Beihong's artistic beliefs, advocacy, and teaching principles have influenced China's overall art development up to the present. During the 1920s, other Chinese artists brought Western art influences to China, such as Post-Impressionism and elements of Matisse. But Xu Beihong's choice of realism and romanticism prevailed because his art encouraged Chinese people who were struggling to master their own destiny.

Figure 2. Xu Beihong (1895-1953), *Galloping Horse*, 1941, 130 x 76 cm, ink and color on paper, Xu Beihong Memorial Museum

Figure 3. Xu Beihong (1895-1953), *The Foolish Old Man Who Removed the Mountains*, 1940, 143.5 x 424 cm, ink and color on paper, Xu Beihong Memorial Museum

Figure 4. Xu Beihong (1895-1953), *Jiufang Gao, Horse Judge*, 1931, 139 x 351 cm, ink and color on paper, Xu Beihong Memorial Museum

Figure 5. Xu Beihong (1895-1953), *Sound of the Flute*, 1926, 79.5 x 38 cm, oil on canvas, Xu Beihong Memorial Museum

Figure 6. Xu Beihong (1895-1953), *Portrait of Mohandas Karamchand Gandhi*, 1940, 20 x 23.8 cm, charcoal on paper, Xu Beihong Memorial Museum. Xu Beihong sketched Gandhi in a few minutes during a gathering in Santiniketan, India.

Figure 7. Xu Beihong (1895-1953), *Spring Rain on the Lijiang* (*Li River*), 1937, 73.8 x 113.8 cm, ink on paper, Xu Beihong Memorial Museum

Figure 8. Xu Beihong (1895-1953), *Wounded Lion*, 1938, 110 x 109 cm, ink and color on paper, Xu Beihong Memorial Museum

CHAPTER 4

Sitting on Father's Desk

Many accomplished foreign guests visited the Xu Beihong Memorial Museum in the 1950s. One was Jaroslav Heyrovský, a Czechoslovakian chemist and Nobel Prize winner. Because he was not in good health, his son accompanied him. Mom offered him a chair to sit in while he enjoyed each painting, examining each most carefully. When he returned to Czechoslovakia, he wrote Mom a letter telling her that his visit to the Xu Beihong Memorial Museum had been his most memorable experience in China. He sent her an album containing beautiful landscape photos of Prague.

While I was growing up in the Xu Beihong Memorial Museum, I met many foreign artists including some accomplished Soviet painters. One of them came to Beijing in the early 1950s to design the famous Soviet Exhibition Center, later called the Beijing Exhibition Center. When he visited the Xu Beihong Memorial Museum, he painted my portrait in watercolor, naming it *Sitting on Father's Desk.* I modeled for him in my summer dress, sitting with my feet dangling from Father's desk in our former living room.

Antoine Allard, a Belgian artist, developed a long-term friendship with me and with my family. I was nine when I met him in 1957 during his first visit to China and to the Xu Beihong Memorial Museum. He was tall with blond hair and a mustache, yet his modest manner put me at ease. His wife had dark hair and a slender figure. She was informally dressed and very friendly.

During his visit to the museum, Mr. Allard drew a charcoal portrait of me sitting in front of a large Chinese brush painting, *Jiufang Gao, Horse Judge*, by Father. From my nine-year-old perspective, I found that Mr. Allard was interested in Chinese people. He said I had the typical facial features of a Chinese girl. Perhaps that was why he enjoyed drawing my portrait. While in

Beijing, he and his wife also invited Mom, Qingping, and me to visit Fragrant Hills Park in the suburbs of Beijing. I remember it was a beautiful sunny day. We walked along the stream running through Cherry Valley and enjoyed the serenity of the surrounding tall pine forest.

I felt that Mr. Allard and his wife were warm towards my family and me partly because we shared the love of art. I think Mr. Allard liked me a lot. He also had a daughter, whom he missed very much during his visit. He showed Mom and me her photo and the lock of her blond hair that he carried with him. Mr. Allard and his wife, although appearing very different from us, were more like us than I had ever imagined in terms of treasuring friendship. This first interaction with Western Europeans from a non-socialist country made me curious about the people of the Western world.

Together with Xie Li, a People's Republic of China diplomat working in the Netherlands, Mr. Allard in 1961 organized an official visit to China by Elisabeth, queen dowager of Belgium, and her daughter, Queen Marie-José. Marie-José had reigned briefly as Queen of Italy in 1946. This high-level visit took place ten years before the normalization of relations between Belgium and China. Mr. Allard accompanied the Belgian queen dowager Elisabeth to the Xu Beihong Memorial Museum. I was very surprised by their visit because during the Cold-War era, royal visitors from a European capitalist country were very unusual.

During that visit, Mr. Allard invited my family and me to spend time in Fragrant Hills Park again. I had just started learning English, and happily spoke a few words of English with him. I think he enjoyed seeing me as a maturing teenager with much curiosity and many questions.

I saw him for the last time in 1978. Aged and not as energetic as ten years before, Mr. Allard still had his gentle smile and friendly manner. Mom and I took him and his wife to dinner in a Hunan restaurant. I had studied English on my own for several years and this was the only time I spoke with him in English, without an interpreter.

As an adult, I was interested in learning more about him and life in Europe. After dinner, Mr. Allard drew my portrait in charcoal again. I looked much more mature in this drawing. To me, the drawing was a landmark, representing the longtime friendship Mr. Allard and our family maintained since he first drew my portrait when I was nine.

• • •

After Father died, Mom still enjoyed certain privileges as Madame Xu Beihong. Like my father, she was often invited to attend high-level government banquets to honor foreign cultural delegations. Our family could also spend summer vacations in beach resort cities in the Ministry of Culture's retreat cabins, reserved for privileged artists, musicians, and teachers. The rooms were free for us. As a little girl, I did not realize that the majority of the Chinese people did not share these benefits.

In order to alleviate her grief and to continue her education, my mother decided to go to Peking University to study Chinese language and literature. Ten years before, she had left Ginling Women's College in order to care for my father. Now thirty, she made the difficult and brave decision to go back to college. She was determined to start a new life for herself and her children. Having donated all her late husband's paintings, his collection, and our house to set up the museum, she would have to rely on herself to raise Qingping and me.

I was almost six years old and Qingping was seven. When Mom left for school a month after Father's death, our home life changed dramatically. We moved to three small coal-storage rooms in the back of the west yard. The dark leaky rooms had ceiling stains. The only familiar sight was the one-hundred-year-old locust tree standing in front of our rooms. It spread its large branches wide, like a grandfather stretching his arms to protect us from rain and wind. We often played on a swing hung from one of its branches.

Mom lived in the Peking University dorms during the week. To help Mom with household chores and babysitting, my grandaunt on my mother's side, Wang Xingying, came from Hunan Province to stay with us. Mom felt comfortable leaving her children and our household with a trusted relative. My grandaunt's husband had died when her only son was a baby. Her mother-in-law had told her that she could remarry only if she gave up her son to their family. Unwilling to leave her son behind, my grandaunt chose to remain single while bringing up her son in her mother-in-law's household. It was fortunate for them that her husband's family had lost much of its land by 1950, because then she and her husband's family were categorized as small-farm lessors rather than landowners.

We addressed her as "Shenpo," the Chinese word for grandaunt. She was about forty when she came to live with us. With only a second-grade education,

Shenpo was nevertheless a loving person with big eyes and short hair. She spoke with a strong Hunan accent. The caring tone in her voice and her gentle smile always warmed my heart. Qingping and I soon became attached to Shenpo, who felt like a second mother to me. For ten years she made comfortable cotton shoes for me, up through my middle-school years. She taught me domestic skills such as cooking and embroidery.

There was no television in China in the 1950s. Every evening Qingping and I huddled around the radio, listening to Chinese classic stories told in serial form. My favorite stories were *Romance of the Three Kingdoms, Water Margin*, and *Biography of Yuefei*, a famous twelfth-century Southern Song-dynasty general who defended China against minority invaders in the north. Using his voice, an articulate storyteller named Lian Kuoru would punctuate his stories' actions with sound effects of battle and the neighing of horses. These exciting stories filled the long lonely winter evenings we spent without our parents.

On weekends Qingping and I were very happy to see Mom. On each visit she taught us a Tang-dynasty poem. We memorized it and recited it for her the following weekend. She also gave us some responsibility for managing our own lives. For example, every weekend she gave us seven candies each, to last the entire week. I usually ate all my candies by Wednesday, leaving me to crave the candies my disciplined brother had saved for the rest of the week.

After school I continued to play on what were now the museum grounds. Through the window I looked into our former living room, now for museum visitors only. I pictured myself and Qingping crawling through the wooden arms of three old black couches lined up in the living room. I imagined our laughter echoing in the house as in the old days. The familiar furniture and artworks remained as they were at the moment of Father's departure. But now the large desk on which Father, early in the mornings, used to reply to letters from art students was empty. The reclining chair covered with Father's old blanket seemed to be waiting for its owner. On the wall hung Father's richly-colored oil study from *Allegory of Fertility* by Flemish painter Jacob Jordaens. Terra-cotta figures from Chinese archaeological digs remained in the glass display case together with a huge abalone shell reflecting colorful hues from the sunlight.

The courtyard where Father and our family had spent so many lovely summer evenings became desolate at night. The dark windows in the surrounding rooms looked like lonely melancholy eyes. Numerous magpies occupied the large tree of heaven. Its many long branches cast a shadowy web across the courtyard.

Whenever I walked there at night, flocks of startled magpies took to the sky. Their agitation often frightened me.

Soon after Father passed away, I encountered a piano for the first time, in the living room of one of my mother's friends. Trying the keyboard with my tiny fingers, I was so fascinated with the instrument that I immediately asked Mom for piano lessons. A supportive mother, she bought me a second-hand German upright piano, a luxury considering our crude living space. Soon Qingping and I were both taking piano lessons twice a week from a pianist working at the China National Theater for Children near our house.

As a child I once asked my mother, "Mama, can Daddy come back to life?" Although he never did, his shadows followed me everywhere around the house. Father's three-foot-tall photo hung in our living room near the piano. It looked exactly like him just before he passed away, with his grey hair and kind smile. When I practiced the piano, I felt as if he were watching over me, and thought I saw his eyes and eyebrows moving slightly, as if he enjoyed my piano playing.

Xu Beihong (left), my brother Xu Qingping, and myself in our house at 16 East Shoulu Street, Beijing, 1949. Paper strips on the windows helped prevent the panes from shattering when the People's Liberation Army besieged the city.

Xu Beihong (right) with his wife Liao Jingwen and their son Xu Qingping and daughter Xu Fangfang in the house at 16 East Shoulu Street, Beijing, 1953.

Liao Jingwen and Xu Fangfang in their small storage-room home at 16 East Shoulu Street, Beijing, 1954. A portrait photo of Xu Beihong is in the background.

Xu Fangfang, Xu Qingping, and Shenpo (Grandaunt) at the moon gate, with the east yard in the background, at 16 East Shoulu Street, Beijing, 1955.

Xu Beihong's living room at 16 East Shoulu Street, Beijing, 1954. On the wall is a couplet by Lu Xun rendered in Xu Beihong's calligraphy. It reads: "Fierce-browed, I firmly defy a thousand pointing fingers; head bowed, like a willing ox, I serve the young."

Xu Fangfang wearing a Young Pioneer's red scarf, Beijing, 1957.

The east yard at 16 East Shoulu Street, Beijing, with its entrance to Xu Beihong's former residence, late 1950s.

Exhibition gallery in the new courtyard of the Xu Beihong Memorial Museum seen through the new moon gate at 16 East Shoulu Street, Beijing, late 1950s.

Xu Fangfang (third from left), her piano teacher, and classmates in the front yard of the Central Conservatory of Music, Beijing, 1960.

Xu Fangfang in 1960. An additional framed print of this portrait was broken by Red Guards during their raid on the family's house in August 1966.

CHAPTER 5

Small Waves on the Sandy Beach

Mom's oldest sister, my first aunt, Liao Xueqi, invited us to spend the summer of 1955 with her family in the beautiful beach resort city of Dalian. This was the first time Mom planned for our family to travel to another city. Qingping and I could hardly wait for summer vacation to begin.

Mom bought three seats in the economy sleeping car. Four years before, Father had refused to take the soft sleeping car CAFA had purchased for him to travel to the water control construction site in Shandong Province. For Mom, this trip was an opportunity to leave behind her sad memories for a while. Qingping and I were happy about leaving our three-room home. A seven-year-old girl with two pigtails, I sat near the window of the train, wearing a white dress with a flowered hem which Mom had made for me. Qingping wore light-blue shorts and a white shirt. We were curious to see the buildings, trees, ponds, and grain fields rushing past the train window.

As the train was chugging along, we started talking to fellow passengers and hit it off with two PLA officers seated next to us. One, named Huang, was a tall, handsome, well-built man of twenty-seven. I shared my illustrated story books with him, and he told interesting stories to Qingping and me and played cards with us. Soon we called him "Uncle Huang." Time seemed to pass quickly before night fell.

Because Mom had bought three bottom-level seats, it was hard for her to watch both Qingping and me at night. In the end, Mom and I squeezed into one bed and Qingping had to sleep on the floor between the two seats. Uncle Huang laid his army raincoat on the floor to make a cleaner bed for Qingping.

Early the next morning, Uncle Huang prepared to get off the train at Jinzhou where his army unit was stationed. He came to Mom and politely introduced himself. We must have told him about Father during our conversation the night before. Uncle Huang expressed to Mom his respect for Xu Beihong. Before leaving, he spent a few minutes writing a note, raising his head from his writing a couple of times, smiling at me as I sat in front of him. After he finished, he folded the note and told me not to open it until I got to Dalian. Qingping and I felt sad to see him go.

The train seemed to have hastened its pace pulling into Dalian. First Aunt Liao Xueqi and Uncle Liao Yunzhang had brought their little daughter, Xiaoqi, to meet us on the platform. Mom and First Aunt fell tearfully into each other's arms. Mom had not seen her since Father had died. We rode in an open horse-drawn carriage to my aunt's house. While the horse trotted along, I watched the buildings slowly pass by in the glorious afternoon sun. The city of Dalian was very neat with wide streets. Many tall buildings showed Russian influence.

First Aunt Liao Xueqi was a high-school teacher, and my uncle, Liao Yunzhang, was a high-level engineer in a large factory. They lived in a single-story two-bedroom apartment. A large upper shelf of their big closet became Qingping's bed, and Mom and I shared my aunt's bedroom. Outside of their house was a large open space with a ping-pong table. Uncle Liao Yunzhang enjoyed playing ping-pong after work.

First Aunt quickly cooked a delicious dinner for us on a gas-fueled stove, something new to me. With the flip of the switch, a blue flame magically appeared. Mom and I envied their convenient gas stove with gas supplied locally via pipes, while all residents of Beijing in the 1950s still used coal stoves.

In the evening after our arrival, First Aunt took us to Qiulin Company, a famous department store where we enjoyed ice cream in the store restaurant. In contrast to Beijing where temperatures could reach one hundred degrees, the cool breeze from the ocean in Dalian made the summer nights comfortable.

That evening I opened the note Uncle Huang had given me. He wrote that he had enjoyed spending time with Qingping and me, gave his address, and asked Qingping and me to write to him. Although I had yet to enter first grade, I proudly wrote my first letter. I told him about my visit to Qiulin Company in Dalian and my tour of its basement, including Mom's remark that workers dug out rat nests to make the basement. Later I found out that Mom had fabricated the rat story to incite my imagination.

The first Sunday after we arrived at Dalian, Uncle Huang appeared unexpectedly at my aunt's door with his usual smile. Qingping and I were very happy to see him. Then he offered to teach us to swim in the ocean. Mom,

First Aunt, and her husband also came along. They rented a sun umbrella and recliners, and sat on the beach the whole afternoon.

The beach was filled with many families, some bringing a basket of snacks and a mat. Although fascinated with the ocean, I was nervous about getting into the water. Uncle Huang was very patient with us. Under his guidance, we learned some simple movements of the breast stroke. We had so much fun that afternoon that Mom let us stay until it was almost dark.

During our month in Dalian, Uncle Huang came every Sunday to take Qingping and me to the beach. That month flew past, our laughter mixing with ocean waves. The morning of the day we were to leave Dalian, Uncle Huang showed up unexpectedly. First Aunt looked apprehensive. But Qingping and I went running over to him. While we were packing, he diligently polished all our shoes. He said that he was going on a business trip and would take the same train to Haiyu on the way.

First Aunt and my cousin, Xiaoqi, held their tears saying good-bye to us at the train station. Mom looked sad. She did not know when she and her sister would see each other again; in fact it would be thirteen years.

On the train, Uncle Huang played games with Qingping and me. Meanwhile, Mom ran into a young female graduate of CAFA who worked for the Navy. Mom looked a little uneasy introducing Huang and her two children to this female artist. She worried about gossip. When the train approached Haiyu, Uncle Huang straightened his uniform and put on his cap. After saying good-bye to us, he turned to Mom and gave her a warm handshake.

From what I observed, Mom maintained her distance. She showed appreciation that Huang had spent time with her children and made our summer vacation more enjoyable.

Uncle Huang continued to write to Qingping and me. He also wrote to Mom frequently. The following spring, he came to Beijing on business. He brought Qingping a soccer ball and gave me a BB gun. I learned to use this exciting new toy to shoot sparrows in our yard. Qingping and I were as happy as if it were Chinese New Year. At a park with a lake the three of us went rowing in a boat he rented. However, Mom never came along on these outings. She was building a wall between Huang and herself, fearing possible gossip about Xu Beihong's widow.

After Uncle Huang's visit to Beijing in 1956, he wrote Mom a love letter. He also expressed deep affection for our whole family. But Mom told him that her love for Beihong was such that she could not love anyone else. If he had developed any feelings for her, he should bury them quickly and not think back, she said. She expressed gratitude for his friendship with her children. Yet after receiving Mom's letter, Uncle Huang took his next vacation in Beijing in order to see us.

He took Qingping and me to Beihai Park to ice skate. I had never skated on ice. He rented a small ice sleigh with a high back, which functioned as a walker. Leaning on the sleigh, I gradually learned to balance on the skate blades. That day I learned to skate.

While Qingping and I were at school, Uncle Huang visited Mom in our three-small-room house. Huddling around the metal stove, he said that he had never loved anyone before and his heart was for her only. Mom said to him, "I am tired of hearing this and do not wish to hear these statements any more. I hope that you will go back to your army unit quickly." Uncle Huang left, discouraged. After that, there was little correspondence between them for a long time.

In summer 1956, we stayed at the Ministry of Culture retreat cabin in Beidaihe, about 180 miles east of Beijing on the northern coast of the Bohai Bay. This small town, with no tourism infrastructure, supported retreat facilities reserved for Party and government leaders and privileged intellectuals and artists. Qian Junrui, vice minister of the Ministry of Culture, and his wife shared the retreat cabin with us. The other guests included Zhang Guangyu, a well-known Chinese ink brush painter. Father had collected one of his paintings, *Affair of the Purple Stone Street,* vividly depicting a flirtatious Pan Jinlian peeking at a man named Ximen Qing from behind a half-opened curtain. Zhang Guangyu was a short old man who liked to joke with me. I remember that his striped pajama pants hung below the cuffs of his dress pants.

All the guests staying there ate meals together sitting around a big table in the dining hall. I most enjoyed eating fresh ocean crabs. Finally at age eight, I learned to eat the "bugs" Mom had always reserved for Father.

There was no running water in our retreat cabin. It was in Beidaihe that Mom taught me how to hand-wash my own clothes.

A few faculty members from CAFA stayed at another retreat cabin: anatomy drawing teacher Wen Jinyang, and oil painting department chair Feng Fasi, an accomplished oil painter. Both had been Father's students. My father had exchanged one of his own ink brush paintings for an oil still life by Wen Jinyang. These artists often enjoyed the beach with us.

After my initial fear of water, I was beginning to like swimming. A CAFA teacher taught Mom to float on her back with her arms stretched out. Soon she was able to do the backstroke. The ocean always fascinated me. Sometimes it acted like an angry lion when the storm raised heavy waves that relentlessly pounded the beach. At other times the ocean was peaceful, glimmering like a huge stretch of floating silk fabric. Small waves gently washed the sandy beach in a slow rhythm. Looking across the ocean to where the water joined the sky, I always wondered what the world on the other side of the ocean was like.

Beidaihe at that time was an underdeveloped small town. I do not remember seeing any restaurants there. We ate boiled corn on the cob sold by peddlers on the beach. Donkeys provided transportation. One day Mom, Qingping, and I, wanting to visit a friend on the other side of town, rented three donkeys to ride. Curious about the donkey, never having ridden one, I touched its tail. Surprisingly it kicked my lower leg hard with its rear hoof. That really hurt. But the donkey rides were comfortable because the owner led the donkey, holding the reins all the way. Mom rode ahead of us wearing a tight-fitting traditional Chinese robe with a striking black and white pattern, with slits up to her knees, and high heels. She perched on the donkey holding a sun umbrella. Qingping and I wore T-shirts and shorts. Riding with her I felt a little embarrassed. Our procession of donkeys amused the local people.

The town's only theater was called the Cultural Theater. We attended singing and dancing performances there, and I practiced on its piano each morning. One night as Mom, Qingping, and I watched a performance, there was a commotion in the back rows. I saw Premier Zhou Enlai walking towards us. He sat down in the same row with us, greeting Mom and the people around him with a smile. Premier Zhou Enlai's demeanor was modest and that impressed me.

I was the only child performer invited to play a piano solo at one performance. Even though I played only elementary-level pieces, the local newspaper praised my talent, identifying me as the eight-year-old daughter of the famous Chinese artist Xu Beihong. I met a teenage girl from the Prep Music High School. The school's full name was Preparatory Music High School affiliated to the Central Conservatory of Music. She also practiced the piano at the Cultural Theater that summer. I really envied her advanced techniques. I dreamed about someday attending the same school she did.

CHAPTER 6

Whatever It Might Take

Father once told Mom, "My father was a painter, and so am I. I hope one of my children will grow up to become a painter."[30] He added, "But it's not easy to become a painter of real capability instead of one with an empty reputation! One must persistently make great efforts to study and improve and must also have great willpower. . . ."[31] At another time he said, "If I pamper my children, then I cannot expect them to become painters."

Qingping and I did not have formal drawing lessons in early childhood. But we each had a stone slab with a wooden frame on which we drew with a white stone pen. This stone slab was erasable, so new drawings could be made. Father often drew an airplane or a cat on our stone slabs. We would turn the slab over and try to imitate his drawings on its other side.

Father began our serious art lessons with calligraphy. He had us practice ink brush calligraphy daily by copying reproductions of work by a sixth-century Northern Wei master calligrapher, Zhang Menglong.[32] Every evening after work, Father evaluated our calligraphy homework. To encourage us, he marked one to three red circles with ink brush around the characters, indicating the good to excellent ones. Very often I got one or two red circles. I continued into my teenage years with this calligraphy practice and felt rewarded.

Encouraged by my parents and surrounded by Father's works in the museum, I enjoyed my daily drawing, and painted landscapes in watercolor. I also did watercolor illustrations for a children's story, *Little Cat Fishing*, which our kindergarten teachers made into a slide show. Every day after school I walked through the museum's exhibition rooms, selecting paintings by Father to copy. His Chinese ink brush painting of water buffalo was my favorite. I would draw in pencil and then embellish it with watercolor. When attending

Beijing Huiwen No. 1 Primary School, Qingping and I took formal art lessons in the after-school program run by the Central Academy of Fine Arts. One summer we took sketching and watercolor from Qian Shaowu, Father's former student and a CAFA sculpture teacher, who had solid sketching skills.

Because playing the piano and drawing occupied a lot of my spare time, I asked Mom: "What will my classmates do when they grow up if they are not going to be painters and musicians?" Mom laughed.

It had been a year since I heard the teenage piano student from the Prep Music High School play at the Cultural Theater in Beidaihe. My first impression of a professional-quality piano performance sparked my dream at age nine to study piano performance and to play as well as the students from the music school. Fortunately an opportunity came for me to apply to the Preparatory Music Elementary School affiliated to the Central Conservatory of Music in Tianjin.

China followed the Soviet model of rigorous training to raise its music performance to a higher level. Piano, string, and some other Western instrument performance majors require years of professional training starting at a very young age. For that reason, the Prep Music Elementary School was established to provide music performance education for children starting in third grade. The goal was to develop pianists and Western string instrument performers who could win international competitions. The Prep Music Elementary School expanded their recruitment in 1957 to include students from Beijing for the first time.

CCOM's newly structured professional-music education system was complicated. Recruited elementary-school students were educated with the goal of entering the Prep Music High School. Graduation from the Prep Music Elementary School did not guarantee admission to the high school; the Prep Music High School faculty decided who would be admitted.

The music school was formally named in 1957 Preparatory Music High School affiliated to the Central Conservatory of Music. It was a six-year, full-time boarding school, covering the equivalent of seventh through twelfth grade. The program prepared students to enter the highly selective CCOM, the college music program. Advancement to CCOM was determined by the CCOM faculty.

The Central Conservatory of Music, established in 1950, was one of the best conservatories in China. Some older faculty members of CCOM had studied with European teachers in old China. In the 1950s, Soviet voice, piano, and violin professors, a German trumpet professor, and experts from other Eastern

European socialist countries taught CCOM students and young teachers. They systematically taught Western European classical music, Russian classical music, and Soviet contemporary music, providing technical training, artistic understanding, and theoretical analysis. The Soviet experts helped establish the school's teaching programs and standards based on a Western classical music curriculum, an important factor making CCOM the prestigious school it is today. CCOM students won numerous national and international awards.

By summer 1957, age nine, I had taken piano lessons for more than three years. I really enjoyed playing classical music. However, my piano studies were not serious and professional. When Qingping and I first started lessons, we were required to practice for only half an hour daily. I remember Qingping practicing the piano, his eyes fixed on an alarm clock on the piano's top, set for thirty minutes, while his friends ran around our living room.

I had dreamed about attending the Prep Music High School since the summer in Beidaihe. But preparing for the audition meant changing my attitude. My piano teacher, Ma, required me to play my audition etudes and sonatas according to professional standards. My practice time increased from half an hour to two hours daily, but I had problems with self-discipline and patience. Mom was very supportive of my interest in music but seldom supervised my practice. Passing the audition became my responsibility. One time after making repeated mistakes, I angrily came down hard on the keyboard with my right foot, breaking a hammer action stick.

During our 1957 summer vacation at the beach resort city of Qingdao, I continued daily practice. A CCOM teacher happened to share with us the same Ministry of Culture retreat facility. After hearing me play, he said that I was not likely to be admitted. This motivated me to work even harder. I said to myself, "I must prove to that teacher that I could get in." I had developed self-confidence, thanks to my mother.

The Prep Music Elementary School audition in the fall of 1957 was held on the campus of the China National Theater for Children in Beijing. By then, my piano performance was much improved. I played my audition pieces with confidence, and believed that I did well on my *solfeggio* (sight-singing and ear-training) tests. I made it to the final few in the last round of selection. However, the other candidates were very competitive. Most had received several years of professional music training from their parents, who were professional musicians or music teachers.

When interviewed by Teacher Ling, the examiner from CCOM, my mother said my musical talent had arisen from a family without musicians. She said that scoring comparably with candidates from professional music families showed that I had more motivation and potential. I believe that my mother's remark played a role in the school's final decision.

When I got my admission notice, I felt honored to be one of the only five children from Beijing admitted to this prestigious music school. But Tianjin was two hours away by train, and I would have to live at school and could come home only during winter and summer vacations. I felt sad about leaving my family and school friends as well as giving up my drawing and painting lessons. At age nine, having never left home, I would now have to live independently.

CCOM had arranged for the five students from Beijing to study general-subject courses such as Chinese and math at the Tianjin Experimental Primary School, a prep school with some boarding facilities. Most students there were not music students. Many came from well-to-do families including those of overseas Chinese and some Chinese Communist Party cadres in Tianjin or other cities.

My step-brother, Boyang, took me to Tianjin by train in the fall of 1957 and helped me settle in, because Mom had to attend the Third National Women's Congress as a delegate. It was my first trip to Tianjin. There were many Western-style buildings, and people on the street spoke a rough Tianjin dialect very different from the standard Chinese spoken in Beijing. The school appeared huge compared with Beijing Huiwen No. 1 Primary School. The campus looked bare, with few trees. In a small yard on one end of the campus, away from the classrooms, was our dormitory. I was assigned to a room in which more than twenty girls slept on iron bunk beds. I climbed onto one of the upper beds, which would be my home for that year.

Life at school was very structured with stringent rules. To ensure student safety, we were basically confined within the campus compound for the semester. Local kids were picked up by their parents on weekends. Students like me, from other cities, were not allowed to leave the walled campus except with special permission and an escort. Guards at the entrance kept track of all the students with bamboo name cards they placed on a wall.

Taking care of myself was my biggest challenge. The bell rang at six every morning and after a few minutes to get dressed and comb our hair, we hurried out to stand in formation on the playground to do morning exercises. At first I was scolded for arriving late to morning exercises because I had problems doing my hair. At home, Shenpo had helped me braid it into two pigtails. In Tianjin, when I tried to braid my own hair, ugly twisted pigtails dangled over my ears instead of neatly on the back of my head.

The cafeteria repeatedly served the same *mantou* (Chinese steamed bun), millet porridge in a huge wooden bucket, and cabbage with some ground pork. Instead of being picky about this food, I had to stuff myself because there were no snacks. Candies would be hard to come by.

When most students went home to spend their weekends with their parents, I felt homesick, roaming around the huge playground by myself or with the few remaining out-of-town students. I hid under the bedcover and cried.

At first, Mom visited me every other weekend. We stayed in a hotel where she washed my hair and rubbed my fingers, cracked in northern China's dry climate, with hand cream. I felt the love and warmth from Mom who shared a double bed with me. She took me to eat Western food in Qishilin, the only fancy restaurant in Tianjin serving Western-style food. I particularly enjoyed their ice cream with chocolate topping. When Mom left me at the school entrance on Sunday evening, I cried. Later, my teacher who had dorm responsibilities told me I should not cry. Therefore at the end of Mom's next visit, I bit my lips and withheld my tears.

Although homesick, I liked my piano lessons and the music program for the Prep Music Elementary School students. Conservatory teachers came to the Tianjin Experimental Primary School to give us our performance major lessons twice a week, and we also had a regular *solfeggio* course and recitals. The primary school had recently built several practice rooms for us near the school entrance, and equipped a few nearby classrooms with upright pianos. This corner of the campus became our "little music school."

My first piano teacher, Lou, was a serious teacher, writing comments in my lesson book and grading my progress after each lesson. My grades were not very good in the beginning, and I was not Teacher Lou's favorite student. Because I had not learned to play the piano professionally in the previous three and a half years, I needed to correct my method. The other two girl piano students from Beijing appeared more advanced in technical training; their mothers were both on the CCOM faculty. I envied these girls. At my first recital, I heard a student comment, "Do you know that she has studied the piano for more than three years, and what a simple piece she is playing!" I was embarrassed. A red-faced piano student from Tianjin claimed she could play *Für Elise* after studying piano for only ten months. I wished I could play that piece which seemed so glamorous with its fast running notes at the end.

There were two boy students from Beijing, both violin majors. Sun, a beginner, seldom practiced. When his teacher arrived for his lesson, Sun's violin case was always covered with dust. I heard that his mother was a schoolteacher in Beijing. The other boy, Chang, had a beautiful Japanese mother, and his Chinese father worked as a scientist for the Chinese Academy of Sciences. They had just returned to China from Japan. Chang looked like a pretty Japanese doll with bangs covering his forehead and slanting eyes with long lashes. He had taken violin lessons for some years and was a very capable violin student.

In spite of the pressure from competition, we music students enjoyed playing games together at our "little music school." In the small yard outside the practice rooms, the two boys and I acted out episodes from a movie our school had taken us to see, *Secret Detective from Guangzhou*. When we played a running game, Chang counted in Japanese the numbers one through five. "Why don't you learn to count in Chinese?" I said. He retorted, raising his pretty eyes, "Can't you recognize the five numbers in Japanese? There is no difference. Let's play!" His roommates were not as tolerant; at the dorm they beat him for defending Japan's invasion of China. He had argued that Japan was so small and the earthquakes and volcanoes destroyed so much land that the Japanese people had to come to China to get more land to live. Because of his difficulties adjusting to the norms in the primary school, he was not allowed to join the Young Pioneers in third grade. Most of my schoolmates and I were already members.

The Young Pioneers of China was a mass organization for children ages nine to fourteen, established by the CCP and run by the Communist Youth League of China. New members pledged their love for the Chinese Communist Party, for the motherland and the people, and pledged to study well, exercise well, and prepare to contribute to the communist cause. At a formal initiation, established members tied red scarves on the new members. We wore our red scarves all the time.

Many children in the 1950s joined the Young Pioneers for the honor. Some did not quite understand the purpose of the organization but followed their friends. We went on outings and collected scrap metal for the steel-smelting plants during the Great Leap Forward. I was elected by my peers and approved by adult authorities to be a medium-detachment leader in the Tianjin

Experimental Primary School. My badge had two red horizontal bars and I proudly pinned it to my upper sleeve.

A couple of months after I entered the music school, Mom stopped visiting me on weekends because she twisted her ankle running to catch the train back to Beijing. I finally got used to school life on my own. Another piano student and I learned a piano duet adapted from the theme song of the popular movie *The Red Kids*. We were asked to record this duet for the Tianjin Radio Station, and our teachers and friends heard it on the radio.

All the music students could take occasional lessons from Soviet experts who had one- or two-year teaching assignments at the Central Conservatory of Music. I remember taking buses, escorted by a primary-school staff member, to these lessons in the evenings. The Soviet experts once invited the Prep Music Elementary School students to a party at their beautiful house with a yard. It was a sunny morning in the spring and their house bustled with many music students and CCOM teachers. I played on their swing set and enjoyed roasted peanuts. We had our group photo taken at the party with an older Soviet piano teacher whom we called Expert Mama. I had seen her at several of our recitals. She was tall with grey hair and smiling eyes.

In my first semester, I was still not very disciplined, particularly in practicing scales and other technical training. But two events in the spring of 1958 made me change my attitude. The music school took all its students to a theater to see a Soviet movie about a musical child prodigy, a war orphan who developed into a fine young pianist with the help of a conservatory conducting professor. For days afterward, the two Beijing piano students and I talked about the boy in the movie and dreamed about becoming a soloist just like him, playing with an orchestra *Piano Concerto No. 3* by Soviet composer Dmitri Kabalevsky.

The audition for the Prep Music Elementary School's first recital in the CCOM auditorium was coming up. All the music students could audition for solo spots. I really wanted to play a piano solo at this recital. I told myself that I had to make it, whatever that might take, and it was primarily my own responsibility. I started paying attention to my piano teacher's instructions and practiced seriously even on weekends, working on *Funny Piece* by Kabalevsky. I felt that I finally found my musical expression for this piece. At the audition I tried to concentrate and let the playfulness of the piece flow through my fingers. The main judge, a female Soviet professor, smiled at me and said "Very good" in Russian. I smiled back, because I understood the words before piano teacher Chen translated them; I had taken private Russian-language lessons in Beijing from a lady who had grown up in Russia.

I was overjoyed to hear that I was selected to be one of the few piano soloists at the recital. On a beautiful Sunday afternoon in May, the stage of the CCOM auditorium was decorated with flowers, and the shining black grand piano there seemed to be expecting me, like a sleek black racehorse eager for his rider.

Mom had made me a new pink dress with small white dots. She was among the proud parents in the audience. The several hundred seats in the auditorium were packed with CCOM teachers, students, and friends. The Soviet experts sat in the front rows. Our repertoire featured many pieces by contemporary Soviet composers.

My first professional solo performance was exhilarating. I entered, bowed to the audience, and smiled at several familiar faces. The grand piano was much more sensitive to my rendering of the playful Kabalevsky piece, and the auditorium acoustics made the clarity of my running notes much better. How excited I was when I finished to loud applause!

Later all the students who played works by Kabalevsky at the recital made a studio recording of their performances, and I was told that this recording was mailed to Kabalevsky in the Soviet Union as a gift.

At this first recital my eyes and ears were opened to the quality of the advanced students' solos, and I was also deeply impressed by an eight-hand duet played by two girls and two boys on two grand pianos. I had heard them play during our dress rehearsals. One of the boys was named Bo Libei, the pronunciation of which sounded like "glass cup" in Chinese, hence his nickname. When he tried to use the pedal, Glass Cup often stepped on the toes of the girl playing next to him. She screamed, "Ouch, it hurts!" The duet they played was adapted from a section in Prokofiev's *Symphony No. 1, "Classical."* The piece's grandeur so lifted my spirit that the music stayed with me for years.

Xu Xin, a college conducting student who later became famous, conducted the children's chorus at the recital. We sang a light-hearted Soviet piece about planting trees at a summer camp. Teacher Xu made our young voices blend into beautiful harmony, the auditorium filling with gentle waves of melody. I fell in love with chorus, which I pursued for the next eight years throughout my music schooling.

This recital opened a window to a wonderful music world with many new musical experiences and a rich selection of pieces to explore. It also offered new music partners to meet and play ensembles with, and the intriguing possibility of a future performance career for me.

During my second year at the Prep Music Elementary School, CCOM moved its campus to Beijing. Some faculty members and students whose families lived in Tianjin remained there to join the newly formed Tianjin Conservatory of Music. The five music students from Beijing were to move with CCOM to Beijing.

I was happy about returning to my hometown, but would miss the classmates and teachers I felt close to. My new piano teacher, Huang, a tall lady with delicate facial features, was a very positive teacher who rewarded my improvements with better grades. I could tell immediately that she liked me. With her encouragement I made notable progress in my piano studies. One incident touched my heart deeply. In summer, Teacher Huang fell ill and had surgery. While recovering, she was not able to come across town to my school, so I took the bus to her house for my lessons instead. She insisted on reimbursing me for bus fare. I held the coins she gave me in my hand all the way back to my school. The few coins became warm, and my heart felt warm too. Years later when I became a music professor in a university, one of my goals was to be a caring teacher. I will always remember the kindness Teacher Huang showed me, a ten-year-old piano student.

The Tianjin primary-school teachers helped the five of us pack our belongings. Because Mom could not come to Tianjin to help me pack, I forgot some of my clothes. I felt upset about leaving behind a green woolen jacket Mom had made and had altered as I grew taller. In Beijing, CCOM arranged for us to complete our general-subject courses for that academic year at Beijing No. 2 Experimental Primary School, a prep school in the West City District, close to CCOM.

As a music student, I was required to live in the dormitory, but I could now go home every weekend and enjoy extra time with Mom, Qingping, Shenpo, and my other relatives.

• • •

More than fifty students, all fifth-graders in 1959, made up the first full-time class of the Preparatory Music Elementary School, a boarding school established on the CCOM campus. The majors were expanded to include Chinese instruments in addition to piano and Western string instruments.

I was very happy to be among a large group of peers sharing my love of music, although most of them were starting from scratch. By comparison, the few of us from the music school in Tianjin were advanced.

Before 1966, the combined student headcount at CCOM, in the Prep Music High School, and Prep Music Elementary School was only around a few hundred. This allowed almost all students from elementary school through college to know each other and form lasting friendships between students and teachers. A few classmates and I made friends with some CCOM conducting students, who acted as our big brothers and sisters. We often visited their dorms and studios. I sometimes imitated their conducting gestures holding a baton while looking in the mirror.

The CCOM campus was once the palace of the last emperor Pu Yi's grandfather. Two grand buildings on opposite sides of the school's front yard had Forbidden City-style tile roofs and decorative motifs. In 1960 one of these buildings became a colorful entrance to the new 999-seat auditorium, said to have the best acoustics in Beijing. Our classroom was nearby. We heard many senior conservatory students' and young musicians' recitals, and auditions for international competitions. I was most impressed with Liu Shikun and Yin Chengzong, Chinese top winners at the International Tchaikovsky Competition in 1958 and 1962, respectively. These young musicians became our role models.

Chen, a very dedicated piano teacher, taught me from the fourth through sixth grades. Teacher Chen was able to uncover my capacity for musical expressiveness, particularly in the rendering of lyrical pieces. At the final exam in the fall semester of fifth grade, I played the first movement of Beethoven's *Sonata No. 19 in G minor, Op. 49, No. 1.* To my surprise, Expert Mama, the Soviet piano teacher, showed up at this final exam, held in one of the CCOM studios. Having missed her for a year because of our move, I was glad for the opportunity to play for her. Fortunately, I was well prepared. She must have noticed the change in me. After all the piano students finished their final exam pieces, Expert Mama got up and gave her comments in Russian. I heard her mention "Fangfang," and nothing could have delighted me more than her praise for my progress. My grade was 5 minus, the top grade for the piano majors. I heard that no one was ever given the full 5 points.

Teacher Chen's husband, Zhu Gongyi, one of the best piano teachers at CCOM, was respectfully called by the students "Mr. Zhu." In the late 1940s, as president of the Beiping Arts College, Father had established the music department there, and Zhu Gongyi had been on its faculty. Although in 1960 Mr. Zhu taught only CCOM college students, Teacher Chen asked him to give me occasional lessons. I remember playing a complicated Chinese piano piece, the *Tea Leaf Picking Song*, for him. He worked with me on the rendering of that piece and opened my eyes to the many musical expressions embodied in its composition. After his lessons, my performances became much more colorful and meaningful.

One morning in the fall of 1960, walking by the fountain in CCOM's front yard, I met Expert Mama, wearing her usual long woolen dress, her eyes still smiling.

Teachers in China did not formally greet their students, so she did not greet me but said, "I am returning to the Soviet Union."

I said, "Hello, Expert Mama," giving her a respectful Young Pioneer salute. Touched by the warmth I saw in her face, I felt very sad that we would have to part.

"It's good we met," she said. "I leave tomorrow."

I could convey my emotions only with the sadness in my eyes. I had read in the newspaper about ideological differences between the Chinese Communist Party and the Soviet Communist Party, headed by Nikita Khrushchev. The former called the latter revisionists. Chairman Mao resisted Soviet attempts at political control over China. Khrushchev then withdrew all Soviet technical experts who were helping China in industrial, educational, and other fields. Chairman Mao responded by announcing the policy of self-reliance and hard struggle.

I said silently, "Dear Expert Mama, thank you so much for teaching me and encouraging me. You watched me grow into a mature piano student in the past three years. I will never forget what you have done for me."

In spite of the political sensitivity, and although such intimate behavior was not to be seen in public in Chinese culture at the time, Expert Mama hugged me while I shyly looked away hiding tears. I felt the warmth as her arms held my thin shoulders in my purple corduroy jacket. Although I never saw her again, I will remember her and our farewell forever.

CHAPTER 7
"I Will Love Him Forever"

While at Peking University, Mom struggled to focus on her studies. Going back to school as a thirty-year-old mother of two was not easy. She worried about Qingping and me all the time. When we fell sick, she rushed home to care for us. She still grieved her husband's death. On weekends she took Qingping and me to visit Zhongshan Park on a tricycle rickshaw, but we all missed the joy we had felt when Father had gone with us. Two years after Father died, Mom took us to an art exhibition there. Several artists, including some of Father's students, were drawing portraits on site. She broke down in tears when she told me, "Your father should be here drawing portraits on these occasions. It would be so natural for him to be here." Her pain was so great that we had to leave after only a short while.

Fortunately, Mom had a great interest in literature and was eager to learn from famous Chinese literature professors at Peking University. She spent all her evenings reading great literature, including famous biographies, in the university library. One of her goals was someday to write my father's biography.

Mom tried to adjust to living in a dorm with half a dozen roommates during the week and eating in a huge dining hall feeding several thousand students. She made new friends, some of whom I came to know. Lulu, a joyful, athletic young woman from Shanghai, had won second place in a national tennis match in the 1950s. With her strong arms, Lulu could elbow her way through the dining-hall crowd to help Mom get her rice.

Immediately after supper, Lulu and Mom always went to the library and put their school bags on empty seats in order to hold them for later in the evening. Then Lulu and Mom often walked around Weiming Lake (Lake with No Name) on the Peking University campus before returning to the library to study. One evening after supper as they strolled through the woods surrounding the lake, dense foliage cast long shadows on the glimmering water. A pagoda behind the trees was bathed in the setting sun.

Glancing at the gentle ripples across the green lake, they talked about the future.

"You are still young," said Lulu. "Do you plan to remarry someday?"

"I will never remarry," Mom answered. "I fell in love with Beihong at age nineteen. I gave my most innocent and sincere love to him. This is a love that is ingrained in my bones and heart. I will not possibly love anyone else." Then she quoted a saying: "'Having experienced a vast ocean, one is hardly satisfied with a small pond.' Beihong is so deep and vast, just like the ocean, with no boundaries. I will love him forever."

During the Peking University's winter break in 1956, Mom visited Xu Beihong's hometown, Jitingqiao, in Yixing County, Jiangsu Province. He had said to her, "The southern China countryside abundant with rivers and lakes is so beautiful. You will like it." But he died just before their planned trip.

During her visit to the Xu family house, Mom stayed in the bedroom in which Xu Beihong had been born. Looking out through the intersecting slats of the window at the soft moonlight cast over quiet fields, she imagined Beihong walking towards her.

Despite her loneliness, Mom felt warmed by the company of Xu Beihong's many childhood friends and his relatives, including Pan Xiangyuan, husband of Xu Beihong's second sister. Mom collected stories from them for Xu Beihong's biography. Uncle Pan Xiangyuan kindly gave Mom keepsakes his family had collected concerning Xu Beihong. She tried to locate Chinese ink brush paintings young Xu Beihong had done while in Jitingqiao. With the Yixing County cultural department's help, some local people brought some of these paintings to her. She paid more than thirty *yuan* apiece for them. The price might seem low by today's standards, but it was more than a quarter of Mom's monthly salary.

She later donated to the Xu Beihong Memorial Museum a few paintings collected on that trip. One was *Portrait of the Elders*, a Chinese ink brush full-figure portrait of four elders, showing Xu Beihong's early figure-painting skills.

Mom also visited several of Father's old friends in Nanjing and Shanghai. In Shanghai, she visited Wu Linruo, president of East China College of Physical

Education. While in Chongqing during the War of Resistance against Japan, Xu Beihong had helped Wu with the Chinese ink brush paintings Wu had done in his spare time. Wu had collected quite a number of paintings by Xu Beihong, the best of which was the Chinese brush painting *Wounded Lion* (Fig. 8), done in 1938 at the beginning of the War of Resistance against Japan when China suffered heavy losses. The lion is the symbol of the Chinese nation. In this painting, the wounded lion turns its head, its piercing eyes filled with determination to strike back against the Japanese invasion. Viewing Wu's collection, Mom could not take her eyes off the *Wounded Lion*. She asked Wu, "Could you donate this painting to the Xu Beihong Memorial Museum?" To honor Xu Beihong's friendship with him, he agreed. His wife, Wu Qingxia, a well-known Chinese ink brush painter, painted a copy of the painting to keep. Mom thanked them from her heart for this valuable donation.

She carefully packed with newspaper the paintings acquired on this trip including scrolls and those not mounted, hand-carrying them on the train. Chinese scroll paintings wrapped snugly around a wooden dowel rod are protected from creases. As for the paintings not mounted, the Xuan paper used for Chinese ink brush paintings could be smoothed out when mounted. In the 1950s after her husband's death, Mom also bought Chinese ink brush paintings by Xu Beihong from private collectors in Beijing. These paintings and some of the paintings she had collected in Father's hometown became her private collection.

The most important painting she collected was an oil, *The Poet Chen Sanyuan,* painted in 1929. Chen, one of Xu Beihong's longtime friends, died in 1937 during the Japanese occupation of Beiping while on a hunger strike protesting the Japanese invasion.[33] This portrait had hung in Chen's living room for many years. Father had told Mom about his satisfaction with this portrait. One day in 1956, a man in a cadre uniform came to the museum, carrying an oil painting by Xu Beihong and asking to see Liao Jingwen. Mom was overjoyed to see that he had brought the oil portrait of Chen Sanyuan, in perfect condition. The man asked for 200 *yuan* for the painting. Although this was a lot of money, Mom was so anxious to get the painting that she did not make a counteroffer but bought it on the spot. The painting vividly illuminates this frail poet's quiet intensity. His firm grip on the armchair reflects strong character. His traditional Chinese robe and the thread-bound Chinese book held in his hand suggest his scholarly status. Mom donated the painting to the museum.

Later she told me that she had had a dream the night after acquiring the portrait. In her dream, Beihong hurriedly came home. He caressed her hair and whispered to her in an intimate voice, "Now that the portrait of Chen Sanyuan is in your hands, I no longer have any regrets."

Another important Xu Beihong oil painting, *Honeymoon*, painted in 1925 in Paris, was later lost. In the mid-1950s, one of Xu Beihong's students, Yu Yunjie, discovered it in a sundry goods store in Shanghai, among the groceries. To help the Xu Beihong Memorial Museum in its early days, he bought this oil painting and donated it. Considering the scarcity of Xu Beihong's oil works, *The Poet Chen Sanyuan* and *Honeymoon* were artistically valuable additions to the museum's collection.

CHAPTER 8

The Anti-Rightist Campaign

Chairman Mao initiated the Hundred Flowers campaign in 1956. The supposed objective was "letting a hundred flowers blossom and a hundred schools of thought contend," a policy for promoting progress in the arts and sciences and developing a flourishing socialist culture. In the same year, Soviet leader Nikita Khrushchev's keynote address at the Twentieth Congress of the Communist Party of the Soviet Union had condemned Joseph Stalin's policies and excesses. His speech became the impetus for a series of grassroots movements in Poland and Hungary demanding democratic reforms. Mao believed that the best way to prevent similar happenings in China was to make the Communist rule more lenient.

Then the Hundred Flowers campaign was linked to a rectification campaign launched on May 1, 1957 against bureaucracy, sectarianism, and subjectivism in the Chinese Communist Party. With this campaign, Mao intended to win the support of non-Party intellectuals and the democratic parties.

In response to the CCP's call to air their views fully, some intellectuals and artists publicly criticized the Party leaders in their work units and higher-level bureaucracy. A mere month into the rectification campaign, the criticism against Party leaders and the demands of the democratic parties greatly exceeded what Mao and the CCP Central Committee were willing to tolerate. They decided that the bourgeois intellectuals intended to rebel against the Communist Party, and in June 1957 launched the Anti-Rightist campaign.

For many artists, the Anti-Rightist campaign was their first experience with navigating the new political system in which the Party could unexpectedly and profoundly change its arts policies, bringing devastating consequences to those unable to bend quickly to policy changes.

Jiang Feng, a communist woodcut artist in the 1940s, became the most controversial visual-art leader in the Anti-Rightist campaign. Between 1949 and 1951, he was the key administrator of the National Hangzhou Arts Academy, soon changed to East China campus of CAFA. Based on the Party's directive to popularize the arts to serve the Party's policies, while in Hangzhou Jiang eliminated from the curriculum traditional Chinese bird-and-flower painting and landscape painting, considering them unsuitable for serving the new socialist China. As a result, some flower painting teachers there were not assigned courses to teach.

While Xu Beihong was president of CAFA, in 1951, Jiang Feng became its Party secretary and vice president. Jiang kept Xu Beihong's sketching course for Chinese ink-brush-painting students, advocating that Chinese painting should reform in order to serve the new era. After Xu Beihong died, Jiang became president of CAFA and also the most influential leader in the art bureaucracy.

Although Xu Beihong and Jiang Feng both supported the sketching course for Chinese ink-brush-painting students, Xu Beihong's view on traditional Chinese painting differed from Jiang's. Xu Beihong highly praised the accomplishments of Chinese bird-and-flower painting and landscape painting. In 1950 he had published an article, "Discussion on Fine Art Heritage—Some Chinese Bird-and-Flower Paintings," in *New Construction*, praising Chinese bird-and-flower paintings as the best in the world. In particular he referred to the eleventh- and twelfth-century Northern Song painters as having reached the pinnacle.

In the early 1950s, some CAFA faculty members who could not paint human figures became part-time faculty. Bird-and-flower painting teacher Li Kuchan suffered from his salary reduction and the lack of buyers for his paintings. Li wrote to Mao Zedong in 1950 about his situation. Mao responded with the following letter to Xu Beihong:

> Mr. Beihong:
>
> I received a letter from Mr. Li Kuchan. He claimed that he was a professor of the Academy of Fine Arts and that he had difficulties in life, intending to ask for assistance. Please consider how his situation is and how it should

be dealt with, and let me know what you will do. Wish you the best with your teaching. Enclosed is Li's letter.

Mao Zedong
August 26

Although Xu Beihong had no administrative power to keep Li Kuchan fully employed, he found employment for Li's wife in the academy's clinic as a nurse.

Xu Beihong also tried to help scholars of classical Chinese literature. He was very impressed with Shi Yongmao's writing, *Correction of the Analects of Confucius*. In Xu Beihong's view, Shi's correction gave a new interpretation of the *Analects of Confucius*. On January 13, 1951, Xu Beihong wrote to Mao Zedong, enclosing two books by Shi Yongmao. The next day, Mao wrote the following ink brush letter to Xu Beihong:

Mr. Beihong:

I received your letter of January 13 and the enclosed two books by Mr. Shi Yongmao. I agree with your opinion that Mr. Shi should be given assistance. The best solution is to find a position in the school which you are currently directing. If this is not possible, please take this letter for discussion with the Central Cultural and Educational Committee in order to carefully resolve this issue. This is my response.

Respectfully,

Mao Zedong
January 14

According to a CAFA oil teacher, some well-known traditional Chinese bird-and-flower and landscape painters in the East China campus of CAFA (Hangzhou) had complained in 1956 about Jiang Feng's leadership at their school in 1950. They accused him of having rejected bird-and-flower and landscape painting and not carrying out the Party policy of collaborating with established traditional Chinese painters. Their complaints were reported to Mao Zedong while he was in Hangzhou. By 1956, the Party's policy had shifted to emphasizing Chinese cultural and artistic heritage, including traditional

Chinese painting. Mao asked Jiang to return to the art academy in Hangzhou to perform self-criticism concerning the traditional Chinese painting issue. But Jiang refused to do so, retorting, "My head is not a paper lantern."[34]

In summer 1957, Mom took Qingping and me to Qingdao for vacation. She planned to spend a month there before taking us to visit her father in Hunan. In Qingdao, she read a report in *People's Daily*, CCP's official newspaper, exposing a major rightist in visual arts who rallied some people to speak at a meeting attacking the Party. Mom's name was listed among the speakers. She cut our vacation short and cancelled our trip to Hunan to participate in the Anti-Rightist campaign in Beijing.

Earlier that year some traditional Chinese painting teachers voiced opposition to their students' studying Western sketching from life. They considered this practice destructive to Chinese painting. Jiang Feng supported the sketching course set up by Xu Beihong for Chinese ink-brush-painting students, but Qian Junrui, vice minister of the Ministry of Culture, was against it. By then, the name of the Chinese painting department had been changed to the color-and-ink painting department because traditional Chinese painting was considered inadequate for the task of portraying life in new China. The name change eliminated its nationalistic connotations. According to CAFA oil painting teacher Hou Yimin, Qian Junrui said in his speech in Beijing's Capital Theater, "If CAFA's color-and-ink painting department insists on having their students study Western sketching, I will order the color-and-ink painting department to be eliminated."[35]

Qian's speech angered some CAFA faculty members. The oil painters from the Soviet professor Maksimov's oil-painting training class were the most vocal. They defended Jiang Feng's sketching requirement for Chinese ink-brush-painting students. They also demanded that the government support the creation of oil paintings with revolutionary historical themes, insuring career prospects for oil painters. In response, the Ministry of Culture organized a meeting to hear visual-art-circle opinions.

Most of the major figures from Beijing's visual-art circle showed up at the meeting along with several hundred attendees. Speakers included CAFA faculty members, such as Feng Fasi, my father's former student and an underground Communist Party member during the late 1940s.

According to my mother, Jiang Feng invited her to speak about Xu Beihong's view on the teaching of Chinese (ink brush) painting. She agreed to speak, considering this an academic issue she believed ought to be debated. During her speech, she presented Xu Beihong's reasons for teaching sketching in the Chinese (ink brush) painting program: "Reflecting life with a focus on human activities was the requirement of the era. Landscapes, flowers, birds, and animals should be painted. But human figures should also be painted. Only by drawing human figures well could artists better reflect people's lives."[36] The attendees applauded her. At that meeting, some oil painters also requested better facilities for creating and exhibiting their paintings. They were worried that the Party's turn toward traditional Chinese painting threatened their careers.

Shortly after the Ministry of Culture meeting, Jiang Feng was labeled "the number one rightist in visual arts" for his rejection of traditional Chinese painting—the crime of "nihilism" in the face of national heritage. This was against the Party's recent emphasis on Chinese cultural and artistic heritage.

In the heat of the campaign, my mother went to the Ministry of Culture. While there, she met Vice Minister Xia Yan, who was in charge of the Anti-Rightist campaign. He said to her, "We and Premier Zhou understand you." Xia Yan also told her not to participate in the Anti-Rightist campaign. But my mother held onto her viewpoints. She often went to CAFA to see big-character posters reflecting activities in the campaign. When asked, she refused to speak against a CAFA teacher who was branded a rightist, believing that he was not anti-Party.

Later at a banquet honoring foreign performing art delegates, my mother met Premier Zhou Enlai. While going around the tables to toast the delegates, Premier Zhou stopped by her table.

He said to her with a smile, "The movement must be going on in your area. A stray bullet can hurt people during a battle."[37]

I believe he meant that some unintended extreme actions were unavoidable during a political movement. He implied that my mother was not the target. She was so touched by Premier Zhou's concern for her that tears welled in her eyes. She believed Premier Zhou protected her from being branded a rightist. Later she realized how much suffering she had been spared. Many artists, such as Feng Fasi, who had spoken at the Ministry of Culture meeting, were branded rightists. Only a few were protected during the campaign, including Dong

Xiwen, who had painted a famous oil, *Inaugural Ceremony for the New Nation*, a Party-leader-approved painting.

The Anti-Rightist campaign may have crushed people critical of the regime, but in some cases personal resentment led to exaggerated accusations. Different academic opinions on art and art education were turned into political crimes targeting certain artists and intellectuals.

According to PRC sources, about five hundred and fifty thousand people, all intellectuals, were branded as rightists. The personal consequences for many alleged rightists were serious. Some artists were sent to rightist labor camps in remote rural areas, without their families. After returning, some were assigned less desirable jobs. Feng Fasi was transferred from the oil painting department of CAFA to teach at the stage setting department of the Central Academy of Drama. After being labeled a rightist, a CCOM violin teacher was assigned to teach the viola, a neglected major with few faculty members. Because most of the violin teachers did not want to teach the viola, being assigned that job was a punishment.

The Anti-Rightist campaign strained the relationships between many rightists and their former colleagues, friends, and even some family members. Such stress brought about divorce and other family problems. Boyang, my father's oldest child from his previous marriage, was such an example.

After graduating from the theory and composition department at the Central Conservatory of Music in Tianjin in the 1950s, Boyang was doing Chinese folk music research at the Chinese Music Research Institute in Beijing. Age twenty-nine in 1957, he responded to the Party's call to speak out freely and air one's views fully. Without any hesitation, he wrote a big-character poster criticizing the Party leader of the Chinese Music Research Institute. Consequently, Boyang was labeled a rightist.

Even though his rightist label was dropped shortly after his return from the labor camp, I could observe the stress this label had brought to his marriage. My sister-in-law, a piano accompanist with Beijing Dance School, felt that her boss did not trust her anymore because of her husband's rightist history. She lost her political responsibilities at work and this created serious tension between the two. Boyang felt troubled and unhappy.

Throughout the entire period when Boyang was labeled a rightist, Mom was very understanding and supportive of him. Although a quiet man who seldom displayed his emotions, Boyang confided in Mom about the constant complaints from his wife. Mom went to talk to his wife to try to help.

Since her marriage to my father, Mom had maintained good relationships with Boyang and Lili, the children from my father's previous marriage. I think she wanted to share my father's love for them. Lili was a sericulture researcher and teacher at the Anhui Agricultural College. She lived with her husband and four children in Hefei, Anhui Province, in southern China, so I did not see her very often. But after his return from the labor camp, Boyang and his family living in Beijing came to visit us almost every Sunday. Mom always cooked a tasty lunch for them.

Boyang and I shared many good times, listening to classical music and discussing concerts and musicians, because I was learning to play the piano. Boyang's son, Xiaoyang, was seven years younger than I. As a three-year-old, he enjoyed playing in our flower garden and throwing my picture books around my room. I remember putting a sign on my bookcase to no avail. The sign, which Xiaoyang was too young to read, said, "Please do not mess up my books."

CHAPTER 9

Our New Home and Family

As soon as she became director of the Xu Beihong Memorial Museum in 1957, Mom applied for funding from the Ministry of Culture to expand the museum. With no storage space, more than 1200 original works by Xu Beihong and more than 1000 valuable artworks in his personal collection were crowded into our family's old garage.

After getting approval for the funding, she talked with the Beijing municipal government about moving two neighbors' houses in order to build the museum's new facilities. Through more than a year of persistent efforts, she was able to persuade our adjacent neighbors to relocate to new homes with government compensation.

There was a *hutong* (alley), adjacent to the museum's south wall and the neighbors' houses, which had little traffic and could be used to expand the museum's entire southern boundary from east to west. In order to apply for the area that the *hutong* occupied, Mom called Peng Zhen, mayor of Beijing. The following day Peng sent two people from the Beijing Urban Planning Bureau to examine the *hutong*. They verified that occupying the *hutong* would not cause traffic problems nor would it affect anybody. Therefore, they made the decision on the spot to let the museum occupy this *hutong*.

Mom was very touched by the speed at which the Beijing municipal government operated. However, because of the Ministry of Culture's budget constraints, funding for the museum's expansion was not provided until 1958 when construction finally began.

Mom and painter Guo Weiqu agreed that the new exhibition galleries should be built in the same quadrangle format as the rest of the museum. The architects from Beijing Institute of Architectural Design followed their recommendation. While attending the music school in Tianjin, I was elated reading Mom's letters describing the construction.

In October 1958, the Xu Beihong Memorial Museum completed its expansion. The new facilities included five storage rooms for the museum's collection, a VIP reception room, four additional staff living quarters, and six additional exhibition galleries, greatly expanding its exhibition area. Although kept in the same single-story quadrangle format as the rest of the museum, the new exhibition galleries were more elaborate. They all had Forbidden-City-style tile roofs, front porches with red pillars, and paintings of colorful flowers with gold highlights above the windows, just under the eaves. The four exhibition galleries around the new courtyard were long one-room buildings along each wall. Mom brought magnolia trees with white flowers from Guangzhou in the south and planted them in the new courtyard. These trees were just the right complement to the elegant architecture.

On China's National Day, October 1, 1958, Zheng Zhenduo, vice minister of the Ministry of Culture, presided over the opening ceremony of the expanded Xu Beihong Memorial Museum. His speech indicated China's central government's support for Xu Beihong and his influential position in China's visual arts. As the artist's old friend, he reminisced about Xu Beihong. Among the attendees were Guo Moruo, Li Jishen, vice chairman of China, and Wu Zuoren, Father's former student. Wu had become president of CAFA earlier in 1958, replacing Jiang Feng after the Anti-Rightist campaign. Guo and Li had both been Father's longtime friends.

All the attendees visited the expanded Xu Beihong Memorial Museum. Then they sat on the lawn of the artist's former residence and chatted for a long time about their shared experiences with Father.

Xu Beihong's large oil paintings, such as *Tian Heng and His Five Hundred Warriors* and *Awaiting the Deliverer*, were able to be displayed in the new exhibition space. A white marble portrait bust of Xu Beihong stood among the fruit trees planted by the artist in the east yard, adjacent to his old home. Sculptor Fu Tianchou was then vice chair of the sculpture department at CAFA. This bust showed windblown hair, suggesting the turmoil Xu Beihong had faced in his efforts to develop Chinese art and art education.

One foreign visitor expressed her appreciation, saying, "I like it so much here that I would like to live here."

The government also planned to build a new house for us adjacent to the museum. Early in 1959, our family moved out of our three rooms where we had lived for six years and stayed temporarily in one of the newly-built exhibition galleries while our new house was constructed. The three rooms were torn down and replaced with storage rooms and one of the new single-story staff living quarters.

I liked our new two-story house. A door through the east wall of Beihong's Former Residence's courtyard led to our yard. Although modest, our new house was much more spacious. Bay windows on the first floor faced south, and a pair of full glass doors opened out to the front porch, decorated with a wisteria-covered pergola. In our new house, Mom was able to receive distinguished foreign visitors properly and invite them to have tea.

Mom, Qingping, and I each occupied one of the three bedrooms on the new house's second floor. My room was the smallest, but I enjoyed its balcony where on summer nights I experienced the fragrance from our flowers. The balcony also served as my escape sometimes. Having once accidentally locked myself inside my room, I had to climb over the balcony, lower myself to the wisteria-covered pergola, and then hang onto its beams to jump to the floor of the front porch.

Brick walls enclosed our yard. To provide privacy from museum activities, we built our own side entrance on a *hutong* named West Kusi. Mom had convenient access to the museum through the new door.

She planted an apricot tree, a pear tree, and a peach tree in our small yard. In a few years, our apricot tree bore sweet yellow apricots which were so juicy that the pits fell out when the fruit was cut open. I remember sharing our abundant apricots with my classmates.

During the Great Leap Forward in 1958 Chairman Mao mobilized the Chinese people to build China's industries and particularly steel-smelting plants. As a child I saw that the Great Leap Forward brought forth ten new showcase buildings in Beijing, including the Great Hall of the People and the History Museum on Tiananmen Square. All these buildings were completed in time for the PRC's tenth-anniversary celebration. The biggest change affecting my family was the new railroad station, which had two clock towers with bell carillons and Chinese tile roofs. Built within walking distance of the museum's entrance, this grand railroad station turned our quiet neighborhood into a bustling place. My classmates and I ran up and down the escalators at the railroad station, a new experience for us. All my classmates leaving Beijing or returning would stop by our house to rest and refresh. At times our house felt like a social hub.

• • •

The year 1959 was difficult. Second Uncle, now living with us, often lost consciousness during his epileptic seizures. Mom, Qingping, and I tried to move him to a bed to recover. But he was six feet tall and very hard to move.

The famine in China began that year and lasted three years. All of our food was rationed through government-controlled, locally-issued monthly coupons for grain, oil, and meat. Our family members were allocated between twenty-five and thirty-two pounds of grain, two ounces of cooking oil, two ounces of meat, and half a pound of cookies per person per month.

Qingping and I, growing teenagers, were hungry all the time. Every morning at the school cafeteria I looked forward to the one *mantou* (Chinese steamed bun) I would get all day. The rest of the meals were pickles, or boiled cabbage with no oil, and rough grain like sorghum, which was hard to swallow. Mom spent some of her savings on high-priced walnut cookies to give us badly needed sugar and oil on weekends.

After Father's death, the government gave my mother a small amount of money, in a lump sum, to raise Qingping and me. That was all her savings, because she had donated our house and all of Father's valuable artworks to the government to set up the museum. But she had to keep most of her savings for our upbringing because the future was uncertain. Mom and Qingping both fell sick from malnutrition. Like many Chinese people suffering from the famine, Mom's and Qingping's faces became swollen, Qingping's eyes reduced to thin slits. Mom's legs were also swollen. They received the standard treatment for swollen people: some soybeans given by special order.

Mom found it hard to take care of her two young children in addition to my disabled second uncle all by herself, particularly during the famine. She must have often felt that a strong man in the family would be helpful.

Uncle Huang had been writing to her for a year. In early 1958, he and Mom had come to Tianjin together to visit me in my primary school. He looked casual without his uniform. Even though we were on friendly terms, I felt a little shy, perhaps because I was three years older than when I first met him in 1955. I did not detect any intimacy between him and Mom.

I believe Mom was hesitant about committing to a close relationship with him. However, in 1959 after I returned to Beijing, Mom received a long-distance phone call from Uncle Huang. He told her that he had reported his relationship with her to the commissar of his army unit. The commissar had sent a cadre to the Ministry of Culture to investigate her background for the army's political check. Uncle Huang urged Mom to support the action that he had initiated. This meant that she had to officially acknowledge their relationship, which the army and her superiors in the Ministry of Culture could consider premarital.

Perturbed that Huang acted so abruptly without consulting with her beforehand, Mom was in a dilemma. Beihong had died six years before but she still loved him deeply. She asked herself, "Could I possibly change my decision never to remarry?" Huang's action exposed a relationship which Mom had not committed to. In fact, she had tried to build a wall between them. She also asked herself, "What will happen to me in the future?" However, now that it was publicized, Huang's action pushed her to commit herself.

Mom went to see Liu Zhiming, vice minister of the Ministry of Culture, to share her thoughts. Liu said to her, "You are still young and should consider marrying again. I support your bringing back the warmth of a family for yourself and your children. But why did you choose an army man instead of someone in the cultural and artistic circle?"

Mom described how Huang and she had met each other. She explained, "I never went looking for another man. Even at this moment, my heart is still with Beihong. My love for Beihong is ingrained in my bones and heart."

Liu sighed deeply and nodded, understanding.

From her later perspective, Mom felt that her relationship with Huang did not have a solid foundation. But in 1959, she succumbed to Huang's proposal partially because she trusted him as a Communist Party member and a PLA officer. Mom had told him that her heart was still with Beihong and that she would always love him. Huang responded, "I respect and love Xu Beihong as much as you do and I will not discourage you from commemorating Xu Beihong." She asked Qingping and me about her decision to marry Huang. As an eleven-year-old girl, I supported Mom's decision. I had always liked Uncle

Huang. Perhaps Huang's warm relationship with Qingping and me helped him win her over. Shortly after he came to Beijing in 1959, Mom and Huang registered to marry. There was no ceremony or banquet.

Uncle Huang brought some happiness to our family. I remember our new family spending a couple of days in a guest house in the Summer Palace. We walked around the lake and enjoyed the crisp air. Mom seemed to have come out of her sadness for a while. Uncle Huang played some simple piano melodies and Mom sang along to "The Beautiful Solo River." Sometimes they went ballroom dancing at the Chinese People's Political Consultative Conference Center on weekend evenings. My thirty-six-year-old mother looked beautiful in her green sweater on the dance floor. While they danced, Qingping and I watched new movies shown at the same center. I felt a little left out when saying good-bye to Mom and Uncle Huang after the movie. Qingping and I went home early in the evening while they danced late into the night.

Father's three-foot-tall portrait photo still hung in our living room. His gentle smile still followed me and warmed my heart. On Chinese New Year's Eve after Mom's wedding to Uncle Huang, we celebrated the passing year with Father, as was our family tradition. Mom lit two long candles in silver candle holders in front of Father's portrait photo. Uncle Huang joined our ceremony and all of us bowed to Father's photo. Mom hung a long string of firecrackers on a stick, and in the joyful atmosphere of loud firecrackers we sent away the past year and welcomed the New Year with Father. The annual Qingming Festival, for paying respects to ancestors and tending family graves, occurs on or around April 5. Uncle Huang came with us to the Babaoshan Revolutionary Cemetery to visit Father's grave and decorate it with flowers.

Through Mom's connections, Uncle Huang left the army and found a human-resource job in Beijing in a unit directly under the Ministry of Culture. Like many soldiers, army officers, and workers, he later got the opportunity to go to college, studying scriptwriting in the Beijing Film Academy. During the week he lived in the school dorm and was home only on weekends.

On the surface, our new family appeared harmonious. My step-brother, Boyang, and his family visited every Sunday. Uncle Huang played well with Boyang's son, Xiaoyang. On Sunday, our extended family, including Boyang's family, crowded around our large round table to enjoy lunch. Everyone seemed happy and Uncle Huang seemed to have blended in. However, deep in her heart,

Mom still missed Father. Only temporarily distracted by Huang, she returned to her grief. She could not help comparing Huang with Beihong. They were so different. She noticed that Huang usually turned the water faucet on full force, while Beihong was always careful to conserve water and electricity.

Although Huang did not notice the change in Mom's feelings, he said to her one day, looking at Xu Beihong's portrait photo, "This home does not look like mine." Our lives were still focused on Father. All our friends were Xu Beihong's colleagues or students. Mom still devoted herself to working at the Xu Beihong Memorial Museum next door. At times she felt that Huang was like a stranger in our home because he was the only one in our closest circle not related to Xu Beihong.

I believe that Mom and Uncle Huang began having problems shortly after they married. One summer afternoon our whole family went to Beihai Park, Mom looking elegant in a white skirt and blouse. We rented a boat. As Qingping and I began enjoying the view from the water, Uncle Huang and Mom started arguing. Qingping was so anxious to leave that before our boat was fully docked he plunged one leg into the water and got his pants wet. I tolerated their quarreling the rest of the evening.

What had happened between Mom and Uncle Huang saddened me, but I could do little to help. Fortunately, he lived in the Beijing Film Academy during the week. In 1963, four years into their marriage, Mom gave birth to my little brother Maomao. However, their marital relationship did not improve.

CHAPTER 10
"I Live for Music"

In my last semester at the Prep Music Elementary School, in 1961, I prepared for my graduation recital. Teacher Chen gave me a very difficult recital piece, *Variations on a Theme of Paganini*. My fingers ran to the last key of the piano on the left-hand side. There are also passages entirely composed of octaves and chords.

At age thirteen I was taller than my classmates, and my hands had grown enough to play the octaves and chords. But I needed to feel comfortable in order to render the music well. In spite of the technical difficulty, I really loved the change of moods with each variation in this piece. Teacher Chen and I both worked very hard on this challenge most of the semester. In the end I felt ready. I scored 5 minus again at my graduation exam and was chosen to play *Variations on a Theme of Paganini* at our school graduation concert to be held at CCOM's new auditorium. Having attended so many recitals by CCOM senior students, I had envied their opportunity to perform in this auditorium with its wonderful acoustics. Now it was my turn.

One evening in June, the red pillars in the lobby of the new auditorium shone with new paint, and flowers and ribbons decorated the entrance. My schoolmates gathered at the lobby, smiling and welcoming CCOM administrators, teachers, parents, and friends of our graduating class. Mom came to school half an hour before the concert with performance attire she had prepared for me. My beautiful mother looked elegant in her tightly-fitting purple Chinese robe with slits opened up to the knees.

I wished Father could have been there to watch my graduation performance. Would he be disappointed that I chose a career in music instead of art? I thought that perhaps he might be touched by my music and proud of me. I had grown to be a tall girl of thirteen with a cute pumpkin-seed-shaped face and features just like his in his youth. I put on my red scarf along with a new white silk blouse and a light blue-and-white patterned silk skirt.

My solo was second to the last on the program, right before the concluding choral piece. I walked to the grand piano with confidence, like a mature pianist. The whole audience waited quietly.

After a few moments of preparation to set my mood, I started *Variations on a Theme of Paganini*. I was a little nervous. But as I got farther into the piece, I started sharing with my audience the rich emotions of this colorful piano piece. Worries about the technical difficulties vanished, and my passion lifted me above the ocean of notes, delivering the musical expression I felt so deeply. As I finished my last note, I felt a great sense of accomplishment. Beaming, I got up to bow.

Since my first formal solo at age ten in Tianjin, I had performed many times, each time with more experience and a better state of mind. I had grown from a beginner to a professionally trained teenage piano student. Shortly after finishing my solo, I returned to the stage again to play the piano accompaniment for the choral piece. I heard someone in the audience murmur, "Here she comes again!" This was the third time I had appeared on the stage that night.

That summer, my school contacted me to perform, as an alumna, *Variations on a Theme of Paganini* for the National Conference for High Schools and Primary Schools, held in Beijing. Its delegates were teachers from all over China. A Prep Music High School piano student and I had been chosen to represent our school. Dressed in the school performance uniform of white silk blouse, red scarf, and green plaid skirt, I proudly showed quality and accomplishment in my performance. Afterward some delegates came to shake hands and congratulate me.

• • •

The year 1961 was the third year of the famine. For every meal, Shenpo measured the exact weight of everyone's portion from our limited monthly ration of rice or flour. We raised a duck and a rabbit for food. The rabbit lived in a pile of coal in our boiler room and its fur got very dirty. The duck was our treasure; she frequently laid an egg for us.

During the summer, my step-sister, Lili, brought her three boys and one girl to stay with us for more than a month because they had trouble surviving the famine in their home town of Hefei, Anhui Province. Her children's ages ranged from five to ten. Lili, my father's daughter from his previous marriage, was eighteen years older than I. In her thirties and thin, she looked attractive with permed hair and a flowered dress.

Lili was talkative and often confided in my mother about the complexities of her family life because she had no one else to discuss these things with. Her family's finances were very tight, because she and her husband had a total of eight children, four of them from her husband's previous marriage. Lili had no access to her own salary; her husband controlled the purse strings.

Mom sympathized and often tried to help her. She sent to Lili bundles of clothing Qingping and I had outgrown. In the early 1950s, Father had often written to Lili. Knowing that she had started a family before finishing college, Father once gave the following advice to her in his letter to her husband: ". . .she really should study a profession because she has a good foundation [in academics]."[38] To honor my father's suggestion, Mom encouraged Lili to go to college even though she had a family.

Mom had verified with the United Front Work Department that Xu Beihong and his ex-wife Jiang Biwei in their divorce settlement had not divided their house in Nanjing. As a result, Boyang was able to claim ownership of the house because our father had died and Jiang Biwei had left for Taiwan in 1949. With Mom's encouragement, Boyang shared with Lili the proceeds from the sale of the house, and with her share Lili went to the Anhui Agricultural College in Hefei to study sericulture, later becoming a professor and expert in that field.

Mom and I took Lili and her children to Beihai Park and the Summer Palace. In the photographs they look very happy. Mom often read to my nephews and niece the Chinese translation of *Grimm's Fairy Tales*. They listened attentively, lost in their imaginations. At the end of the summer, Mom gave them the book to take home to Hefei.

Although our family did not have enough grain coupons, Mom managed to share our flour rations. In Hefei, Lili's family lived on thin porridge mixed with wild leafy vegetables the children searched for and gathered every day. But in our house my nephews and niece really enjoyed the wheat flour flat pancake rolled up with plum sauce and green onions, a treat Mom made for them, not available back home. Mom also spent her limited savings to purchase high-priced cookies for Lili and her children. Our monthly ration of meat was too meager to feed our family and Lili's, so Mom went to a "free market" and bought frogs from peasants. That summer, stir-fried frog legs became our main course for dinner, and Lili's family enjoyed this very much.

Lili used her agricultural knowledge to nurture the corn and pumpkins Mom had planted in our small yard. That fall the harvest bolstered our insufficient diet.

As a mother, Lili took a hands-off approach to her four children. She jokingly told me that they grew up "in the sun and rain," meaning that they occasionally slept outside. This contrasted sharply with my mother's controlling ways. I found my little nephews and niece very lively, sometimes wild. When they first arrived, they liked running around the museum courtyards, shaking the dates off the trees. A museum staff woman complained to my mother about them. The boys had pulled the flowering lotus plants out of the large earthenware bowls containing goldfish and scribbled on the museum's whitewashed walls. When the staff woman tried to stop them, one of the boys retorted, "This is my grandfather's home. It is none of your business." To my surprise, Lili got serious with her kids this time and required them to apologize to the staff woman. I was impressed with her ability to make them behave.

At the end of the summer vacation, Mom took Lili's family, Qingping, and me to a restaurant serving Peking duck, a one-time event for us after two years of famine. It must have cost Mom a fortune. For Lili's children, this was their first taste of crisp juicy roasted Peking duck.

I treasured getting to know my sister and being "little aunt" to her children. But I worried about how they would survive when they returned to Hefei. Mom said to Lili, "You are always welcome in my home if you need to come back."

• • •

Mom had had a serious talk with me before my graduation. Although I had been admitted to the Prep Music High School, she wanted me to consider switching to a general middle school. This would allow me to continue painting lessons and prepare for entering the Preparatory Art High School affiliated to the Central Academy of Fine Arts, starting in tenth grade.

I understood her desire for me to pursue my father's career. I told her I loved painting and would continue studying art, such as calligraphy, during my summer and winter vacations. But I said to her, "Why do you live? I live for music."

Although disappointed, Mom allowed me to continue my piano studies. She had told me that Dad loved music. He said to her, "When I was near the end of my resources in Paris, I chose to go hungry so I would not miss a good concert."[39] I believed he would have been happy with my choice. His artistic dedication always inspired me.

My mother had good writing skills and I attribute my passion for literature to her. She had a large collection of Chinese translations of Western novels. While my schoolmates napped in their dorms after lunch, I sat in the classroom reading history books and the novels I had brought from home: *David Copperfield, Jane Eyre*, and *War and Peace*. I also had a strong interest in current political events. To me, maturity meant understanding current as well as historical events. In the summer I read *Eugene Onegin*, a novel in verse by Russian poet Alexander Pushkin, in one day. The poetic expressions and vivid descriptions of the characters opened my teenage eyes to another art form that draws characters' portraits, except with words.

Nineteenth-century romantic stories in literature and movies fascinated me. On summer nights, I often stood on the balcony under the moonlight, looking at my reflection in the glass balcony door. It showed a young girl's face with delicate contours, upward-curved eyes, and a slender figure. I imagined meeting a handsome young man who would fall in love with me, just as in the stories.

My father believed artists should be educated in liberal arts including sciences. Encouraged by Father's example, I read science fiction, history, and literature. My Chinese literature teacher and teachers of other general subjects at the Prep Music High School were very good, but I thought that the courses' contents were inadequate. In our textbooks we had only limited chapters on classical Chinese literature. I begged my mother to help me expand my understanding of classical Chinese writings. With her help, I willingly learned and memorized the first half of the *Mencius* (*Mengzi*), a collection of anecdotes and conversations by Mencius, one of the major Chinese Confucian philosophers. I also studied *Nine Songs* by Qu Yuan, a third-century BCE poet, and works by ancient writers such as Ouyang Xiu, Fan Zhongyan, and Su Shi.

However, what I enjoyed most was memorizing and reciting Tang-dynasty poems by Li Bai, Du Fu, and Bai Juyi. With five hours' piano practice daily and about ten required courses including music and general subjects, I had little time, but memorized a few lines right before sleeping each night. In due course, I learned several poems by Bai Juyi. His "Pipa xing," a poem about a female *pipa* (Chinese plucking instrument) player, describes the clarity of the notes from her *pipa* playing as "Pearls, large and small, on a jade plate fall." I was particularly fascinated with the poetic line, describing the music coming to a temporary pause:

> The resentment hidden in the heart arises.
> At that moment, the silence brings more emotion than musical sound.

This verse set me thinking about traditional Chinese painting in which even the empty space in a landscape is deliberately chosen and has meaning.

My mother had spent most evenings supervising Qingping's homework. Because I had been self-disciplined since first grade, Mom never thought to ask me about my homework, and I almost felt ignored. Later during my literature learning experience with her, I came to understand her better and we became closer. Mom also helped me embellish my frequent writing assignments. I expanded my vocabulary and learned poetic expression and figurative speech from her. Most importantly, she taught me to take notes while reading. I collected well-written passages and phrases in the Chinese novels I read. This helped me improve my writing, which I became more interested in.

My Chinese literature teacher often chose my compositions to read to my classmates as model compositions. During my second year in the Prep Music High School, I submitted an essay, "My Musical Instrument," to the High-School Student Essay Competition in Beijing. My essay was selected to be included in the *Excellent High-School Student Essay Collection*.

CHAPTER 11

Between the Notes

My first-year Prep Music High School class had fifty-six students, most from my Prep Music Elementary School. There was unprecedented pressure and competition. We learned that at the end of our first academic year, some students would be eliminated from the program.

My new piano teacher, Chen, had the same last name as my Prep Music Elementary School piano teacher. She zeroed in on weaknesses in my technical training and set higher standards. I was eager to take on the new challenges and made progress. But Teacher Chen fell ill in the middle of the first semester and I was assigned a temporary teacher for the rest of that semester. Then, in the next semester, I had another temporary teacher, not dedicated to teaching me because I would be her student for only one semester. She spent more time with her regular students while putting me off until the very end of her schedule, leaving little time for my lesson. Disappointed, I resorted to my own resources to supplement the limited instruction. One of my final-exam pieces that year was Mozart's *Piano Sonata No. 10 in C Major, K. 330.* I listened to recordings of this sonata by accomplished pianists to learn the proper style. Some phrases with many grace notes were particularly hard to finesse. Another classmate playing the same sonata for his final fortunately shared with me his fingering and other tricks he had learned to tackle those grace notes. We both relished uncovering the emotions in these phrases. With advice from him and other classmates, I did reasonably well on my first-year final exam. At least the result was good enough for me to survive the elimination process.

At the end of my first year, eighteen students, about one-third of our class, were asked to leave. They were transferred to general middle schools in Beijing. Principal Yu from our Prep Music High School said, "There is a difference between a vase and a spittoon. We certainly should not keep the spittoon type of students in our school." This sounded very harsh. But I reasoned that China was a poor country, and to provide free education for the conservatory and prep students, our school had to be very selective to reach its goal of producing star students. Many who stayed were from elite families.

Later, I found out that the school administration stuck to their professional standards in the elimination process regardless of students' family backgrounds. For example, the students eliminated included a famous composer's son and a CCOM trumpet teacher's son. However, I felt sorry for two peasant girls who also had to leave. One of them was an *erhu* (Chinese two-string fiddle) major and the other a violin major. The *erhu* student had bad hygiene habits. Elected to be in charge of student well-being, I advised her to change her habits. The peasant violin student impressed me with her vivid composition describing catching fish near her village. However, she was not able to play Western classical music with emotion because she could not relate to it. I saw her crying while she waited to perform at her final exam recital. She was the only violin student to play at that recital without a piano accompanist, probably because her teacher neglected to arrange one for her. I found that out only at the recital and therefore was not able to play the accompaniment for her.

These two girls came from Yongfengtun, a village in the rural suburbs of Beijing. In 1959 following the Great Leap Forward, CCOM had set up an after-school music program there, enabling scores of the children to take musical-instrument lessons. Some entered the Prep Music High School in 1960 and 1961. Unfortunately, during the elimination process, most were deemed untalented. Only one girl, nicknamed "Big Turnip," survived the elimination and later graduated in violin performance.

At the end of my first year, the Prep Music High School moved to a nearby campus converted from a factory. The dormitory buildings were being remodeled, so there was a student housing shortage. As a result, at the beginning of my second academic year, 1962-63, my classmate Jian and I were asked to commute from home. Jian lived close to school. I lived in the eastern part of Beijing. But there was a direct bus No. 10 from the railroad station near our home to the Guohuijie (Congress Street) bus stop, a five-minute walk to the school.

Following the end of the famine, the years 1962 and 1963 saw tolerance for some bourgeois arts. Later Mao criticized this tolerance by China's cultural authorities.

Living at home that year gave me the freedom to pursue my passion for music, art, movies, and literature, away from the controls on campus. This short-lived opportunity broadened my perspective as a musician. My father had wanted that for his students.

Because I did not have to go to bed on schedule, I immersed myself in classical music late into the night, turning out the light to listen to my favorite, Rachmaninov's *Piano Concerto No. 2 in C minor.* The strings' deep, rich rendering of a Russian melody accompanied by the piano's rolling waves of arpeggios inspired me to imagine a broad seascape and a Russian soulful strength. I was lost in my imaginary world, traveling through the passages of this concerto. A couple of my classmates also shared my excitement about this concerto. We dreamed of someday playing it with an orchestra.

My second-year assigned piano teacher, Wang, was strict and sometimes impersonal. But she was a very good pianist and teacher who had studied at CCOM with Mr. Zhu Gongyi, who occasionally had given me lessons.

Teacher Wang put me on a good study plan. While helping me master the style of *Three-Part Inventions* by J. S. Bach, she demonstrated how to differentiate tones for three different voices. This allowed me to begin studying the more difficult Bach piano music such as the preludes and fugues in *The Well-Tempered Clavier.* Bach's piano works were a challenge for students in our early teens, but I began to appreciate the fine structure of Bach fugues.

Teacher Wang believed in rigorous technical training. Through practicing many demanding etudes, I made significant progress in dexterity and the independence of my fingers which were required to perform Mozart and Beethoven sonatas. I also purchased a recording of Mozart's *Piano Sonata No. 13 in B-flat Major, K. 333*, and through careful listening, tried to imitate the pianist's exquisite performance style. This turned out to be a successful learning experience. After my recital of that Mozart sonata, Teacher Wang wrote comments, stating that I was musically expressive, meaning that my performance could convey emotions implied in compositions and touch listeners' hearts. Her encouragement gave me more confidence to pursue a piano performance career.

CHAPTER 12

A "Politically Incorrect" Family

Living at home, I also saw Qingping more often. He decided to follow in my father's footsteps and become a painter, starting in 1961 at the Preparatory Art High School affiliated to the Central Academy of Fine Arts.

Qingping showed me some high-quality prints of paintings by major nineteenth-century Russian painters such as Repin, Surikov, and Levitan. These reproductions were among the limited number of images of European artworks available to us. We both marveled at the vivid oil paintings, such as Repin's *Barge-Haulers on the Volga* (*The Volga Boatmen*) and *They Did Not Expect Him*. The latter shows a family surprised by the return home of a political exile. Each figure has a different facial expression captured very dramatically by the artist. I was also impressed with Surikov's *Morning of the Strelets' Execution*, an emotionally powerful painting depicting the suppression of soldiers who came out against the reforms of Peter the Great, and people's reactions to the execution. But what triggered my romantic imagination most were Levitan's richly-colored landscape paintings of the Russian countryside. Qingping helped me select a printed *Portrait of the Composer Modest Mussorgsky* by Repin to decorate my bedroom. He framed the print and hung it on the wall next to my own photo, a smiling teenage girl in a woolen plaid jacket. The adjacent portrait of Mussorgsky was a stark contrast, showing the intense eyes and unshaven face of this Russian composer, who wrote the piano suite *Pictures at an Exhibition*.

After entering the Prep Art High School, Qingping had suddenly turned into a mature and caring older brother. He seemed to enjoy listening to my Western classical music records as much as I enjoyed looking at his Russian painting albums. He often sketched me playing the piano. His drawings captured the liveliness of my playing. During his art high school years, Qingping's drawing skills progressed to a higher level with the help of private advanced drawing lessons from Li Hu, Father's former student and head of the figure painting specialty at CAFA's Chinese painting department. The closeness and trust that Qingping and I built at that time has lasted.

The summer vacation of 1965 was the last summer our family spent in our beautiful quadrangle-style Xu Beihong Memorial Museum. In the morning, Qingping and I sat on the front porch of the exhibition gallery near the grapevines in the east yard, studying foreign languages. From there I could see the white marble portrait bust of my father among the dense foliage. I enjoyed the serenity of the garden and the intimate atmosphere because so much of my father's life still remained there. All the fruit trees he had planted bore abundant fruits as he had wished.

That summer Qingping painted my portrait in oil. I wore a dark green dress tightly fitted around my small waist, with short sleeves bloused around the shoulders, a dress Mom had outgrown. To add a contrasting color, I put on my red scarf even though I was already seventeen, three years older than the maximum age for Young Pioneers. Every morning for two weeks I posed on that front porch. That was the only oil portrait Qingping painted for me. As the teenage girl's innocent face gradually appeared from a sketch to full color, I pondered the events of our growing up together. I remember what Father told me when I was five: "You will grow up to be a beautiful lady, wearing a fur coat and high heels." How happy he would have been to see his teenage daughter with maturing feminine features in that oil portrait! He would have been proud to see me pursuing my piano performance study in one of the best music schools in China.

At eighteen, Qingping had just graduated from the Prep Art High School, where after four years of solid training he had become a good painter. My father had painted my mother's portrait with similar tenderness. As Qingping observed my face carefully, I was also studying him. He was a tall, well-built young man with long bushy eyebrows like two forceful brush strokes across his forehead. His eyes behind glasses often showed shy consideration. The hint of a mustache was apparent. His broad lips looked like our mother's, usually carrying his genuinely kind smile.

Qingping was preparing for his college entrance exam. Unfortunately he was not able to apply to the art school of his choice, the Central Academy of Fine Arts. The academy stopped recruiting students in 1965. All the existing students and faculty members went to the villages in Xingtai, Hebei Province, to conduct the "Four Clean-ups" full-time. "Four Clean-ups" was a term for the Socialist Education Movement, originally aimed at cleansing the bureaucracy of new bourgeoisie in the political, economic, ideological, and organizational fields, to prevent the restoration of capitalism. This movement was carried out between 1963 and May 1966 in rural areas and a small number of urban factories and schools.

Planning to study art in France, just like our father, Qingping decided to apply to a foreign-language institute and major in French. He had studied Russian for four years in the art school. But to compete with general high-school students, he made special efforts to prepare to pass a foreign-language exam, which was part of the college entrance exam. Mom asked Brother Chen, a professional Russian interpreter from the Ministry of Metallurgy, to tutor Qingping that summer. Brother Chen was the nephew of a close family friend from Sichuan Province who had known my parents from the 1940s. When his nephew first came to Beijing to study Russian in 1950, my parents let him stay with us for a few months. As little kids, we called him Brother Chen.

With Brother Chen's help, Qingping's Russian vastly improved. During that unbearably hot summer we did not have an electric fan, and air conditioners were unheard of. Every night Mom fanned Qingping using a big palm-leaf fan while he studied late into the night. I believed he did very well on his Russian-language exam. His first choice of college was the Beijing Foreign Languages Institute, one of the best foreign-language universities in China. However, at the end of that summer, he was admitted to the English department of the Beijing Teachers' College, a second-rate university for training school teachers. This was actually his very last choice, and everyone in my family was shocked. Mom was devastated. Believing the decision unfair, she could not eat or sleep for days.

Finally, Mom decided to talk to Premier Zhou Enlai, requesting reasons why the Beijing Foreign Languages Institute denied Qingping admission. At the west gate of Zhongnanhai, she asked the guards to call Premier Zhou Enlai regarding an urgent matter. In a little while, Zheng Siyuan, Deputy Secretary General of the State Council, came out and talked to her.

Holding back her tears, Mom said in a serious voice, "Secretary General Zheng, I am not trying to come in through the back door, seeking special privileges. I am only hoping to find justice. If Qingping's college-entrance exam scores are as high as other applicants being admitted to their first choice of universities, he should be admitted to the university of his first choice as well. Although Beihong made a great contribution to China's art development, I never asked for any special treatment for our children's school admission. At least they should be treated fairly and not discriminated against." She insisted on obtaining Qingping's college-entrance exam scores, not usually released to applicants in the 1960s.

Through complicated bureaucratic channels, we learned that Qingping's college-entrance exam scores were more than excellent. He had actually earned extra points on his Russian-language essay writing, bringing his total score to 106 on a scale of 100. The problem was his family's political background. Applicants from politically incorrect families were rejected from colleges particularly if family members had been jailed or executed by the CCP. Having relatives in Hong Kong, Taiwan, or overseas jeopardized an applicant's chances. A top university for training diplomats, the Beijing Foreign Languages Institute stringently screened students' families.

We found out that during the political check, a personnel affairs cadre from the Xu Beihong Memorial Museum had claimed that our family had overseas connections. Quite a few of Xu Beihong's overseas Chinese friends had in fact come to the Xu Beihong Memorial Museum. Therefore Qingping was not to be trained for foreign affairs work. I suspected that Wang Shuxiao had construed the above connections to raise suspicion. She was the only Party member and the only cadre responsible for personnel affairs in the museum. That summer I had seen two women walk into the reception room with Wang Shuxiao and remain there behind closed doors for a couple of hours. I sensed from their demeanor that they might be government cadres.

I heard that Premier Zhou Enlai had spoken with the leaders of the Beijing Foreign Languages Institute and the Beijing Second Foreign Language Institute, saying, "Xu Beihong is a world-famous artist. Of course he had many foreign friends. How can this be considered a political problem, even affecting his children's college admission?"[40] With Premier Zhou Enlai's endorsement, both foreign-language institutes expressed willingness to admit Qingping. Finally, Qingping enrolled at the Beijing Second Foreign Language Institute, a newly established college.

By the time Qingping's admissions paperwork was finished, classes had already started. I sewed a bed sheet around a blanket and gave it to him to take to school. The day he started college, carrying his bedding I accompanied him to the campus in the eastern suburbs of Beijing. That morning many students were standing among the trees away from the classrooms, reading foreign languages aloud. I wanted to be part of that environment. Qingping would be taught French by teachers from France. I hoped that in two years I would also be able to attend a college of my choice.

The events around Qingping's college application made me think seriously about my own future. Job prospects for musicians in China were quite uncertain. We might have to relocate to rural areas to do elementary music training for common people. There was a great demand for improving education in rural areas. Whatever job prospects there might be, I was determined to go to college to become an educated person.

CHAPTER 13

The Exhibition at Hangzhou

Chinese literature teacher Ning in the fall of 1963 was assigned administrative duties over our third-year class at the Prep Music High School. He was a short man whose name means "peaceful," although he was anything but peaceful. To improve our discipline, he required all the students to live at school. My friend Jian and I both moved to the school dormitory. Teacher Ning also asked each student to submit a personal profile including the family members we felt closest to. Then he talked with each student individually about any issues that he felt required attention. Most likely he ruffled some feathers.

I adjusted to the school's rigid schedule, but kept reading for an hour after lunch while most of my classmates napped. I also continued learning Chinese poetry before the lights went out at 9 p.m. The previous year in class, whenever our former Chinese literature teacher read a Tang-dynasty poem or ancient prose aloud, I jumped in and gave him the next line. This earned me the cynical nickname "Learned Scholar." This reputation was good and bad for me. I was sought after as a scriptwriter for our choral performance narrations. Yet pursuing knowledge outside of our curriculum distanced my classmates, who thought I was aloof because I did not work only on music performance courses. In fact, quite a few of my classmates ignored or even flunked their general-subject courses such as math and science.

Some of my classmates started gossiping about me, even to Teacher Ning. They envied my family's living standard and our summer vacations. I had written about these trips in my compositions which the teacher had read to my class.

Teacher Ning, hoping I would blend in with the other students, said to me, "In old China, some intellectuals ignored repressive authority to uphold their own morals and beliefs. Did you get your aloof attitude from those old-China intellectuals like your father?"

"No. I just want to follow my own interests," I said.

Aware of Father's sincere efforts to serve the new China, I was offended when Teacher Ning categorized my father as an old-China intellectual. This was my first clue to the coming political forces that would affect my family and all intellectuals.

In my third year at the Prep Music High School, I played Beethoven's sonatas and Chopin's waltzes and nocturnes with competence. In one semester, I was the only student in my class to earn the maximum score of 5 in all required courses I took including music courses and general-subject courses. I understand now the heavy pressure placed on me to conform. Then, my individualistic quest for knowledge meant I would have few friends. Later in life I realized the value of having pursued a well-rounded education on my own. This gave me confidence to seek out career opportunities that average conservatory students would not have.

In the spring semester of my third year, I followed my mother to Hangzhou, a beautiful city near West Lake, two hours by train from Shanghai. She had gone to Hangzhou in April 1964 to hold an exhibition of paintings by Xu Beihong. I joined her during the five-day spring break in early May. On my first twenty-four-hour train trip by myself, at age sixteen, I met fellow passengers and shared my experiences with them. The train conductor saw my music-school badge. At his request, I sang several cheerful folk songs I had learned in my Chinese folk music course. My fellow passengers applauded me and I was elated.

In Beijing, trees had only started to show the pastel greens of spring, but as I traveled south, stretches of green rice paddies and other greenery gradually expanded. I arrived in Hangzhou at night. The next morning before breakfast with Mom in the hotel restaurant, I opened an exit door to find myself standing on the bank of West Lake. A vast expanse of calm water blended wondrously with the morning mist, just as in a Chinese ink brush landscape painting.

During my three-day visit to Hangzhou, Mom and I took the boat to Gushan (Solitary Hill) on the other side of West Lake, where the exhibition was being held. The Xu Beihong Memorial Museum had limited funds and staff to hold exhibitions in other cities. However, in the early 1960s art-exhibition arrangements were not as formal as today. Through persistence and resourcefulness, Mom and one of Father's friends, Zhou Jianren, governor of Zhejiang Province, made it happen in Hangzhou. Zhou Jianren arranged the use of the exhibition facility in Gushan free of charge. According to Mom, the Zhejiang provincial government paid for her and her staff member's train tickets and the shipping of one hundred scrolls of Chinese brush paintings by Xu Beihong. Mom and her staff member accompanied Xu Beihong's artworks on the train to Hangzhou. Students from the Zhejiang Academy of Fine Arts in Hangzhou served as attendants at the exhibition, and in return the entrance fees collected were given to the art school.[41] Many people came to this first exhibition from the Xu Beihong Memorial Museum. Among the visitors was Pan Tianshou, a well-known Chinese ink brush painter and president of the Zhejiang Academy of Fine Arts.

I left Mom in Hangzhou, and on my return trip to Beijing, I met someone who spoke good English. I told him that I was Xu Beihong's daughter and a student at the Prep Music High School. He happened to be carrying an illustrated English adaptation of the novel *Robinson Crusoe* by Daniel Defoe. This was the first story in English that I had encountered. I tried reading the story but my English was not good enough. I realized that my two years of English studies at the Prep Music High School had been inadequate for me. The man on the train was kind enough to give me the book so that I could look up all the new words in a dictionary when I got home.

I decided to improve my English on my own and eventually learn to read English stories. At Wangfujing in downtown Beijing I purchased my first English-Chinese dictionary by Zheng Yili, which I still have. With the help of the dictionary, I read *Robinson Crusoe* and also simplified versions of English novels such as *David Copperfield*. Even though the stories were shortened adaptations, the language sounded much more natural when compared with the Chinese translations of the works. I also studied a more advanced English textbook on my own, hoping to build my English vocabulary while I was young and quick to learn.

CHAPTER 14

The New Repertoire

Jiang Qing initiated the revolution in Peking opera in 1964, causing massive changes in our music curriculum. Western classical music was to be de-emphasized in favor of Chinese music. At a school-wide meeting, CCOM leadership announced the Ministry of Culture's new policy on performances and art-school curricula: The content must promote revolutionary spirit, incorporate Chinese artistic styles, and be understood by the masses.

The Central Committee of the CCP and the State Council, in September of the same year, issued a notification to universities, requesting liberal arts teachers and students to participate in the Socialist Education Movement. The notification reads: "In some institutions, leading power is not in the hands of the proletariat. Many bourgeois experts are competing with us for young students." The following February, university science and engineering teachers and students received a similar notification. I think that some university students' studies might have been affected by the Socialist Education Movement, but I was not aware of any large wave of college students settling in the countryside as early as 1964 and 1965.

A musicology student from the Central Conservatory of Music, Chen Lian, wrote to Mao Zedong in 1964, reporting problems in the conservatory's teaching and performances. In response Mao wrote instructions including, "Make the ancient serve the present and the foreign serve China."

These instructions had a major impact on the arts. CCOM, which had earlier been modeled after the Soviet system, now revolutionized the school's teaching program and built connections between its students and workers, peasants, and soldiers. The school re-evaluated China's musical heritage and European bourgeois music, criticizing the elements harmful to the new era, and incorporating useful elements in order to develop a new socialist, Chinese music teaching system. In reality, the leftist line prevailing at CCOM from 1964 to 1965 criticized most Western classical music, prefiguring the coming Cultural Revolution when all Western classical music would be banned.

Studies in Chinese voice and Chinese instruments were separated from the Central Conservatory of Music and incorporated on a new campus, China Conservatory of Music. The Western instrument performance students remained at CCOM, but our Western classical music curriculum was eliminated except for etudes because no Chinese music etudes were available for technical training. We broadened our repertoire of Chinese music, but the lack of Western classical music curriculum meant less development of our technical skills. The Chinese repertoire written for Western instruments was limited. Some violin students wrote Chinese violin pieces themselves to create the new curriculum.

The new direction required us to learn from workers, peasants, and soldiers, which was now part of our schooling. Starting in the late first semester of our fourth year and throughout our fifth year in the Prep Music High School, every semester our class spent three to four weeks in a factory or the army, interrupting all music lessons and other academic courses.

Near the end of 1964, my fourth-year class and the fifth-year class spent three weeks in the Beijing Printing Factory, a government-owned large-scale printing shop, producing large-format pictorial publications. We spent our days there checking the finished publications for defects. We also held discussions about how to adopt for ourselves the selfless quality of the workers. Our master workers were straightforward and kind. Factory work was a new experience for me, but I found it monotonous and anxiously waited to get back to music studies.

At the end of the three weeks, we performed a Chinese-song-and-dance show for the workers. Eleven piano classmates and I learned a brisk dance named "Harvest Song," depicting the joy of rural people harvesting grain. Wearing straw hats, we danced with cardboard sickles as if we were cutting crops in the fields, and waved long silk streamers, mimicking the work of threshing. The workers seemed to enjoy the show. Later we performed the same show at CCOM. Although it was the first time I had learned a Chinese dance, I liked its lively spirit. To my surprise, my piano teacher, Wang, complimented me, saying, "Your sense of rhythm was very good when you danced."

When we returned to the music school, we did not have enough time to study our music majors because of the busy rehearsal schedules for the song-and-dance show. In addition to performing the dance, I also wrote and helped direct a skit about a poor peasant family who suffered under their landlord and became homeless beggars.

In the remaining semester after the factory work, I learned only one piano recital piece, *Celebrating Fanshen*, adapted in 1964 from a Chinese instrument ensemble piece by Zhu Jian'er. The melody, played on the *banhu* (Chinese two-string fiddle), was familiar, having been used as a theme song for a radio program broadcast to the countryside. The piano adaptation retains much of the Chinese flavor. The percussive technique and lively rhythms create a festive atmosphere. I played this newly published piece for my final recital that semester and have kept it in my repertoire. When I played this piece in the U.S., some American friends called it Chinese jazz.

In 1963, the Communist Party had called on all the people to learn from Lei Feng, a soldier who became the model for everyone in China. Lei Feng, an orphan, brought up by the Communist Party, studied Chairman Mao's works and learned to lead a selfless life. He joined the PLA where he did many good and self-sacrificial deeds, such as washing his comrades' clothes when they were away on long marches. Very frugal about his own needs, he gave his savings to the needy. At age twenty-two he died in an accident, leaving a diary recording his revolutionary thoughts and actions. We were encouraged to put aside our personal interests and dedicate ourselves wholeheartedly to the nation and the people, following his example. My schoolmates and I competed to do good deeds around the school, such as sweeping the classroom floor and doing chores during lunchtime in the school kitchen.

Then, in 1965, our fourth- and fifth-year students and some teachers from the Prep Music High School were sent to the 4680 People's Liberation Army unit in the mountains in the remote rural suburbs of Beijing for one month. At that time, Mao Zedong favored and supported Lin Biao, defense minister, who had indoctrinated the armed forces in Mao Zedong Thought. A campaign, "Learn from the People's Liberation Army," was in full swing, calling on the entire nation to learn from the PLA's political thought work. The purpose of our month in the army was to reform our thoughts, discipline ourselves, and learn politics and military skills from the PLA.

We lived in barracks. Each class was assigned a platoon leader from the army unit, who directed our political studies and military training. We attended political lectures about the army's political thought work. This made the PLA a powerful army which followed the Party's leadership closely and successfully accomplished its tasks.

Ages sixteen and seventeen, pampered in the music school, we found military training harsh and strenuous. Students and teachers marched together in the same formation every day, sometimes singing in rhythm with the marching. The platoon leader singled out my respected piano teacher Wang and ordered her to march back and forth in front of the students. She was embarrassed and I felt much sympathy. But I kept my feelings to myself because obeying orders was the army's top priority.

Sometimes we ran long distances in the morning in the cold March wind, leaving me exhausted, with frozen hands. Our platoon leader, Xu, ran ahead tirelessly.

One day when all the students gathered in formation on the training ground, the battalion leader said, "Comrades, Chairman Mao told us to weather the storm. Today is a real test. Let's see if you can stand still for two hours." He gave us all a stern glance and then walked away with his hands crossed behind his back. I saw my classmates' reluctant faces.

Time had never ticked by so slowly. After one-and-a-half hours, a couple of the students' faces turned pale. They almost fainted and had to be taken away with assistance.

A more stressful exercise was emergency mustering of troops in the middle of the night. The most painful task, however, was night watch. We took one-hour turns to patrol the barracks alone near a graveyard. It was close to the Qingming Festival. Local people had put white paper flowers and strips on grave mounds. The wind rustled the paper flowers and I imagined ghosts of the dead flying from the graveyard.

One night, a fifth-year student named Gaoqiang had an accident. That night as he dreamed about the endless marching exercises, he responded to his drill officer's command, "Eyes right," and fell from the upper berth of the bunk bed. He lost his front teeth and was taken to a hospital the next morning.

During that month Mom wrote me a letter calling me "little soldier" and expressing her worries. I was a little homesick. Lacking true enthusiasm for the political studies, marching drills, and discipline, I followed orders. I was interested only in our mountain climbing and target shooting. We learned to take apart and reassemble a semiautomatic rifle. During target-shooting practice, we lay prone on the ground for hours. Some of my female classmates were not able to close one eye in order to aim, so they covered an eye by tying handkerchiefs around their heads. I thought this made them look like pirates. I did well in my target shooting and physical training, probably because of my sports experience in school.

At the end of our one-month training, a few of us were awarded "good soldier" titles for having good political thoughts and military skills. I felt rewarded by the recognition, but in my heart I knew that my piano skills were slipping. That was what I cared about most.

The momentum of our piano technical training was lost because of the one-month interruption every semester. Continuous daily practice is crucial for building technical skills at our age, when time is irreplaceable. It usually took a month simply to recover from those off-campus periods. Just as I was making progress, we had to go to a factory again.

Because I had experienced the direction change only for a few months, I could not predict its length and its serious political implications for my career, for my father's legacy, and for the rest of my family.

During my fifth year, many new required courses were thrown together quickly, such as songwriting, choral conducting, accordion, and piano accompaniment improvisation. The school intended to train us to be multi-skilled musicians to serve the masses. But these courses only scratched the surface of the subjects and did not teach us any applicable skills. Later when I worked as an accompanist, I realized the importance of learning to improvise accompaniment, but the sketchy course in piano accompaniment improvisation had not helped much.

The only new course which I found useful later was accordion. I learned one accordion solo piece, *Cavalry March*, which made me popular while performing with a Mao Zedong Thought propaganda team, a performance group during the Cultural Revolution.

The practice rooms in the Prep Music High School's new campus had been converted from a factory. Each room was open to the outside, giving exposure to cold and much dirt in Beijing's windy climate. We were required to wipe down with wet rags the thick dirt accumulated on the window frames and doors of our practice rooms. The dry skin on my right thumb cracked, but I carried out the task to show that I was not a pampered aristocratic girl. Consequently my thumb got badly infected. To drain the infection, the doctor made a deep cut on the tip of my thumb, and I could not play the piano for several weeks. At my final exam for piano accompaniment improvisation, we were given a song on the spot and about thirty minutes to develop an accompaniment before playing it for the exam. My thumb was not healed, but I managed to pass that exam using nine fingers only.

After we came back from the month in the army, Teacher Wang assigned me a final exam piece, *Happiness of People's Commune Members,* composed by Liu Shikun, a famous Chinese pianist. However, after a couple of lessons, Teacher Wang stopped coming to lessons. I thought that she might be sick. I faithfully waited for her during the scheduled lesson time for the next few weeks, but she never showed up. Because the final exam was approaching, I was very worried.

One day I waited outside the studio of the piano department chair, Teacher Liu, a beautiful and reserved lady. When she finished all her lessons and was on her way out, I caught up with her and said, "Teacher Liu, my piano teacher, Wang, has not come to teach for four weeks. What happened to her? Will she come next week?"

Her only reply was, "Oh, really?"

Teacher Liu did not seem to know what was going on with Teacher Wang. I was disappointed at her complete lack of response. She certainly did not indicate that she would find another teacher for me.

My respected teacher Wang, the Prep Music High School piano teacher whom I learned the most from, disappeared from my life. She had cared about me, encouraged me, set challenging goals and helped me achieve them. I missed her and cried over the keyboard in the practice room. I was also disappointed and angry at her for being irresponsible and leaving me on my own for half of the semester with no instruction for my final exam. I remember agonizing in the hot stuffy practice room in June 1965, trying to figure out how to prepare for my final exam. What happened to me that semester was unheard of in our music school, known for its rigorous teaching program. I did try to learn from three classmates who were learning the same piece for their final exams. But I did not think that they had much to offer. We were all equally inexperienced at interpreting this new Chinese piece.

At the final exam recital, I was not well prepared and felt embarrassed. I watched my twenty or so classmates repeat three or four Chinese piano pieces, and some, as if bored, played their pieces hurriedly. The advanced-level Chinese piano repertoire was apparently very limited. Quite a few students played *Ode to the Great Leap Forward*, accompanied by a second piano. That final exam did not seem as rigorous as previous exams consisting mostly of Western classical music. Performance standards for the new Chinese piano pieces were not clearly defined while both teachers and students tried to interpret the new repertoire. I passed that piano final exam without my teacher's instruction.

Later I heard from a student that Teacher Wang's husband, an art teacher from the Central Academy of Drama, had been in political trouble and was consequently sent to Lanzhou in China's interior. Teacher Wang, given no advance notice, had to follow her husband. Looking back, I am still grateful to Teacher Wang for helping me immensely with many aspects of my studies.

Thirty-five years later, in 2000, we met again. She came to visit me at Renmin University of China. I was the music department director in the newly established Xu Beihong School of Arts. As I showed her around the campus, I said, "Teacher Wang, I think that I learned the most from you in my piano studies. Thank you for teaching me for three years at the Prep Music High School."

She looked embarrassed and said, "I felt much guilt."

I did not want to ask for details about her state of affairs during that semester. I had come to understand her special circumstances.

• • •

By the end of my fourth year, three of my classmates had already joined the Communist Youth League of China, a mass organization of advanced (model) youth led by the CCP. The main task of the CYL was to unite and lead young people to follow Chairman Mao and the Party's directives. In my view, a CYL member ought to study Chairman Mao's works thoroughly and do many selfless deeds. Envious, as most students were, of the Youth League members chosen and trusted by the Communist Party, I was determined to become a member.

To show dedication, in mid-1965 I volunteered to publish the school's wall newspaper. Our goal was to raise student awareness of national and international events. With a couple of assistants, I wrote in chalk on exterior wall surfaces designated for campus announcements, selecting content from newspapers, mainly political news. Taking advantage of my drawing skills, I highlighted the news in stylized characters. Periodically I organized tests about current events and published the average score of each class.

For more than two months I worked on the wall newspaper after lunch when most students were napping. The newspaper was in addition to my tight class schedule, leaving me exhausted at the day's end.

I talked with the Communist Youth League leader, Teacher Wu, showing her my diary containing my self-criticisms and study notes on Chairman Mao's works. I stated my desire to follow Chairman Mao, to be selfless, and to criticize the bourgeois influence from my family, primarily my mother, a bourgeois intellectual who instilled in me the bourgeois dream of artistic fame common among my classmates.

At that moment I felt that making these criticisms was the correct thing to do. However, deep in my heart, I missed Western classical music and literature. I did not like some of the Chinese piano pieces that I was assigned to learn, but had to follow the current sweeping across China. I had also become aware of my tendency to self-centeredness. Joining the Youth League seemed to me the bold step that I should take toward the selfless model of Comrade Lei Feng. I tried sacrificing my self-interest, giving up my own study time to help my classmates improve their English.

Several months later I was told that I had "passed the test." My application was finally approved on November 23, 1965, by the Communist Youth League branch at the music school. I was happy to be part of this honorable organization and looked upon as a model youth by my peers. Our fifth-year-class Youth League group met every Saturday afternoon and shared our revolutionary thoughts.

One member, a frail girl in a neat and stylish polyester blouse, said, "I think that I will be happy living a rural life and doing manual work in the fields. I do not think that kind of physical labor will kill me."

I thought to myself, "Did she really mean what she said? Would she be happy, living that way all her life?" I knew that I myself might not be happy.

My artistic dream remained in the shadows of my heart. The dream surfaced often when I returned home on weekends and strolled the gardens and courtyard of our old family house, now part of the museum. In the serene summer nights, the moonlight shed silvery hues on the trees showing the silhouette of the persimmon tree's low branches, the tall walnut trees, and the mimosa trees' broad-reaching flowering branches. Their flowers scented our yard with their familiar sweetness. I had grown up with these trees, planted or cared for by Father, and they seemed like family. They still stood faithfully by his portrait bust.

The living room of our former family house remained the same as when Father had died more than a decade before. Looking at the reclining chair Father used to rest in and the large desk with his ink brush and ink slate, I often asked myself, "Would Dad be happy to see Qingping and me grow up, following his artistic dream?" However, his dream was not in line with the Party's objectives. To become accomplished artists could conflict with the Party's expectation that we dumb down to serve the people.

But what really tormented me was the government's plan to demolish the Xu Beihong Memorial Museum to make way for subway construction. Mom had appealed to government authorities to keep the museum and the house where my father had spent the last few years of his life. But she received no response.

Under normal circumstances, the construction design could have been revised to bypass the museum. But in 1965, the CCP Central Committee redefined the target of the Socialist Education Movement as Party persons in power taking the capitalist road—a portent of the coming Cultural Revolution. In this ultra-leftist environment the Xu Beihong Memorial Museum stood out as "bourgeois" cultural heritage. The Xu Beihong Memorial Museum was the only art museum in China dedicated to exhibiting a single artist's works and the only art museum in China with artworks on permanent display. In 1965, the political movement was marching to its climax, and many efforts to preserve cultural heritage were ignored. Nevertheless, I cherished the museum which kept my memory of my father alive. They could tear down the buildings, but they could never remove these cherished childhood memories from my heart.

• • •

In the following spring, my whole fifth-year class was sent to the Two Seven Locomotive Factory in Changxindian in the rural suburbs of Beijing where we worked for one month. I followed a female master worker, Liu, learning to use various tools to repair machine parts. Sometimes when the key in a machine shaft was worn out, I was required to find a key stock and file it down to fit the keyway in the round shaft.

Master Liu was patient. After I turned out a defective key, I said, "Master Liu, I am sorry I filed down the key stock too much. It is loose in the keyway."

"Don't worry," she said. "Here is another key stock. Try to work carefully this time and check the fit more often so you do not file off too much." I felt better when I finally made the perfect fit with her help.

The job was physically very demanding, requiring me to stand all day and bend over to work on parts, sometimes for hours. By the end of the day I was exhausted. The factory was loose about safety regulations. One day I saw a small hammer fall from the second level of the adjacent workshop, narrowly missing my female classmate's head. I could not imagine myself working in this environment for the rest of my life.

In the second half of the month, I was transferred to the locomotive workshop, not to labor but to interview workers in order to put together a show depicting the workers' dedication to their jobs. I was able to sit for a change. For the performance at month's end, two grand pianos were moved from the music school to the factory. Cui, a talented piano student, adapted an orchestral piece into a piano piece named *Locomotive*, played by two pianos. The music simulates the sound and the rhythm of a locomotive accelerating from slow chugging to smooth running as a steam engine laboriously built its momentum. The workers applauded this piano piece performed by Cui and a female piano student.

Although our show was a worthwhile attempt to serve the workers, I was glad when it was time to go back to my music studies. Most of my classmates, I am sure, felt the same way.

On the return trip to our school, we stopped near the famous Lugouqiao, also known as Marco Polo Bridge, over the Yongding River, where the Japanese had launched their full-scale invasion into China in July 1937. We took off our shoes, rolled up our pants legs, and paddled in the cold water of the swift running Yongding River in April. We had one picture taken as eight classmates and I held each other's hands to create a chain while standing in the middle of the river. With broad smiles, supporting each other in the swift current, we shared optimism. I had just turned eighteen.

Xu Fangfang (front row, far right), classmates, and CCOM teachers at the Two Seven Locomotive Factory in Changxindian where they worked in April 1966.

Xu Fangfang (fourth from left) and classmates standing in the Yongding River at Lugouqiao (Marco Polo Bridge), April 1966, supporting each other in the swift current, feeling they could stand up to the challenges ahead.

Xu Fangfang playing the piano score of the model work, the piano-accompanied cantata *The Red Lantern*, in the house at Haibo Hutong, Beijing, 1968.

Xu Qingping and Xu Fangfang at Tiananmen Square, 1968. The slogans in the background read: "Carry the Proletarian Cultural Revolution to the end. Wish Vice Chairman Lin Biao good health."

CHAPTER 15
A Wave of Fists

After returning to the school, we were busy preparing for an important concert to be performed in the Forbidden City Concert Hall on June 1.

All the girls from the first-year to our fifth-year classes were asked to sing a children's choral piece in order to make up for the shortage of younger students. A CCOM composition student wrote this choral piece to promote a model Communist Party leader, Jiao Yulu, Party secretary of Lankao County, Henan Province. Even while suffering from terminal cancer, Jiao was leading the people in his impoverished county in planting more paulownia trees.

At that concert in the Forbidden City Concert Hall, our youth orchestra performed a piece which also sounded like a locomotive with accelerating rhythm, albeit one that was a little out of synch. Someone joked that the train seemed on the verge of derailment. This remark later appeared prophetic.

Returning to the music school that night, we heard on the radio the shocking text from a big-character poster by Nie Yuanzi at Peking University, claiming that Peking University was controlled by bourgeois anti-revolutionaries. It called for all revolutionary intellectuals to "resolutely, thoroughly, cleanly, and completely eliminate all demons and monsters, and counterrevolutionary revisionists like Khrushchev." *People's Daily* printed the text on June 2, calling on true revolutionaries to follow Chairman Mao's leadership.

The Great Proletarian Cultural Revolution had begun in mid-May 1966, but most people did not know about this until June 1 when the radio broadcast of Nie Yuanzi's poster announced the movement to the entire country.

According to Mao, the moment had come for eliminating enemies within the Party, and their ideology. Chairman Mao condemned Party leaders who were following the capitalist road and cautioned against "a Khrushchev in China," who might turn China into another revisionist society like the Soviet Union.

Students in other universities and high schools rallied in support of the action at Peking University. They were encouraged to openly criticize their teachers and expose school administrators for not following Mao's directions. On June 2, 1966, students at CCOM and the Prep Music High School suspended classes, formed revolutionary organizations, and seized control of the campus. They vowed to expose every enemy of the revolution.

CCOM had been overseen by the Ministry of Culture whose leaders Mao deemed responsible for promoting feudal and capitalist art. Mao had made an accusation against arts leaders in December 1963, saying, "The 'dead' still dominate in many departments." He added, "Isn't it absurd that many Communists are enthusiastic about promoting feudal and capitalist art, but not socialist art?"[42] We interpreted Mao's statement as saying that all leaders in the arts, and most intellectuals, academics, and artists were bourgeois, because they all deviated from Mao's teaching that the arts should serve only proletarian politics.

Mao believed that an anti-Party "black line" dominated the arts field, allowing feudal and bourgeois arts to pervade society, serving only the bourgeoisie. In June 1966, students in my music school followed Mao's call to write big-character posters to expose the bourgeois direction of our school. In the first few days, it was like the rehearsal for a big show, except no one was practicing. The only music on campus was revolutionary songs played on a loudspeaker. We were allowed to sing only "Sailing the Seas Depends on the Helmsman," "The East Is Red," and a few other songs praising Mao and the Communist Party.

The lyrics of "The East Is Red" say:

The east is red; the sun rises.
From China arises Mao Zedong.
He strives for the people's happiness.
Hurrah, he is the people's great savior!

On the surface the movement looked exciting, with different big-character posters put up on campus weeding out bad people every day. But classes and lessons were suspended, and deep down I felt empty, thinking of my education, my beloved music, art, and literature all taken away from me. I wondered how long it might be before we could go back to our music studies. It would be ten years, during which there would be no formal teaching in all universities, including CCOM and other conservatories in China.

I was trying to keep my head above the water as threatening waves were about to engulf everyone around me. In the Cultural Revolution, most famous professors, artists, and musicians were considered bourgeois academic authorities to be struck down. Although my father had died ten years earlier, his influence remained, making him the foremost bourgeois academic authority in visual arts.

One day my schoolmates and I met to prepare accusations against our principals. I was quiet, trying not to attract attention. But a student from a revolutionary cadre family sneered at me and at an orchestra conductor's daughter, saying, "You children of reactionary bourgeois stinking intellectuals, go and look at your parents' big-character posters. Then criticize them. Why don't you?"

Saying nothing, I simply felt humiliated. Having few friends, I kept to myself, fearing that anything I said could be used against me.

Overnight, respectful students became a hateful mob. Some male students dragged our three Prep Music High School principals and some teachers outside the school buildings and forced them to dig in the surrounding ground while their students watched. Principal Yu, who had once made the memorable comment about the difference between a vase and a spittoon, received severe criticism. Some students hung a brick around a principal's neck to force his head down at a criticism meeting. Another student put a wastebasket over the head of an administrator so that she was blinded while being pushed to a criticism meeting. The students accused the principals of employing a pyramid structure for the purpose of developing a small number of award-winning stars. They denounced the administrators for poisoning them with bourgeois music in their curriculum containing mainly large, foreign, and ancient works.

The principals were held captive for days in a school jail. One piano student wrote a song, "Cow Demons and Snake Spirits," for the captives to sing. The student composer intentionally ended the song on the leading note, the most unstable note, to ridicule the singers. The principals were forced to sing solo, "I am a cow demon and snake spirit. I am guilty. I am guilty." Because Principal Zhang had had no music training, his singing, with its odd intonations, sounded like spoken Shandong dialect. I could not bear to see our respected principals so humiliated. I wondered how these formerly sensitive music students now had no tenderness left in their hearts. Principal Yu used to tell us that we musicians were engineers of the human soul.

Many of the students must have lost their souls during this period. Some were sincere revolutionaries, but most, in my opinion, were afraid because many came from politically problematic families. Some demonstrated their loyalty to Chairman Mao through brutally abusing the teachers and administrators. A plump, formerly shy male student used to bow to his piano teacher with a timid smile, not knowing what to do with his hands. But now, this very boy angrily pushed his piano teacher out of her studio and forced her to dig in the ground with a shovel. He punched his fists into the air and painted "black element," meaning reactionary, in big characters on the back of her shirt.

In June, mass-criticism rallies were held in our campus's largest open space where our principals and some teachers, including our Youth League leader, Teacher Wu, were abused. My most vivid memory of a mass rally is the public interrogation and punishment of CCOM president Ma Sitson, whom I had never seen before. A famous violinist and composer, Ma, a non-Party member, was the school's honorary president and not involved in directing the school. At that rally I was curious to find out more about him.

Ma was solidly built, with a big head the students had shaved clean. When the student representative yelled, "You big blood-sucker, confess your crimes against socialism," Ma spoke in a low voice with a strong Cantonese accent, "I did not do anything to sabotage socialism." At that, one fierce-looking boy struck Ma's head with a brick. Immediately, a stream of blood dripped from his bald head. Shocked and saddened, I lowered my eyes so as not to witness this brutality. Nonetheless, I forced myself to join the crowd in chanting, "Down with reactionary academic authority Ma Sitson! Long live great leader Chairman Mao! Long live the Great Proletarian Cultural Revolution!"

With each repetition of the slogan, a wave of fists thrust toward the sky.

Later in June, work teams were sent to universities to supervise the Cultural Revolution. Ordinary teachers who had been abused in the beginning of the Cultural Revolution were not targets anymore. The plump male student felt really embarrassed when he saw his piano teacher, who was no longer in disgrace. The boy reassumed his humble manners.

For a few weeks, some order was restored in CCOM. Zhao Feng, Party secretary of CCOM, did self-criticism about the bourgeois direction of the music school under his leadership.

In early August, the Cultural Revolution took another turn. On August 5, Mao Zedong put up his famous "Bombard the Headquarters" poster, criticizing leaders from the central down to the local levels, accusing them of suppressing revolutionaries and striking down the surging Great Proletarian Cultural Revolution. Mao's writing indicated that bourgeois headquarters existed within the CCP Central Committee. Without naming names, he was actually singling out the actions of Liu Shaoqi, chairman of the PRC and Mao's major rival within the Communist Party. Liu had sent the work teams who supervised the raging Cultural Revolution at universities and colleges. I believe that Mao considered the work teams an obstruction to the Cultural Revolution.

After the Eleventh Plenary Session of the Eighth CCP Congress held in August 1966, Lin Biao became sole vice chairman of the Party, replacing Liu Shaoqi as Mao's unofficial successor.

On August 8 the Central Committee of the CCP published the Sixteen Articles targeting those authorities within the Party who were taking the capitalist road. Mao's real target was again Liu Shaoqi. The Sixteen Articles also stressed the need to criticize the "four olds": old ideas, culture, customs, and habits. This would eradicate the negative influence of intellectuals, artists, and academics, and strengthen the socialist system. This was the thrust of the Red Guards' first campaign.

Only students from families of the "Five Red Types," including revolutionary cadres, revolutionary martyrs, revolutionary soldiers, workers, and poor and lower-middle peasants, were allowed to join the Red Guards. These students, wearing Red Guard armbands, were encouraged to destroy the "four olds." The police cooperated, giving them private information about people in the neighborhood. These Red Guards conducted home raids called *chaojia*, which means search and ransack.

Thousands of Red Guards gathered on Tiananmen Square on August 18, 1966, and Chairman Mao appeared on the Tiananmen gate tower, where he allowed a Red Guard to fasten a red armband to his sleeve. This signaled that Mao was authorizing the new movement's launch. Some Red Guards got to shake hands with Mao.

Overnight, red terror swept across Beijing. To eradicate the "four olds," the Red Guards destroyed old books and artworks and physically attacked and denounced perceived "bourgeois" elements: intellectuals, former landowners, rich peasants, capitalists, rightists and former rightists, counterrevolutionaries, and bad elements, meaning those who disrupted social order. "Counterrevolutionaries" could include innocent people framed politically in the Cultural Revolution. Later some Red Guards rooted out CCP cadres taking the capitalist road. Violent actions spread to other cities when the Beijing Red Guards traveled for free all over China during the "exchange of experiences" movement Mao had authorized. The only places the Red Guards were not permitted to enter were Zhongnanhai, the Forbidden City, and PLA areas.

I was shocked. My father certainly represented "old culture." Although many of his works expressed his patriotism during the War of Resistance, in my view they did not explicitly serve Mao's current political position. My father's works and his collection of ancient masterworks were definitely among the "four olds." I felt sad, confused, and began fearing for my life because I belonged to a group labeled "children of dogs."

The red terror took the life of our family friend Professor Yu Dayin of the department of Western languages and literature at Peking University. She spoke perfect English and had tutored me in English, and I felt very grateful for the privilege. Peking University students broke into Professor Yu's house, ransacked it, and forced her to kneel out in front. Unable to bear the humiliation, she committed suicide the next day.

Within our school, the most violent group of Red Guards was the "Maoist Red Guard" group, consisting of more than ten CCOM students from revolutionary cadres' families. Before the Cultural Revolution, most of them had dressed stylishly and hoped to become accomplished musicians of Western classical music. The "Maoist Red Guard" group at CCOM followed the Beijing high-school Red Guards in conducting home invasions and beating those they considered bad elements in society.

Frequent announcements of mass rallies from the campus loudspeaker unnerved not only me but other CCOM students from problematic families. All students on campus were expected to gather in the auditorium to witness the Red Guards' revolutionary actions.

One night the campus loudspeaker woke me up. I was on my feet immediately, following my schoolmates into the crowded auditorium where "Maoist Red Guard" members held the stage. The leader, Yan, wearing a yellow army uniform with a Red Guard armband, was a heavy young woman who had worn a long blue dress at her piano recitals. But at the mass rally she wore shorts, and stood arrogantly with her portly legs apart. One hand pressed against her waist and the other brandished a leather belt. Her fierce eyes searched the audience, and everyone shuddered.

She yelled, "We found Guan, a reactionary in our school! His family hid a gun under the grapevine in their yard. But our Red Guards uncovered the gun. We have brought the enemy here for you to see!"

Guan, a quiet bassoon student in his fourth year at the Prep Music High School, was then dragged on stage with his hands tied behind his back. He was forced to kneel and Yan and her fellow Red Guards whipped him with their belt buckles. Blood oozed from beneath his T-shirt and bruises colored his fair-complexioned face. During this violent show, Yan raised her fist and yelled, "Down with reactionary Guan! There is no wrong in revolution. It is right to rebel. Long live the Proletarian Cultural Revolution! Long live Chairman Mao!"

The crowd repeated her slogans with a thunderous voice.

PRC citizens were not allowed to possess arms. The Cultural Revolution leaders required everyone to turn in any type of arms, including hunting rifles, to the authorities. I turned in my BB gun, the only "weapon" in our household, to our school's revolutionary committee in early June 1966. Guan served as an example of the punishment dealt out to any who dared to resist orders. I heard that Guan was later sent to his home village to be brainwashed through forced labor.

One day in August, we were informed that large numbers of Beijing high-school Red Guards were coming to smash the Prep Music High School, considered an aristocratic school with most of its students coming from well-to-do bourgeois families. In response, my schoolmates closed the school gate and reinforced it with a barricade made of sections of tree trunks. Meanwhile, male students patrolled the campus for intruders, while I observed nervously. But after several hours of apprehensive watching, the rumored Red Guard attack did not come.

Beijing high-school Red Guards did flood the CCOM campus, not to smash it but to publicly debate with CCOM students a political couplet written in July by some high-school students from CCP cadre families: "The son of a heroic father will be a good man. The son of a reactionary father will be a rotten egg." In Chinese, "rotten egg" is a very derogatory epithet. Tan Lifu, a student at Beijing University of Technology and head of the university's Red Guards, provided his theoretical support, making this couplet a mobilizing force for a nationwide faction of Red Guards defending their CCP cadre parents, who had now been targeted as capitalist roaders inside the Party.

For this event, more than one thousand Beijing high-school Red Guards and CCOM students and Red Guards crowded our 999-seat auditorium. High-school Red Guard speakers took the floor, surrounded by CCOM students shoving each other for a chance to speak. Each CCOM speaker was questioned by the high-school Red Guards about his or her family background before being allowed to air his or her views. Most CCOM speakers voiced their opposition to the viewpoint expressed in the couplet, while all the Beijing high-school Red Guard speakers spoke in its favor.

This searing debate lasted throughout the night. One of our young piano teachers, Liu Shikun, who had won second prize at the International Tchaikovsky Competition in 1958, spoke against the viewpoints of the couplet. When questioned by the Red Guards about his family background, he answered confidently, "National bourgeoisie."

National bourgeoisie were Chinese capitalists who established their businesses in China independent of foreign powers. According to Mao Zedong, they were friends of the CCP during the revolution because they had been economically oppressed by foreign powers which tried to dominate China's industry and commerce. I had heard that Liu Shikun was married to a daughter of Ye Jianying, an influential PLA marshal.

Despite the angry Red Guards' interruptions, Liu delivered an eloquent speech, arguing that a person from a reactionary family could choose to revolt against the family and follow the Party. After his speech, a gang of female Red Guards pushed him out of the auditorium, bombarding him with political accusations. One pulled his shirt so hard that she tore off a sleeve.

Personally, I thought that the couplet was created to propagate the superiority of a faction of Red Guards who came from revolutionary family backgrounds. The couplet was also used to reject those from politically problematic families. A couple of months later, I heard a leading member of the Cultural Revolution Small Group denounce the couplet, arguing that the blood-lineage theory contradicted Marxism. The Cultural Revolution Small Group was the highest authority appointed by the CCP Central Committee to direct the Cultural Revolution. Thus the debate on the couplet finally ended and the heyday of this faction of Red Guards was over by the end of the year.

In August, after Mao's "Bombard the Headquarters" poster criticized Party leaders for suppressing revolutionaries, the work team sent to CCOM to direct the Cultural Revolution was withdrawn. After that, CCP organizations from the top level to the local and unit levels stopped functioning. Red Guard organizations at universities had no formal chains of command with the CCP Central Committee. It was left to the masses to conduct the Cultural Revolution in universities and in work units.

Two major rebel groups were formed in CCOM, representing conflicting political viewpoints, and for the first time in my life I would have to choose one. The "August Eighteenth Red Guard" group ("August Eighteenth") honored the date Mao gave an audience to the Red Guards on the Tiananmen gate tower. This group aimed to defend the Party leaders in power. The other group, much smaller, was the "Mao Zedong Thought Fighting Regiment" ("Fighting Regiment") of CCOM students and teachers, who had been suppressed earlier by the work team in charge of the school's Cultural Revolution. The "Fighting Regiment" advocated the right to fight against Party leaders obstructing the Cultural Revolution. It was aligned with the Red Guard Third Headquarters, one of the citywide alliances initially composed of minority-faction Red Guards from seventeen universities in Beijing.[43] The "Fighting Regiment" accepted students from politically problematic or "black" families as followers, although those students could never become Red Guards.

I had been on my own since the beginning of the Cultural Revolution. As with other decisions, I had to make this one independently. If I chose incorrectly, I could be singled out as a target by an opposing rebel group.

To figure out the most current political direction of the Cultural Revolution, I studied the newly published Sixteen Articles and important editorials in *People's Daily*, trying to read between the lines. I went to Tsinghua University and Peking University to read the big-character posters on campus because these universities played leading roles in the Cultural Revolution. I also talked with members of both rebel groups in CCOM. Based on my investigation and analysis, in September I decided to join the "Mao Zedong Thought Fighting Regiment." Although not as powerful or numerous as the "August Eighteenth" group, the "Fighting Regiment" seemed to be heading in the direction advocated in important CCP Central Committee documents.

At that time I truly believed in Chairman Mao and the Party. I wanted to follow Mao in wiping out the class enemies in the Cultural Revolution. I applied for Red Guard membership in the "Fighting Regiment" but my application was rejected because my family did not belong to the "Five Red Types." I loved my parents, but how I wished then that my parents had joined the Communist Party before 1949 so that I could be among the trusted revolutionaries! Even though some rebel groups labeled me the child of dogs, I did not believe my parents were reactionaries; my father had kept a close relationship with Premier Zhou and the Communist Party. However, my parents' expectations for me to become an accomplished artist or musician were considered bourgeois in the Cultural Revolution, which swept away their dream as well as mine. My only choice was following Mao and the Party as a way of trying to survive.

Quite a few of my classmates also joined the "Fighting Regiment" headed by Xin, a college-level double-bass student. I developed friendships with some classmates and teachers in this organization.

CHAPTER 16

Spreading the Revolution

All college students, revolutionary teachers, and high-school students received in early September permission from the government to travel free throughout the country, a movement called the "exchange of experiences." I believe Mao's objective was to spread Beijing Red Guards' revolutionary practices to the rest of the country, using the Red Guards to implement his ideas nationwide. At the same time, Red Guards and students from all over China traveled to Beijing to see Chairman Mao and learn from Beijing Red Guards.

A group of ten or more "Fighting Regiment" members decided to take the opportunity to travel to southern China. Our travel plan included visiting revolutionary sites, with some sightseeing in the backs of our minds. We hoped to support some revolutionaries along the way, but did not have specific plans for that mission.

Very excited about the opportunity to see the country, I was a little nervous about my first long journey on my own, an unpredictable adventure while the Cultural Revolution was evolving. I also worried about Mom, who could be harassed by any intruders although the most violent Red Guards from Beijing No. 8 and No. 4 High Schools had left our house by late September. I discussed my travel plans with Qingping, the only family member I could depend on. Because Mom's monthly salary had been cut from 120 *yuan* to 60 *yuan*, I had little money for the trip. Qingping kindly said, "Xiao Mei, don't worry. I will stay with Mom while you are traveling. Here, take this 15 *yuan*. It's my monthly allowance for school meals. I will not need the money if I eat at home with Mom." At the time this kind of support was rare even among family members. Most people were concerned only about their own survival.

I bundled a blanket and tied it on my back. I had Chairman Mao's red quotation book, my Prep Music High School student I.D., and a few necessities packed into my school bag. When we set out on September 27, the weather was getting cooler. But I wore plastic sandals and a sweater, not thinking about the cold weather ahead.

Our first destination was Guilin, two days and two nights away. During this long train ride, my need for sleep overcame any concerns about hygiene, and I slept on the floor under the benches in the economy car.

Finally I saw Guilin with my own eyes. In all of China this city enjoys a deserved reputation for its uniquely beautiful landscape. It was also where my parents first met at the end of 1942 during China's War of Resistance. The mountains along the Li River have abruptly steep sides and rounded tops, and in the autumn mist they reminded me of Father's famous Chinese ink brush painting *Spring Rain on the Lijiang* (*Li River*).

After Guilin, our group traveled to Chengdu and Chongqing in Sichuan Province. In Chongqing our group leaders decided we should help the local Red Guards with their Cultural Revolution. Our "Fighting Regiment," formed by students suppressed by the work team in CCOM, aligned itself with a similar faction in Chongqing. With our portable mimeograph, we printed slogans such as "There is no wrong in revolution. It is right to rebel," and took the flyers to a couple of schools. After talking with both factions at a school, we aired our support for the smaller group, suppressed by the leaders in the Chongqing Municipal Party Committee of the CCP. We spent only half a day there, distributing flyers and encouraging the smaller group to press on with their struggle. We promised support from the Beijing Red Guards. I even donated ten *yuan* to them, half of my entire travel budget. Shy at first, the students gained confidence after we showed our support and were sad to see us leave so soon.

The hospitality station in each city we visited assigned us lodging in a school. I slept on the concrete floors of classrooms covered with some straw. My thin blanket could hardly shield me from the cold and dampness in Chongqing. I had heard about the Sichuan specialty dessert, Laitangyuan, "glutinous rice balls from Lai's original recipe" with sweet sesame fillings, but could not afford one. Because my ten *yuan* had to last for more than a month, I lived on plain restaurant noodles with free hot pepper sauce. Fortunately, my travel group helped me. One night our "Fighting Regiment" leader suggested that Teacher

Guo, a young CCOM piano teacher, share his salary with some of the poorer students. Guo was one of the sons of Guo Moruo, a prominent poet and a friend of my parents. Teacher Guo gave me ten *yuan*, allowing me to visit several other cities I had dreamed of seeing. Guo's generosity came just in time during the most difficult period of my life.

I was proud to spread the revolution to the schools in Chongqing. While traveling I did not have to fear being attacked because of my problematic family background. A male voice student named Zhang and I also worked to help some local students go to Beijing to fulfill their dream of seeing Chairman Mao in Tiananmen Square. Zhang and I took advantage of our Beijing student status to get train tickets for these students.

On a different note, I felt a special attachment to the foggy city of Chongqing. I learned from Mom that she and Dad had developed love for each other in Panxi on the north side of the Jialing River, in the suburbs of Chongqing. The night view was unique, with lights dotting the mountain city on both sides of the river. Chongqing's roads were hilly. In my mind's eye, I saw Father taking the long series of steps to the top of the riverbank in the morning fog, working his way from the river to his teaching job at Central University. He had painted there a Chinese ink brush painting, *Water Carriers of Sichuan*. The narrow vertical format accentuates the long path of stairs on which the water carriers climb to the top of the riverbank. It was in Chongqing that my mother overcame many difficulties to finally marry my father. There they saw the victory of China's War of Resistance in 1945.

Our group's next destination was Guizhou Province. We visited Zunyi, a small town where the historic Zunyi Conference had been held in January 1935 during the Long March. At that meeting, Mao Zedong's guerrilla strategy was confirmed and his leadership in the CCP was established.

Our group traveled next to Kunming, the capital of Yunnan (South of the Clouds) Province. To me, Kunming was like a foreign city, with its light-colored buildings and big fountain in the center of downtown. The lush green all over the city and suburbs contrasted sharply with Beijing.

The most interesting part of our visit to Yunnan was our trip to the Labor University, attended by ethnic minority people working in the neighboring communities. A free ride on the back of a truck took us to the university in four hours. We stayed in the crude dirt-floored dormitory for one day. Upon arrival, we were invited to a gathering that evening where a few female ethnic minority students took turns singing folk songs. This was the first time I had encountered folk singing by ethnic minorities. I really enjoyed the melodies and the free style of their soft singing. When I asked a student where she had learned her song, she said, "I just made it up."

As a music student, I was really intrigued and asked, "Does it take long to compose a song?"

She answered, "I had thought about what I wanted to sing for a few minutes before I composed the music and lyrics." This showed me a new facet of music making.

On our return trip to Kunming, we walked on the beautiful Yunnan Plateau covered with yellow and red flowers. A light drizzle had just stopped. I paused and took note of the large-petaled flowers, the yellow showing vibrantly through the moisture left by the rain. I breathed deeply and took in the colorful landscape stretching to the horizon. We sang "Sailing the Seas Depends on the Helmsman" while walking, and our voices floated on the gentle breeze across the plateau.

Teacher Guo and some other students took a different route after our Chongqing visit and now our group consisted of only two male students, Xin and Zhang, and several female students. Our group decided next to visit Chairman Mao's home village in Shaoshan, Hunan Province. I was interested in learning about Mao's early revolutionary activities, including developing peasant movements in the area. The exhibits unfolded many stories I had not learned from my history books. Our group took a photo in front of Mao's residence. Zhang looked like a Red Army soldier with his army uniform and a broad coolie hat on his back. The female students all looked happy and proud.

At Nanchang in Jiangxi Province we visited an exhibition about the Nanchang Uprising of August 1, 1927, considered the CCP's first action against the Kuomintang's anti-Communist-Party purges. August first was later remembered as the anniversary of the founding of the People's Liberation Army.

In Nanchang, we discussed what to do before returning to Beijing. For me the tour of revolutionary sites was complete. I appreciated the one-month free-travel adventure shared with my schoolmates. The warm friendships we built lasted many years.

I told my group about my desire to visit my father's hometown in Yixing, Jiangsu Province. At the Nanchang train station I was finally on my own, trying to get on a train to Shanghai where my second aunt, Ren Youchun, and her family lived. I hoped that Second Aunt would help me connect with relatives in Father's hometown. But by late October, trains were already packed with Red Guards and students going north to Beijing. I was not able to get a ticket to go to Shanghai that day. That night I lay on the sidewalk outside the Nanchang train station, waiting for the next train. Fortunately the sidewalk was not too cold because Nanchang was south of the Yangtze River, where the weather in October was still mild.

I got on a train to Shanghai the next day. All I had was Second Aunt's address, which my mother had given me. Second Aunt had stayed with us twice in Beijing and Mom had treated her well. At the Shanghai train station, I got directions to her house in Danshui Road (Fresh Water Road).

The widow of my father's younger brother Shou'an, Second Aunt had in the late 1950s worked in a factory to support her young children. She now lived with her two daughters and a maid named Shaoma (Mother Shao), who had been with their family for years.

I had not told Second Aunt I was coming. A small thin lady in her sixties, she was surprised but happy to see me. Their apartment on two floors was small and crowded. Instead of a flush toilet they had wooden buckets. Every morning they emptied the buckets into a wagon which had a daily route passing their building. Except for the bathroom, I felt very comfortable. For the first time on my trip I had a chance to sleep in a bed and have my clothes washed. Second Aunt was very warm and talkative, but I could not understand her Yixing dialect, which my cousin had to translate.

Second Aunt made delicious fresh vegetable dishes for me, a rarity on my trip. We chatted late into the night. I felt the warmth from her, a relative who did not shy away from me because of my mother's political trouble. During the Cultural Revolution some family members turned against each other in order to save themselves. Since that visit I have always cherished her help during that difficult time in my life. I told her I planned to visit my father's hometown in Yixing and she gladly wrote a letter to introduce me to my cousin there, Pan Nansheng, son of my father's younger sister Xu Aizhen.

• • •

I had always dreamed of visiting Father's hometown. I grew up proud of my father and always wondered what in his childhood had made him a great artist. In late October I was finally able to trace my roots in Father's native region.

My cousin Nansheng, a quiet gentle person, an accountant for the Yixing Tax Bureau, lived with his wife and their little son and daughter in the city of Yixing. Nansheng kindly took me to visit my father's hometown, Jitingqiao, about ten minutes by bus from the city of Yixing.

Ten miles to the west of Lake Tai, the area around Jitingqiao was crisscrossed by streams and rivulets. This quiet township had about fifty families, mostly peasants and fishermen. In contrast to the grey northern China plain in late fall, the land around Father's hometown was fresh greenness stretching out for miles, covering the rolling hills like a velvet blanket. What a sight it was to see the junks with their snow-white sails widespread against the clear blue sky in nearby Lake Tai! I was fascinated by the tall smooth bamboo plants growing in clusters alongside the rivers. As breezes rose, rustling bamboo leaves and rippling streams made gentle music together. My grandfather, Xu Dazhang, had nurtured my father so he could enjoy unity with nature. His love of the green hillsides and the meandering streams had later in life given him endless sources for his creative artworks.

Father's family house, made of wood and brick, was about one hundred years old. It was built on the bank of the Tang River, a major canal connecting the medium-sized cities Wuxi and Changzhou, and others. Nansheng's father, Pan Xiangyuan, used to live in the Xu family house. After his father moved in with him in the city of Yixing, they asked an agricultural production-team leader to take care of the Xu family house in exchange for living there rent-free. When the production-team leader learned that I had come a long way from Beijing to visit, he kindly treated me to a bowl of rice porridge and showed me around the house.

Father's family house had rooms partially surrounding a yard and threshing-ground. This design closely integrated their daily lives as farmers and painters/scholars. The family had raised their own vegetables in a fenced garden, and Father, as a child, had planted two peach trees. In a corner of the living area next to the threshing-ground was a pig sty. Above the study, on the second floor, was a large bedroom. I was told that Father had been born in that bedroom. The windows of the study were divided by an arrangement of intersecting slats which helped secure strong paper that could be painted on. The wooden door of the study had flowers carved into it. In the quiet atmosphere of the study, I imagined Father spending hours in his childhood focusing on classical Chinese literature. In the same study, Grandfather had given Father his first painting lessons.

After a few days in the city of Yixing, I took a boat to Dacheng, a neighboring town where Father's favorite uncle, Lu Shunchuan, and his family lived. I remembered the old man with a long white beard who had visited our home in Beijing in the early 1950s. Unfortunately, he had died during the famine. His eighty-two-year-old widow lived with her sons in their two-story house. Even with her bound feet she actively did some farm work and housework. I saw her threshing soybeans out of their shells in the kitchen in the back of the house. Also in the kitchen was a large bath pot. Family members sat in it, their feet hanging out, and bathed in water heated by firewood. A lamb stood in a dark corner of the kitchen, watching me with eyes that appeared blue.

During the couple of days I stayed with Father's aunt, her sons treated me to a special dish which Father had enjoyed as a child: a bowl of boiled green-colored glutinous rice balls with ground pork filling. Marinated ramie leaves were mixed with glutinous rice powder to make it green and add fragrance. I was told that Father had raised ramie in his family vegetable garden specifically to provide this ingredient.

Granduncle Lu Shunchuan had made the downstairs of the house into a teahouse. During festivals, Granduncle invited Peking opera performers and folk storytellers there, and crowds gathered for this free entertainment. Father was always invited. The heroes in the operas and stories like *Water Margin, Biography of Yue Fei*, and *Romance of the Three Kingdoms*, with their determination to fight for the oppressed, inspired Father so much that he drew them from memory and imagination.

I also visited Nansheng's younger sister, Pan Ximei, and her husband, Tang Tingchuan, in Tangdu of Dingshan Township, not far from Father's hometown. The couple worked for a pottery trade school for which Pan Ximei was a worker and Tang Tingchuan a teacher. Tang had a cheerful disposition and a tanned face with a broad smile. At his school he showed me the process of pottery and porcelain making. Although some machines were used to make the initial models, many steps were hand-done to create exquisite teapots.

Tang's family, with three young children, lived in one room shared with their pigs. At night I crowded into bed with the children while the pigs snorted in the corner. I had never before slept in the same room with pigs. Father, as a child, had probably tended pigs in his family's yard. Tang and his family did not have much but they seemed to love their creative pottery making. I liked the warmth and honesty of Father's relatives. I imagined Father living his daily life with people like these.

Before leaving Yixing, I went to Jitingqiao again. At the family cemetery, I paid my respects at the graves of my grandfather Xu Dazhang and my great-grandfather Xu Yangeng. Seeing the two untended mounds covered with weeds, I held back tears. My grandmother Lu's coffin still lay above ground in another cemetery nearby. She had died in January 1938, the year after the Japanese occupied their hometown. She had wanted my father to come home to bury her. But his complicated life ended before he could fulfill her wish.

I also met distant relatives who told me they all belonged to the extended Xu family. They described my grandmother, Lu, as a kind, soft-spoken woman who gave her last ration of rice away to beggars. For years she had allowed migrant farmhands to camp in her vegetable garden. My artistic grandfather and my kind-hearted grandmother, during their short lives, had guided my father and developed his artistic talents, enabling him to become a great artist.

Sitting by Father's family house, listening to the water streaming past, I felt that Father was still with me although he had left me thirteen years before. Here in Jitingqiao I touched the soil Father had tilled. I saw the surroundings that had nurtured him, and came to know the people among whom he had taken root. The river flowed past insistently. The water never ran dry because spring water from a faraway mountain was continuously welling up. Likewise, these were inexhaustible sources from which Father drew inspiration for his paintings. His hometown people had given him personal qualities that guided his later life.

It was early November when I left, and Nansheng lent me a padded jacket against the cold. I thanked Nansheng's family for their hospitality. Although obstacles awaited me in Beijing, where Mom was still in political trouble, I was now a stronger person, having found my roots and support from my extended family. I had also conquered many hardships on my adventurous trip around China.

Returning to Beijing turned out to be a nightmare. I first took the bus to Nanjing, where the trains were even more crowded than before. Youths from all over China were trying to get to Beijing to see Chairman Mao before the end of the "exchange of experiences" movement. I waited for a day and a night in a long line at the Nanjing train station, sitting on the ground, shivering in the cold wind. With only four *jiao* left, I began to worry. If I could not get on the train the next day I would be starving. I bought two *mantou*, which was all I had the entire day. In the middle of the second night, I finally got onto the platform. But the Red Guards already on board refused to unlock the doors. I followed a student who found a window slightly open and scrambled to squeeze my body through the window.

There was not even a place to stand. Some people sat on the tea-tables. I squeezed through the packed car to the junction between the cars, where I stood for eight hours. After Jinan Station in Shandong, the crowd diminished a little, and I could finally sit down. I began feeling nervous, not knowing what to expect at home. At last the train pulled into Beijing. My heart was warmed by the sight of the familiar twin clock towers on the train station. The streets were filled with Red Guards from other cities.

When I reached our house, I decided to be cautious and use the museum entrance, from which I could first phone home next door. I was relieved to hear Xuezheng, Mom's younger step-brother, on the phone, who said, "Xiao Mei, there is no problem. Come right home." I happily reunited with Mom and Qingping. As soon as I relaxed, my physical strength gave out. I ran a fever from flu for more than a week.

• • •

The warm welcomes from Father's relatives helped me face the persecution of my parents. After Father's death, Mom, Qingping, and I visited the Babaoshan Revolutionary Cemetery twice a year: on September 26, the anniversary of his death, and during the Qingming Festival around April 5. On September 26, 1966, Mom was in political trouble, and for the first time we missed our visit to Father's grave.

Father's tombstone loomed larger than those adjacent. A bronze profile relief of Father was fixed to the tall white marble tombstone. Poet Guo Moruo, Father's friend, had written the calligraphy inscribed on the tombstone, "Artist Xu Beihong's Grave." Our family, friends, and relatives gathered there on the anniversaries of his passing to share our memories. There we also met art students, art lovers, and leaders from the Chinese Artists Association. I had always been touched by the appreciation they showed for Father.

On a cold day in December, Mom, Qingping, and I decided to visit Father's grave despite the risks. It had just snowed and the bitter north wind cut through our padded overcoats. It took us two hours by bus and walking to get to the Babaoshan Revolutionary Cemetery. I was relieved when the cemetery guards let us in after we explained that we were family members of Xu Beihong, who was buried there.

During the summer, Red Guards had vandalized many tombstones in the Babaoshan Revolutionary Cemetery. Most destroyed tombstones belonged to non-Communist Party people identified by the prefix of "Mr." instead of the Party designation "Comrade." We finally arrived at Father's grave. My heart sank when I saw that the grave had been leveled. Several other tombstones nearby were also broken. I thought to myself, "Father was not spared the Cultural Revolution even after his death."

His white marble tombstone was broken into three pieces we found some distance from his grave. The bronze profile relief of Father was gone. I closed my eyes and remembered our many visits here. I could smell the tall cypress trees and see the blue sky between their thick green leaves, providing seclusion for his resting place. I spoke silently to Father during each visit. Perhaps he could sense our arrival as we cautiously stepped on the flat white marble base that covered his grave. Perhaps he felt happy to see Qingping and me growing taller year after year.

Now the only permanent place where Mom, Qingping, and I had shared memories of Father had been destroyed. The wind whistled, twirling powdery snow across the desolate cemetery as if to echo the sadness in our hearts. The broken pieces of Father's tombstone lay quietly in the thick snow. Many art students had come here to pay their respects to Father. I believed that their love for Father's work was silently hidden, just like the broken tombstone buried in the snow. I wondered when this injustice would be rectified. I tearfully murmured, "Dad, I wish that you could see me. I just turned nineteen. No matter what is happening to you politically, I will always love you."

CHAPTER 17
Justice Is Served

One bitterly cold day in November, Mom, Qingping, my "little uncle" Xuezheng, and I had all huddled around the metal stove in the living room, our only heated room. We could not afford the coal to fire the radiator system in our two-story house; Mom's salary could hardly buy us food. Qingping used a small hand-wagon to haul coal for our metal stove. It cost eight *yuan* per wagonload and we used it sparingly.

We had to sell our furniture very cheaply. I remember selling Mom's large real wood wardrobe to a second-hand store for 120 *yuan*. We also sold a beautifully crafted set of stacking tea tables for about 50 *yuan*. I was greatly disappointed that we did not have meat for our 1967 New Year's celebration meal.

For some, it was worse. While their parents were detained for months, some children of problematic families stole from grocery stores to survive. A sixteen-year-old female student from the Prep Music High School moved in with a male classmate; although not socially acceptable, it kept her alive. Another female schoolmate had been living with her mother, who during the summer had been beaten publicly every day by the rebel group at her work unit. Unable to tolerate further abuse, her mother drowned herself in a well. My schoolmate, distraught, attempted to leap from her fourth-floor apartment window, but neighbors were able to stop her.

Within my realm of observation, most intellectual families attacked for political reasons during the Cultural Revolution simply tried to endure the persecution. They had no power to fight back. Whatever actions they might take, they could not be sure of the outcome.

With our family gathered around the half-fueled metal stove, I thought about my mother's political persecution. Although without a definite plan, I resolved to fight for our survival. That day I confidently told Mom and Qingping, "I am an optimist. I believe that things will get better for us."

In winter 1966, the Cultural Revolution switched its main focus to the capitalist roaders within the Party, targeted by the Sixteen Articles. In line with this new direction, I thought that the target at the Xu Beihong Memorial Museum should be the Party leader Wang Shuxiao, and not my mother, the non-Party member director.

I had reason to believe that Wang was behind the Red Guards' brutal beatings of my mother. In September, when the No. 8 High School Red Guards were leaving the museum, a Red Guard named Jiang had said to Mom, "Wang Shuxiao is not a good person. The Red Guards beat you up because of Wang Shuxiao's claim that you had guns and ammunition and that you were a spy." Finding no guns, ammunition, or spies at our house, Jiang had torn up Wang Shuxiao's white silk scarf because he felt cheated.

He returned to Mom a few small souvenirs they had taken from our house, but not Chairman Mao's four personal letters to my parents. As long as we did not have those four letters, Mom was vulnerable to abuse from other Red Guards whom Wang might call on.

I wanted to find evidence of Wang Shuxiao's crimes and expose them. I believed she would use any means to persecute my mother for her own gain. With the confidence gained from my travels around China, I started my secret investigation.

Conversations Mom had overheard among the No. 8 High School Red Guards that summer had revealed that Jiang's mother, Chen, was a cadre at the First Ministry of Machine Industry in Beijing. Based on this information, one day in December, I disguised myself as a Red Guard from the Red Guard Third Headquarters in a yellowish-green army coat and hat, and walked into the big First Ministry of Machine Industry building. I soon identified Chen in one of the offices; she and her son had a family resemblance. I assumed a manner of authority and said, "Comrade Chen, I am from the Red Guard Third Headquarters. Could we have a private talk, please?"

Chen looked a little nervous. She led me into the hallway. I said, "I hear that your son, Jiang, from Beijing No. 8 High School, got involved in the Cultural Revolution at the Xu Beihong Memorial Museum. We need a few facts about his actions there. I hope that you will cooperate with us." I paused for a second and then asked casually, "How did he decide to go to the Xu Beihong Memorial Museum?"

Chen responded with a forced smile while her eyes were searching elsewhere, and said, "Well, one day in summer we were looking at the print of a horse by Xu Beihong hanging in our apartment. Jiang suddenly got the idea of going to the Xu Beihong Memorial Museum to carry out their Red Guard actions."

"I see. When he was in the museum, did he get any information from anyone there?"

"Yes, a woman comrade named Wang Shuxiao with Party responsibilities gave him information about Xu Beihong's wife, Liao Jingwen."

"What did she say about her?"

"She told Jiang that Liao Jingwen had guns and ammunition."

This clicked with what Jiang had told Mom. But I followed Chen's answer a step further. "Did Jiang uncover any guns and ammunition from Liao Jingwen or her home?"

"No, he did not."

Now I knew what Jiang and his fellow Red Guards had been digging for in our yard, and why the Red Guards had beaten my mother so violently when they found no guns and ammunition. I asked a few minor questions just to pretend I did not know anything about the Cultural Revolution situation at the Xu Beihong Memorial Museum. We talked for about half an hour. Then I thanked her and said I might come back and question her further if necessary.

Chen's statement confirmed my suspicions.

At that time there was no justice system or police force to chase criminals and serve justice legitimately. I could either watch Mom be abused incessantly by Wang Shuxiao, who might have stolen Chairman Mao's letters and could commit more crimes without anyone to stop her, or take action against Wang myself and protect my mother. I chose the latter, although this would not be easy. Wang was a sneaky woman with many more years of experience than I had. But as a teenager, I was not afraid to take risks. Our family had lost so much, and Mom's life was at risk.

By myself I had no power to take the steam out of Wang's rampages. But in winter 1966, power existed in rebel groups, particularly those in colleges and universities. I needed strong evidence and a legitimate rebel group action to expose her crimes. I thought that our "Fighting Regiment" at the Central

Conservatory of Music was in a good position to help me, and that the new direction, targeting the capitalist roaders inside the Party, was in our family's favor.

By December, our "Fighting Regiment" had grown from a small group to a dominant organization in our school. Our opposition had collapsed. The "Fighting Regiment" was aligned with the Red Guard Third Headquarters, backed by the Cultural Revolution Small Group. I thought that this powerful alignment would give "Fighting Regiment's" future actions legitimacy and mass support.

I decided to ask my classmates within the "Fighting Regiment" for help. Mengli, a violin student, my classmate since fifth grade, was empathetic and responsible. I visited her at her home, consisting of one large room. Her living quarters was behind a tall dresser. I poured out the story of what Wang Shuxiao's actions had brought to my mother. I also described Chairman Mao's four letters to my parents. I told Mengli I suspected Wang Shuxiao had stolen these letters. Also, Wang might have taken artworks by Xu Beihong from the Xu Beihong Memorial Museum, because she had mentioned that Xu Beihong's paintings had value overseas.

Mengli listened attentively. After our conversation, she took a few of our classmates to visit Mom. They saw the scar on her forehead. Mom's personal description of the violence against her brought tears to my friends' eyes.

Next I talked with classmate Tian Sheng, a cello student, also my classmate since fifth grade. A young man willing to take risks when necessary, Tian Sheng was one of the earliest members of the "Fighting Regiment" and one of its leaders, possessing genuine leadership skills. He had visited our house one evening in 1964 and left with a very good impression of Mom. That evening a Chinese massage doctor, Old Lady Wang, had come to visit Mom from Shuangqiao (Double Bridges) in Beijing's suburbs. Dr. Wang was well known for treating bone and muscle injuries using traditional Chinese therapeutic massage. I had called Tian Sheng and a female student to come over and have this doctor check them out.

Tian Sheng decided to take action against Wang Shuxiao to serve justice and recover the cultural relics from the museum. Mengli and my other friends joined in for the same reasons, and also for recovering Chairman Mao's personal letters to my parents. We planned a surprise search of Wang's apartment to retrieve those letters and find other evidence of her crimes to be used during a mass-criticism meeting against her at the museum the following day.

I had not asked my classmates what they thought about my father politically. At the time, none of the top leaders in China had publicly cleared Xu Beihong politically. So clearing the name of his widow might not be viewed favorably. But none of my friends questioned my father's political status. Many years later I asked Tian Sheng if he had been worried about Xu Beihong politically in 1966. Tian Sheng said that as a teenager he had been curious about fine art. He particularly appreciated the humanism expressed in Xu Beihong's paintings and considered him an influential artist in Chinese art history. Therefore he never questioned Xu Beihong politically. However, Tian Sheng did have valid concerns about the consequences of our planned actions. Because we were acting only on my suspicion and his judgment, Tian Sheng was afraid that if we found no evidence against Wang we could not justify searching her apartment. Despite his worries, he decided we should go ahead, partly because he trusted me.

We got Wang's address. She lived on the north side of Beijing. One cold December night, Tian Sheng assembled a dozen "Fighting Regiment" members, mostly my Prep Music High School classmates. He wanted them to be able to outnumber Wang's family members in case there was resistance. They secured a truck and a driver from CCOM and drove to Wang's apartment in the dark. Tian Sheng and some female students in army overcoats crowded the second-floor hallway outside Wang's apartment. One knocked loudly at the door. Wang Shuxiao opened it and appeared surprised. Tian Sheng's group rushed in and filled her apartment.

"How dare you break into my home?" Wang yelled.

Tian Sheng spoke. "Wang Shuxiao, we are members of the Mao Zedong Thought Fighting Regiment from CCOM. Listen. We are taking a revolutionary action because we believe that you stole cultural relics from the Xu Beihong Memorial Museum. We must search your apartment."

Wang laughed and said, "Aha! Xu Fangfang must have sent you here." Then she barked at Tian Sheng, "Shit! I didn't steal nothing. You rotten egg! Get your stinking fingers off my things."

Wang did not resist the search, instead putting all her efforts into cursing. Tian Sheng's group was in control. Their purpose was retrieving the cultural relics and not to harm Wang physically. Therefore they left her alone while she cursed incessantly.

Tian Sheng went ahead, searching her two-bedroom apartment. In about one hour our suspicions were confirmed. He found Chairman Mao's letters to my parents, handwritten in ink brush with Mao's personal signature. Tian Sheng then felt confident about searching further. He also found a number of scrolls and other original artworks by Xu Beihong. Faced with the stolen goods, Wang did not try to argue in her own defense. All she did was use her dirty mouth, which never shut up.

Later that night Tian Sheng brought the confiscated items to our house for Mom to identify. Mom confirmed Chairman Mao's letters and the original artworks by Xu Beihong taken from our house and the museum. I had been nervously waiting for the search results. After seeing the evidence of Wang's crimes, I felt relieved that my friends' actions had been justified.

From the present day's legal point of view, Tian Sheng and my other schoolmates did not have the right to search Wang's apartment because China's legal authority had not approved the search. However, without the timely action, Wang could have destroyed Chairman Mao's letters, or transferred the original artworks by Xu Beihong to other hiding places for her personal interests. We would never have been able to expose her crimes and Mom's life would have remained in jeopardy.

That night we prepared the mass-criticism meeting against Wang Shuxiao. One student wrote in thick ink brush strokes, "Down with reactionary Wang Shuxiao." The horizontal slogan was put up at the entrance of the large mounting room in the museum. The next morning more than twenty students from the "Fighting Regiment" escorted Wang Shuxiao to the mass-criticism meeting in the mounting room.

Museum staff members and our neighbors crowded in, many standing around the entrance. Although the room was unheated, the emotions there were intensely heated and my heart was beating fast.

The students kept the order of the meeting. They displayed on the table the evidence of Wang's crimes, including the original artworks by Xu Beihong and other cultural relics from the museum retrieved from Wang's apartment. The Xu Beihong Memorial Museum people spoke up, identifying the items displayed. Lao Ma spoke against Wang, criticizing her for bullying staff members. My "little uncle," Xuezheng, told the audience how Wang had threatened him and Mom's other family members.

Finally Mom spoke. Her appearance had once been stylish, but was now very different. She wore a bulky padded blue overcoat and her hair was short and cut straight at the bottom. Not fully recovered from the violence she had suffered, she looked pale and haggard, yet her speech was confident and convincing. She exposed Wang's repeated verbal attacks on the socialist system which had punished her rapist husband. Mom also described how Wang had instructed the Red Guards to demand from her Chairman Mao's four personal letters. Wang then kept the letters that the Red Guards had stolen for her.

Mom pointed to Chairman Mao's letters, the original artworks by Xu Beihong, and other cultural relics recovered from Wang's apartment and said that the presence of Chairman Mao's letters could have protected her from Red Guard violence. That was why Wang had taken the letters at the start of the Red Guard movement. Wang had wanted Mom to suffer with no means to defend herself.

Mom also exposed Wang's false allegation about her possession of guns and ammunition, and Wang's having instigated the Beijing No. 8 High School Red Guards to beat her. As the wife of a convicted rapist, Wang had targeted Mom because she wanted to shield herself. Mom stated the revolutionaries had finally seized Wang Shuxiao, a capitalist roader inside the Party and the real target of the Cultural Revolution.

Mom commended the justice brought to the Xu Beihong Memorial Museum. As she finished her speech, I looked around the room. The audience seemed moved by Mom's story and angry at Wang Shuxiao. Lao Ma and other museum staff appeared satisfied. The students from the "Fighting Regiment" looked strong and proud.

At the end, Mom raised her right fist and shouted, "Down with reactionary Wang Shuxiao!" The audience chimed in. Although Mom's voice seemed a little short of breath, her big eyes shone with fury. For the first time during the Cultural Revolution, I felt a sense of reward because Mom was finally able to stand up to her abuser. Justice had been done and I felt proud to have helped.

Wang Shuxiao seemed defiant, but when faced with the evidence of her crimes did not try to defend or excuse herself. She was not physically abused.

The two students escorting her only held her head down a few times, an expected practice at mass-criticism meetings during the Cultural Revolution. Even with her head lowered, Wang's small eyes continued to stare angrily up at the speakers. Nevertheless, she was finally reprimanded publicly for her crimes. The swiftness of our student group's actions impressed me. Tian Sheng and his group had collected evidence, presented the evidence, and exposed Wang Shuxiao's crimes publicly within twenty-four hours.

Tian Sheng knew that the Xu Beihong Memorial Museum was to be demolished soon. Therefore keeping the confiscated items in the museum office would not be safe. He decided to take these items to the Beijing Municipal Bureau of Culture, the department in charge of the Xu Beihong Memorial Museum. The bureau people were at first hesitant to take the confiscated items, but Tian Sheng persuaded them. One bureau cadre brought out a large wooden trunk bound by metal strips. The items filled the trunk. Tian Sheng requested a receipt, but the bureau cadre refused to write one for fear of getting involved. Tian Sheng made a list of all the items and left the list on the trunk. He sealed the trunk and wrote his signature on the seal. The bureau cadre took the trunk with the list and promised to keep them.

After Tian Sheng and his group's actions, Wang Shuxiao lost her influence. Besides Mom's safety, our greatest satisfaction was recovering the letters Chairman Mao had written. They were safe and out of Wang Shuxiao's hands. My schoolmates from the Prep Music High School had taken risks and brought justice to my family. Their actions made me believe that people of principle still existed, and I was very grateful.

In 1973, when order was restored in Beijing, the Beijing Municipal Bureau of Culture contacted Tian Sheng, who opened the trunk and found all the listed items intact. After the checking and verification process, a Beijing Municipal Bureau of Culture cadre thanked Tian Sheng for protecting government-owned cultural relics. Later in the 1970s, the items were transferred to the Xu Beihong Memorial Museum preparatory group, whose task was overseeing the new museum construction and preparing for its opening.

I think Wang Shuxiao should be prosecuted for stealing government-owned cultural relics, making false charges against Mom, and instigating the almost deadly beatings. In present-day China such crimes could bring jail sentences. But Wang's crimes and worse atrocities committed during the Cultural Revolution were not prosecuted because the legal and public security system at the time ceased to function in the face of red terror. After the Xu Beihong Memorial Museum was demolished in 1966, I heard that Wang Shuxiao later went back to the rug factory to be a worker again. At least she was no longer able to abuse her power in cultural institutions.

• • •

By late January, all of our neighbors' houses and most of the Xu Beihong Memorial Museum were already torn down to make way for the subway construction. Our two-story house became the only house left in our neighborhood and the subway construction authorities pressured us to move out.

Packing our belongings was very painful. With tears in my eyes, I swept up my broken classical music records, which amounted to thirty pounds when sold to a recycling station. While I had traveled in southern China, Qingping had burned all my compositions, including my award-winning essay. He was afraid that the Red Guards might use these compositions against me.

Qingping and I picked through piles of torn paper and debris the Red Guards had strewn all over the floors. We had left things this way to discourage any additional searches. We found the oil portrait of me wearing my green dress and red scarf which Qingping had painted in summer 1965. One corner was torn, but the image was intact.

To our delight, Qingping found one charcoal drawing of Sheng Peiyu by Father. Her husband, poet Shao Xunmei, while studying literature in England, had traveled to Paris where he met Father. In Shanghai in 1930, Father did a pencil portrait of Shao Xunmei and a charcoal drawing of his wife for them. The Shaos had financial difficulties in the 1950s, and in 1957 Shao's wife sold these two drawings to Mom for one hundred *yuan* each. The pencil drawing of Shao Xunmei was unsalvageable, but the charcoal drawing of Shao's wife, Sheng Peiyu, was undamaged. I was overjoyed to see this drawing which had once hung in our living room. It beautifully captures her quiet strength.

Mom's books included Chinese classical and contemporary literature and novels by famous Russian and European writers. These books had remained inside our bookcases, their glass doors sealed by the Red Guards in August

1966. I also discovered the Linguaphone English-language phonograph records with their textbook. Mom had bought these records for Qingping and me. Somehow these and Mom's books miraculously survived the raids.

As our truck with all our belongings drove away from No. 9 West Kusi, I looked at our house standing alone in rubble. Leaving behind my childhood in the debris of the Xu Beihong Memorial Museum, I bore in my heart forever the beautiful memories of my life with Father and Mother in our family's former home where my artistic dream had taken shape.

CHAPTER 18
Battle the Waves

A couple of months before our move, Tchaikovsky Competition winner Liu Shikun and Teacher Guo from CCOM assumed leadership of the "Mao Zedong Thought Fighting Regiment." Liu worked with the rebel group led by his wife Ye Xiangzhen at the Central Academy of Drama. They expanded their struggle beyond their schools.

This couple together with rebel group heads from the Beijing Film Academy and the Central Philharmonic Orchestra led raids on the houses of three important CCP leaders who were considered anti-Mao and had been dismissed from their positions several months before. The Lius and the rebel groups acted swiftly one night in December 1966, seizing the three CCP leaders including Peng Zhen,[44] the mayor of Beijing. The three CCP leaders were detained that night in the rehearsal hall of the Central Philharmonic Orchestra. A few days later the rebel groups held a mass rally against them and Yang Shangkun, director of the General Office of the Central Committee. This event demonstrated that CCOM's "Fighting Regiment" was capable of radical actions against selected high-level CCP leaders. I heard later that members of the Cultural Revolution Small Group, including Jiang Qing, had prompted the rebel group heads such as Ye Xiangzhen to take actions against the four CCP leaders.

Afterwards, Liu Shikun bragged that he and his wife had been very familiar with the houses of the three CCP leaders, and had therefore, without any trouble, scaled their walls and seized them in their sleep. "Fighting Regiment" members said they had caught Mayor Peng Zhen in his pajamas and stopped him from using his special phone.

On January 19, 1967, Liu Shikun, his wife Ye Xiangzhen, and core members from the "Fighting Regiment" led the seizure of the Ministry of Culture, which controlled major segments of visual arts and performing arts in China. I did not participate in seizing the CCP leaders, nor was I part of taking over the Ministry of Culture. I heard "Fighting Regiment" leaders announcing these actions after they had happened. A few months later, Liu Shikun was denounced at CCOM mass rallies as an anti-Party counterrevolutionary and consequently jailed for six years. Afterwards I heard that Jiang Qing had ordered the actions against Liu in her attempt to strike down his father-in-law, Marshal Ye Jianying.

Several leading members who were CCOM string students strongly opposed the seizure of the Ministry of Culture. They split from the "Mao Zedong Thought Fighting Regiment," and, with composition student Wei, formed the "Red Rock Struggle" group. Quite a few classmates and I left the "Fighting Regiment" to join the "Red Rock." I thought that the split was because of a power struggle within the group, not because of any real differences concerning political direction. My decision was mainly based on the friendships I had developed with some "Red Rock" members during the "exchange of experiences."

At mass rallies we voiced our opposition to the January-nineteenth takeover of the Ministry of Culture. My classmates and I camped in the Ministry of Culture for several days. We hung a couplet at the entrance of our opposition's office: "The monster's wind is big in the small temple. The turtles are abundant in the shallow pond." Here, "turtle" was a derogatory term directed at our opposition.

The "Red Rock Struggle" group gave us propaganda assignments. A few classmates and I went to the trolley-bus terminals one evening and painted "ANTI-JANUARY-NINETEENTH SEIZURE OF THE MINISTRY OF CULTURE" in big ink characters on all the trolley buses. These slogans traveled everywhere in Beijing the next day.

In May, Jiang Qing, a leading member of the powerful Cultural Revolution Small Group, replaced the paralyzed Ministry of Culture with the Central Cultural Revolution Literature and Arts Group (Literature and Arts Group). As head of this group, she now controlled the performing and visual arts. Other members included Zhang Chunqiao, Yao Wenyuan, and Qi Benyu. After Mao's death in 1976, Zhang Chunqiao and Yao Wenyuan, along with Jiang Qing, were recognized as three of the members of the group referred to as the Gang of Four.

The "Fighting Regiment" and the "Red Rock Struggle" group were united under a new name, the "Red Fighting Regiment." One of its leaders was

Wei, a CCOM composition student. He and a male cellist from the Central Philharmonic Orchestra were appointed to head the department of music and dance under the newly formed Literature and Arts Group. In addition to directing the Cultural Revolution in the work units, the new department also organized performances including concerts of the symphony *Shajiabang*, adapted from a modern Peking opera of the same title. This Peking opera portrays Communist guerrillas and a female underground Communist liaison officer fighting the Japanese invasion in southern China. Both the Peking opera and the symphony *Shajiabang* were model performing works developed under Jiang Qing. In summer 1967, the "Red Fighting Regiment" performed the symphony *Shajiabang* with their orchestra and chorus. I was not present; I had gone to Nanjing to perform in a Mao Zedong Thought propaganda team. At least they were making music instead of fighting each other.

A new rebel group named the "Beijing Commune" appeared in CCOM. Their members did not like Qi Benyu and the new establishment in the arts. They particularly disapproved of Wei's music and dance department, which suppressed different opinions such as theirs. Thus there was a new factional struggle in CCOM, between the "Red Fighting Regiment" and the "Beijing Commune."

Jiang Qing's new establishment in the arts soon switched focus, and CCOM students led by Wei surrounded Zhongnanhai, put up tents around its entrances, and attempted to harass Premier Zhou day and night. These radical students together with thousands of Red Guards from other Beijing colleges also besieged and forced their way into the Soviet embassy. Their excuse was that the Soviet Union had published an article by Chinese composer-violinist Ma Sitson titled "Why I Left China," first published in the U.S.A. in *Life* magazine. Ma Sitson had suffered during the Cultural Revolution before escaping from China in January 1967. The students' sieges of the Soviet and other embassies disrupted China's diplomatic ties with other countries. Years later I learned that these activities were Jiang Qing's initial attempt to attack Premier Zhou, who was in charge of China's diplomacy. I did not participate in any of the above actions.

I thought that the radical actions by the dominant "Red Fighting Regiment" were not justified. I particularly hated their relentless harassment of Premier Zhou. Yet I was afraid to voice my opinions in school. In order to stay away, I traveled with a few classmates to Nanjing where we stayed at the dorms of the Front Drama Troupe.

We formed a Mao Zedong Thought propaganda team. I played the accordion, a heavy red 120-bass accordion lugged on my back.

The songs we sang all praised Mao and the Cultural Revolution. Our dances involved thrusting fists into the air, balanced by a downward punch to the ground. In Ma'anshan, a few hours by car from Nanjing, the audience at the Ma'anshan Steel Works applauded my accordion solo of *Cavalry March*, the only solo accordion piece I had learned at the Prep Music High School. Playing this popular political music was as close as I could come to the kind of performing I had dreamed of. I was glad to have that opportunity.

On July 16, 1966, Chairman Mao, age seventy-two, swam for an hour in the Yangtze River at Wuhan, a feat cheered by the whole nation. A year later, while in Nanjing, I decided to swim across the Yangtze River, which at Nanjing was about three miles wide and swift-running. A year before, Chairman Mao had set an example for all of us to battle the waves of the revolution and face the world. I wanted to prove to myself that I could do this despite the difficulty and danger. One afternoon some Beijing college students and I left for a meeting in the suburbs of Nanjing near the Yangtze River. When we arrived at the meeting, I took off my sandals and asked a male student to keep them for me for a couple of hours. Then I took a boat across the Yangtze River to the dock of Pukou, on the opposite side of Nanjing.

In my red T-shirt and shorts, I jumped into the river, announcing that I was going to swim across. Someone at the dock said, "What a Tomboy General!" To my surprise, two young men at the dock followed me into the river. Near the shore the water was peaceful. But as we approached the middle, the current became so strong and swift that it carried all three of us downstream. Endless waves rushed over me. One of the men yelled, "Keep swimming. We must cross the current!"

I pulled all my strength together to battle the waves while trying to keep my head above the water. All three of us were washed downstream beneath the Yangtze River Bridge, at that time under construction. I had heard that the strong turbulence around the bridge support columns could drown us. Fortunately we were not caught in the worst of it. Although very nervous, I kept pushing across the current for about another hour.

The sun was beginning to set when I pulled my body up on the muddy riverbank at Nanjing. Exhausted, I could barely walk through the fifty yards of knee-deep mud on the shore. In the golden sunset near the river was my friend, the college student from Beijing, dangling my grey plastic sandals from his bicycle's handlebars.

I must have looked awful with my muddy T-shirt and shorts sticking to my body. But sitting on the back of my friend's bike I felt relieved. He pedaled us on the long trip back to the city of Nanjing, complaining that I had kept him waiting too long. I had swum for almost three hours. People must have looked at my friend suspiciously while he stood on the riverbank by himself with a pair of ladies' sandals. Despite his complaint, I felt triumphant.

• • •

A year before the Cultural Revolution, Mom had planned for another residence to replace our current house, which we knew was to be demolished. She bought a small quadrangle house in Haibo Hutong, Xuanwu District, in Beijing. It had belonged to Ye Shengzhang, a well-known Peking opera performer. However, just as Mom completed renovations on that house, the Cultural Revolution broke out. Based on the government's new policies eliminating private property ownership, she was forced to turn in her title to the Haibo Hutong house, and it was vacant during the latter half of 1966. By early 1967 when we were required to move out of No. 9 West Kusi, the housing authorities controlled the allocation of the Haibo Hutong house. They gave our family only the north-side rooms to live in while planning to allocate the remaining rooms to different families. To fight for more space, our family sent Qingping and Xuezheng to negotiate with the subway construction authorities. As college students, Qingping and Xuezheng were not afraid of anything; they had nothing to lose. They argued that the allotted north-side rooms could not hold all the belongings from our two-story house. They demanded that our family be given the two west-side rooms in addition to the north-side rooms; otherwise we refused to move. In the end, the subway construction authorities talked the housing authorities into giving us one additional west-side room instead of two. We accepted that compromise.

In our Haibo Hutong house, we now had no privacy, because three other families shared it. In our shared yard, our neighbors' three young girls made noise and commotion. I could hear the policeman in the west-side room arguing with his wife. The other tenants were not interested in upgrading and beautifying the flagstone courtyard. Every family put up a clothesline, displaying wet laundry in front of their rooms. Cohabitation like this was common in Beijing, where tenants tried to tolerate each other. We paid a low rent of forty *yuan* a month.

An older stern-faced woman headed the street committee, a low-level organization under local government, whose main responsibility was keeping the neighborhood orderly and secure. Suspicious, she often burst into our house and harassed us, even in the middle of the night. Her excuse was always that she needed to check our *hukou* (residence cards).

Shenpo lived in the west-side room with her daughter-in-law and her newborn granddaughter. Her son worked in a city in northeastern China and visited only during his two-week annual vacation. Mom lived in the only bedroom on the north side while Qingping and I slept in our large living room, partitioned by my piano and our red wardrobe cabinets. It took me a while to get used to sharing limited living space.

In spite of the crowded living conditions, life for our family was less stressful because no violent students intruded anymore. Several speeches Premier Zhou gave in late 1967 and early 1968 showed his political support for Xu Beihong. On August 16, 1967, Premier Zhou said to some overseas Chinese representatives, "Among artists, Xu Beihong is the one who is politically strong enough to withstand any tests…I wrote inscriptions for Lu Xun's former residence and also for the Xu Beihong Memorial Museum."[45]

The Beijing Municipal Bureau of Culture in charge of the closed Xu Beihong Memorial Museum paid Mom all the back salary they owed her for two years, from the time the Cultural Revolution began in 1966. When Mom's situation improved, Uncle Huang moved from his office back to our house. But Mom felt distant from him. Trying to maintain an appearance of harmony, they each hid their feelings.

Because of the physical confrontations between the "Red Fighting Regiment" and the "Beijing Commune" at the CCOM campus, I stayed home more, so as not to get involved. My artistic dream resurfaced. However, all the conservatories and universities were now closed. It was considered a crime to seek any knowledge besides that found in Mao Zedong's works.

Pursuing a piano performance career during the Cultural Revolution years was difficult because the politically correct repertoire was limited to a few revolutionary songs, some songs from Albanian movies, and episodes from the ballet *The Red Detachment of Women*. The ballet was adapted from a movie of the same title, portraying a peasant girl's rise in an all-female detachment of the Red Army fighting the Kuomintang. The ballet was a model work developed under Jiang Qing's direction.

In our Haibo Hutong home, I seldom played my piano, fearing that my neighbors would complain. It was easier to study English undetected. I decided to listen to the Linguaphone course phonograph records salvaged from our old house. The course lessons included examples of spoken English used in restaurants, theaters, shops, or doctor's offices. I had to keep my studies secret from the street committee woman and our neighbors in the adjacent rooms. My mother's bedroom had a large walk-in closet holding our suitcases, where I set up aerial wires and tried to listen to BBC broadcasts on my transistor radio. This was very risky. If caught, I could be jailed. But having battled the Yangtze River's turbulence and survived, I was not afraid of taking risks in the name of education.

For several months, I listened to the Linguaphone course records carefully, trying to identify each syllable. I discovered how words in spoken English ran together. Our English course in the Prep Music High School had not taught us this. I imitated the spoken English on these records and was beginning to sound somewhat like the British people. While listening, I visualized upper-class London where a well-dressed lady ordered oxtail soup in a restaurant, and a couple went to the theater in formal dress. In that world, educated people could enjoy Western classical music, art, and civilizations of the past. I hoped that someday I would be able to visit England.

I could read English and Chinese books only in my hiding place. I feasted on Chinese and Western classics from Mom's library. I read the Chinese classic, *Dream of the Red Chamber*, by Qing-dynasty writer Cao Xueqin, fascinated by the vivid description of numerous characters in the declining aristocratic family and the many poems reflecting each character's personality. I often read throughout the night because during the day I seldom had a quiet place to study. Mom's bedroom was the only private room. I studied in that room only when she was not there.

My favorite books included *Cousin Pons, Eugénie Grandet* by Balzac, and *Anna Karenina* by Tolstoy. I admired Balzac's insight into human weaknesses and his sharp ridicule of the evil characters in high society. I was back in my old dream world, traveling in my imagination. But when faced with my real world, I saw no practical future for my literary or artistic pursuits. I only hoped I might be assigned to a factory job that would leave me some spare time to pursue my artistic interests at the end of each workday.

Although I lived at home, I still went to CCOM occasionally to keep up on the latest news about the conflicts between the rebel groups. In July 1968, I was shocked to see that Building No.1 had now become a battlefield. Most of the practice rooms were sealed and the pianos moved into the hallway. Some were used to blockade the entrances to the building, now the "Red Fighting Regiment" stronghold.

Qi Benyu, a Cultural Revolution Small Group member, was arrested as a counterrevolutionary at the beginning of that year. The news of this powerful arts-world leader's downfall confounded me. Later I heard that Mao had ordered the arrest of Qi and two other members of the Cultural Revolution Small Group for sabotaging the Cultural Revolution.[46] However, CCOM's "Red Fighting Regiment" remained dominant until the summer of 1968 when the "Beijing Commune" started taking action. They took Wei, the former "Red Fighting Regiment" leader and head of the music and dance department, and kept him in isolation for investigation because of his close relationship with Qi Benyu.

After the "Beijing Commune" took Wei, the "Red Fighting Regiment" seized "Beijing Commune" leaders, locking up a few of them in small windowless practice rooms on the third floor of Building No. 1. There they beat and interrogated them in order to find out where the "Beijing Commune" was keeping Wei.

One "Beijing Commune" leader broke through the soundproof boards to get to an adjacent classroom where he escaped from a third-floor window and ran to the barracks of the Motor Battalion of the People's Liberation Army, close to the CCOM campus. The soldiers there believed that this escaped leader was not a counterrevolutionary but had been locked up because of factional fights. So the PLA soldiers kept the "Red Fighting Regiment" students from entering the barracks to seize him. Later, the soldiers treated the leader's wounds, gave him a PLA uniform to wear, and drove him to his friend's home in the Central Academy of Fine Arts where he hid until the violent situation ended.

The intense physical violence at CCOM really scared me. For the rest of July, I stayed away. I heard that gun battles took place between the rebel groups on the campuses of Tsinghua University, Peking University, and other universities where some students were killed. Starting in late July 1968, the CCP ordered worker Mao Zedong Thought propaganda teams to take control of major universities. Industrial workers made up most of each team, with some PLA participation. In the following few months, these propaganda teams entered all universities and colleges in China. The violence on college campuses finally ended. So did the leadership role of college students in the Cultural Revolution.

In August, a Mao Zedong Thought propaganda team of workers and PLA officers took control of CCOM. The rebel groups were forced to stop fighting each other and to form a great revolutionary alliance under the worker propaganda team. All students were notified to return to school, where we spent most of our time every day studying Mao's works. The worker propaganda team required us to memorize three famous articles by Chairman Mao: "Serve the People," "In Memory of Norman Bethune," and "The Foolish Old Man Who Removed the Mountains." Cultural Revolution leaders in work units challenged everyone to recite these articles, often referred to as the "three old articles," which promote selfless dedication to the cause of communism.

Three months after the worker propaganda team entered the Prep Music High School, all the students from the 1966 and 1967 graduating classes were given diplomas. As a member of the 1967 graduating class, I had completed five out of six years of the piano performance program. Although I missed my last year of formal music training, I was happy to receive my diploma with my straight-faced photograph and the music school's official seal.

CHAPTER 19

The Making of a Model Opera

My classmates and I faced limited job prospects. Except for a few foreign musicians' performances in the 1970s, Western classical music was banned in China between 1966 and 1976. Traditional Peking opera was also banned. In 1968, a few model performing troupes were the only performing groups of any kind. They were authorized by Jiang Qing to perform the few model works developed under her guidance.

Jiang Qing had been a movie actress in the 1930s. Backed by Mao Zedong, Jiang in 1964 initiated her attack against China's cultural leadership, whose high-level advocate was Liu Shaoqi. She denounced most of China's theater for depicting feudal and bourgeois content dominated by emperors and princes, generals and ministers, and scholars and beauties, the main subjects of traditional Peking opera. In the same year, she started what is known as the revolution in Peking opera. She defined the role of the arts, which was to serve the CCP under Mao's direction, and insisted that the main figures portrayed in performing arts be workers, peasants, and soldiers.

Since then she had directed the development of model Peking operas and other model performing works which represented Mao's specific political lines throughout recent revolutionary history. This was Jiang's attempt to ensure total control of the arts, promoting Mao's political direction and his leading position only. In 1966 she defined the standard for model works as "the unity of revolutionary political content and the highest possible perfection of artistic form."[47]

The model works that met Jiang Qing's criteria included five modern Peking operas: *The Red Lantern, Taking the Tiger Mountain by Strategy, On the Docks, Shajiabang, Raid on the White Tiger Regiment*, the ballets *The Red Detachment of*

Women and *The White-Haired Girl*; and the symphony *Shajiabang*. These were the only performing works allowed onstage from June 1966 up to 1968. I heard that spoken drama and local operas were banned.

In visual arts, the model work approved by Jiang Qing was the oil painting *Chairman Mao Goes to Anyuan*, painted in 1967 by Liu Chunhua, an art student from the Central Academy of Arts and Crafts. The painting was created with a clear political purpose: discredit Liu Shaoqi, a well-known leader of the 1922 Anyuan coal mine labor strike but now the target of the Cultural Revolution, and portray Mao Zedong as the only leader of the Anyuan coal mine labor strike which initiated the CCP-led labor movement. Mao was well known as a rural organizer, but the painting portrays him, in addition, as the urban industrial proletariat's leader.

In 1968 pianist Yin Chengzong composed a piano-accompanied cantata, adapting twelve arias from *The Red Lantern*. Jiang Qing approved this as a new model work. *The Red Lantern* describes the story of three unrelated people adopting the same family name. Li Yuhe, a railroad switchman, Granny Li, and Li Tiemei (Iron Plum Blossom), a young girl, are united into one family fighting the Japanese invaders during the War of Resistance.

I was very happy to have the politically-approved piano-accompanied cantata for us piano students to use as repertoire. The arias adapted from this modern Peking opera include:

1. All Have a Red Heart (Li Tiemei)
2. I Should Be Such a Person (Li Tiemei)
3. A Poor Child Learns the World Earlier (Li Yuhe)
4. Nothing in the World Could Overcome Us Communists (Li Yuhe)
5. I Am Filled with Braveness (Li Yuhe)
6. Learn Father's Red Heart, Courage, and Iron Will (Granny Li)
7. Blood for Blood (Granny Li)
8. We Never Leave the Battlefield until We Have Killed the Wolves (Li Tiemei)
9. Red Lantern Light Gives Me Direction (Li Tiemei)
10. Hatred in My Heart Will Sprout (Li Tiemei)
11. The Party Taught Me to Be an Iron Man (Li Yuhe)
12. My Aspirations Take Me to the Sky (Li Yuhe)

In late summer, I asked around until I found the scores of the piano accompaniment and started learning them. The Peking opera melodies, so different from any of the Western classical music I had learned, intrigued me. I particularly liked two arias sung by Li Tiemei, "All Have a Red Heart" and "I Should Be Such a Person." The accompaniment for the first aria is very lively and bright with most of the notes on black keys. The piano music depicts the young girl's light-hearted humor very well. The piano accompaniment for the second aria is lyrical, its harmony adding more emotional depth to Tiemei's understanding of her father. However, I found some of the accompaniment for Li Yuhe's arias hard to play, especially the aria "My Aspirations Take Me to the Sky," with its heavy chords and fast octaves. In the first few months, I learned the accompaniment alone without knowing what it might sound like with singers.

In November, soon after my official graduation from the Prep Music High School, I heard that both the Beijing Peking Opera Troupe and the China National Peking Opera Company in Beijing needed pianists to play the piano-accompanied cantata *The Red Lantern*. The criteria, determined by the worker propaganda team at our music school, included a clean political background of the student and his or her family, and the student's performance capability. After much discussion, the worker propaganda team announced that six piano students from the 1966 and 1967 graduating classes had been assigned to the accompanist jobs. I was lucky enough to be one of two piano accompanists for the China National Peking Opera Company, a model performing troupe. Twenty-one, I was overjoyed to get this job.

The China National Peking Opera Company had been reorganized under the new leader, Qian Haoliang, who acted the major role of Li Yuhe in *The Red Lantern*. The sole objective of this troupe was to create and perform Jiang Qing-approved model Peking operas. The company had a new and spacious location near Weigongcun in the western suburbs of Beijing.

Life in the China National Peking Opera Company compound was almost military. We wore government-issued army uniforms and army overcoats while working. Monday through Saturday all the employees, including married couples, lived either in the all-male or all-female dormitories, with two to four people sharing a room. Weekends were the only time we could go home. We ate all our meals in the troupe's dining hall. This lifestyle must have been hard for married people, but I was used to living in a dormitory shared by twenty students.

I felt honored to wear the green army uniform and enjoyed the job's benefits. As a professional-school graduate, my monthly salary was thirty-two *yuan*. Twelve *yuan* was deducted each month for meals, which were subsidized with another twelve *yuan* by our government employer. Compared with the canteen food at the music school, the troupe's food was very good, with eggs or meat at every meal.

During the political studies which occupied a few afternoons a week, all the orchestra members discussed learning from Mao's works and Jiang Qing's speeches to guide our making of model operas. Jiang Qing's leadership role in the arts was emphasized repeatedly. Our Party leader, Qian Haoliang, indoctrinated us to follow Jiang Qing's leadership with the same "absolute dedication" as we followed Chairman Mao's. Like most of my colleagues, I never questioned Jiang Qing's authority over the making of model operas.

Our meetings began with reciting quotations from Mao's works. Common people performed this as a daily ritual. One evening a performer in the troupe got married and I attended the wedding. Waving the little red books of *Quotations from Chairman Mao Zedong*, the young couple first recited a quotation by Mao, "From all corners of the country, we have joined together for a common revolutionary objective." Then they bowed to Mao's portrait, pledging their loyalty to the great leader. That was their wedding ceremony.

Except for the political studies, I was happy with my new job. We had four hours of practice time in the mornings. I played modern Peking opera piano accompaniment for Peking opera performers' practice sessions. At least I was using some of my piano performance skills and developing as an accompanist.

The Cultural Revolution still had momentum in the winter of 1968. Some former Party leaders of the China National Peking Opera Company were kept in isolation for investigation, watched twenty-four hours a day while they confessed their supposed counterrevolutionary crimes. The second week I was working there, a Party person responsible for the Cultural Revolution asked me to take the night shift to watch the female detainees. I felt very uncomfortable about this. It would take time away from playing the piano, and I hated losing sleep. Nevertheless, I agreed to do it. I slept in the detention building, and on a bitterly cold December night they woke me up just in time for my shift. There was no time for me to return to my dorm to get warmer clothing, such as a heavy overcoat with padded sleeves. Shivering, I went to my post to watch a fifty-year-old detainee. I managed to stay awake although the freezing room chilled me to the bone for eight hours. My arms were particularly cold. I had never been as thoroughly chilled as I was that night.

The next day I felt very tired. But I used some of my designated sleeping time that afternoon to practice the piano accompaniment for Li Yuhe's aria "My Aspirations Take Me to the Sky." I worked for about four hours on the heavy chords and octaves in the piece. At the end of the day, I felt terrible pain shooting through the muscles and tendons in my arms. I thought that my arms must have caught cold the night before, and practicing strained my arms and made it worse.

I went to see a doctor immediately. He diagnosed a pianist's playing injury. Some classmates in the music school had suffered similar playing injuries, and usually took one semester off to undergo treatment and recover. The doctor said that to fully recover I needed to rest and gradually increase my practice time to build my muscle strength.

I had, however, just started my new job and to build credibility, despite the pain in my arms, each morning I continued to accompany the Peking opera performers. I reduced my practice time from the assigned four hours to two. I tried applying steam from brewed Chinese herbal medicine to my arms every morning before work. This helped a little. But I could not follow the doctor's advice, so I never regained my strength and endurance. Two hours of playing a strenuous accompaniment hurt my arms.

I felt devastated and hopeless. My dream of becoming an accomplished pianist would never come true. "What is the point of living my life?" I asked myself. But that thought was momentary. I had so much passion for music, art, and literature that I would live for my passion. Perhaps I could learn to write music and help with revising *The Red Lantern.*

In the new orchestra for *The Red Lantern*, sixteen Western string and wind instrument players were integrated with a traditional Peking opera ensemble. The Western instruments included four violins, two violas, one cello, one double bass, two trumpets, two French horns, one flute, one oboe, one clarinet, and one bassoon. The Western instruments provided more harmony and potentially richer expressions for more powerful portrayals of proletarian heroes. The

Peking opera performers, however, were not used to Western instruments and harmony. They were trained to coordinate their singing with the Peking opera fiddle, and follow percussion instruments in their acrobatic fighting and acting.

The harmony in a traditional Peking opera ensemble is very simple, mainly doubling the voice line. The leading instrument for the singer is the *jinghu* (Peking opera fiddle). The *jing'erhu* (Peking opera two-string fiddle) plays an octave below the *jinghu*. The *yueqin* and *xiaosanxian*, both plucking instruments, together with the fiddles are the four major instruments in an ensemble. A plucking instrument provides some bass support. The *bangu* (wooden clapper and drum) player acts as conductor, using his *bangu* to lead an ensemble and direct the interaction between ensemble and performers, setting the tempo and rhythm for singing and acting. Rhythmic patterns of percussion instruments, including the *bangu*, small gong, large gong, and cymbals, give cues to performers' movements or serve as preludes to arias. They punctuate certain acting and dance-like movements, highlighting what a character expresses at a given moment in the drama.

I found that the Peking opera performers were as ignorant of Western musical instruments as I was of Peking opera. Singing in Peking opera is unique. A singer can temporarily alter the music's tempo or change the rhythm in the middle of a phrase, like stretching a rubber band at will. Peking opera singers call this style "rubber band." I felt that even the most difficult *rubato* (a temporary disregard of strict tempo to allow expressive quickening or slackening) in Chopin's piano music could not come close to the difficulty in accompanying the "rubber band" style of singing in Peking opera. While Western opera singing is smooth, Peking opera singing often contains "angles," emphasizing certain rhythms and notes. This exaggerated singing style allows the portrayal of powerful characters such as the heroes in *Water Margin*. Perhaps this special feature is why Jiang Qing selected Peking opera to create proletarian heroes, while other local operas and spoken drama were banned.

Some passages in modern Peking operas did not have piano accompaniment scores. I had to improvise accompaniments to the melodies. Sometimes I also had to change keys to suit a performer's voice. The Peking opera singers did not understand that Western musical instruments use twelve major keys which include different scales and harmonies. They wondered why I could not simply tune the piano to suit the range of each singer's voice, as the two-string fiddle player could.

I was determined to learn from the performers, *jinghu* players, and *bangu* players. But breaking into their network, made up of closely-knit family or apprentice-master relations, was not easy. The old *bangu* player was quite authoritarian. The older ensemble players liked to gossip and used a language I was not familiar with. But the young performers and musicians trained at the School of Chinese Theater Arts, later renamed the National Academy of Chinese Theater Arts, were easier to talk with. Soon I made friends with a young *jinghu* player, Xiao Lin (Little Lin). He had small eyes and a smiling face. With his *jinghu* propped up on the thigh of his crossed leg, he played very skillfully. I watched him coach performers and remember him rocking his head from side to side and using his voice to show a singer specific expressions of an aria. Xiao Lin worked like a modern-day Western opera artistic coach, directing a singer while playing accompaniment not on a piano but on a fiddle.

I found more musical interaction between singer and accompanist in Peking opera than in Western opera. Peking opera singers rely on the *jinghu* player during their performance, while a Western opera artistic coach usually does not participate in stage performance. I learned to sing a few arias from *The Red Lantern* and asked Xiao Lin to accompany my singing in order to experience authentic Peking opera accompanying style. I could have lost face in the presence of experts, but I was determined to try.

In time my sincerity and eagerness to learn won over the older players and performers. I was fortunate to meet some who were famous, including Li Shaochun, well known for his singing and acrobatic performances. Zhang Junqiu, a man who played leading female roles in traditional Peking operas, had delicate skin and his behavior was quite feminine, as if influenced by his stage acting. When he demonstrated singing for me, he turned his face halfway and covered his mouth with one hand, as if shy.

I also watched well-known traditional Peking opera excerpts, such as *Lin Chong's Night Escape*. With Jiang Qing's approval, the *Red Lantern* group adapted some elements from these excerpts to create heroes in the model opera.

After a year, the Peking opera performers and I reached some mutual understanding. This experience opened me to the rich heritage of Peking opera, which combines speech, singing, instrumental music, dance, mime, and acrobatic depiction of martial arts. While Western opera features new songs for each opera, Peking opera keeps a pool of aria formats and instrumental melodies for all operas. I learned to identify various aria formats and how different renderings add uniqueness to a character. Watching many Peking opera rehearsals I learned the characteristic rhythm patterns of percussion instruments. I gradually mastered the challenge of accompanying the "rubber band" style of singing and became quite skillful at improvising an accompaniment for any voice melody.

To help the performers get used to the harmony of Western instruments, I composed some music for them to use with their dance-movement exercises, collaborating in this with a young performer, Xiao Liu (Little Liu), a graduate from the School of Chinese Theater Arts. He was short with a fair complexion and dark hair combed up high on top and back. I had been impressed with his pantomime acting in *Lin Chong's Night Escape*. Agile and sure, his dancing expressed Lin Chong's fluid strength.

His face lit up when I told him about my composition idea. For the next few evenings, we worked in the rehearsal studio, simultaneously composing the music and choreographing the dance movements.

I asked young drummer Xiao Tang (Little Tang) to suggest tunes from traditional Peking operas to be adapted to the exercise music. In a couple of weeks, I tried out my piano accompaniment music with performers who had learned the dance movements from Xiao Liu. They appreciated the piano music with their daily practice because there had been no accompaniment before. Because some of the tunes were familiar, they easily learned to coordinate with the piano music which included Western harmonies.

After many revisions, the model opera *The Red Lantern* was finalized in May 1970. Its script stresses the leadership of Mao Zedong and the Party.

An earlier version was devoted to underground work. Jiang Qing suggested portraying armed struggle, but opponents insisted on depicting underground work only. Before 1949, Mao Zedong led armed struggles while Liu Shaoqi headed the underground work in Kuomintang areas. Jiang Qing's emphasis on the portrayal of armed struggle stressed Mao's leadership. The completed and approved model opera's final scene depicts guerrillas defeating the Japanese soldiers, added to reflect Mao's view that the Party's underground work should coordinate with armed struggle—the highest form of revolution.

Jiang Qing gave other instructions for revising the script of *The Red Lantern*, making Li Yuhe stand out from the other heroes and dominate the negative characters. Jiang Qing also demanded that any imperfection found in an episode, an aria, or a minor movement that might be construed as detrimental to the revolutionary heroes should be altered over and over until her required standard was met. Achieving the highest possible perfection of artistic form, as defined by Jiang Qing, was an important element in making model Peking operas. However, in the case of *The Red Lantern*, I believe that this artistic standard was achieved mainly through the sincere efforts and creative insights of many professionals in our *Red Lantern* group. From what I observed, Jiang Qing's artistic instructions were only minor points, such as suggesting different placements for the patches on Granny Li's clothes. She came a few times to the Xidan Theater to review dress rehearsals of the revised *Red Lantern*. Her instructions were relayed to the whole group the following day and acted upon immediately.

Our entire music group worked enthusiastically and very hard revising *The Red Lantern* during the summer of 1969. Because the bourgeois composers had all been sent to the countryside, two composers from the Air Force Singing and Dancing Troupe wrote music for the Chinese and Western instrument combined orchestra. They composed some powerful interludes and preludes leading up to the stage appearance of Li Yuhe.

The Western instrument players spent a lot of time learning to follow the *bangu* player's conducting. After they could play together with the traditional Peking opera players, the whole orchestra still had to rehearse with the performers. To relieve some of the pressure on them, I played piano accompaniment for certain episodes during the rehearsals. But still the orchestra players were exhausted. My schoolmate Wu Li, playing the cello all day long, injured her right wrist. But she was the only cello player, so she continued to rehearse with a bandaged wrist. Instead of sitting in the orchestra pit, the orchestra was crowded behind a screen on the right side of the stage with the percussion instruments close to the other players. Wu Li said, "The cymbals and *bangu* were so deafening that my ears hurt."

I was impressed with the performers who went through equally difficult adjustments. For example, Sun Yue acted as the alternate for Li Yuhe's role. In the beginning, we admired his masterful singing skills and a rich voice but were puzzled by the noticeable distortion of his lips while singing. I found out he had developed the habit when acting major older-male roles in traditional Peking operas, in which long beards hide the performer's mouth.

Sun made a great effort to loosen up his facial muscles, sometimes making funny faces backstage. During performances, with his lips now controlled, his rich voice, complemented by the strength of character shown in his face, portrayed a powerful hero.

Another major performer I came to know was Li Weikang, who was my age and had started working at the China National Peking Opera Company about the same time. Li Weikang acted as the alternate for Tiemei's role. She came to my studio to practice Tiemei's arias with my accompaniment. She had a beautiful voice and exquisite singing techniques. However, she had been trained for the traditional Peking opera roles of virtuous proper women. In general, Peking opera performers stay with the roles they were trained for. But to portray Tiemei, the lively girl of seventeen, Li Weikang focused on adjusting her singing and acting style. I was delighted by the quality of her first performance of *The Red Lantern*. The audience applauded her after her aria "I Should Be Such a Person."

Among the performers of *The Red Lantern*, I was most impressed with Gao Yuqian, who acted Granny Li's role. Gao had also been trained for roles of virtuous proper women in traditional Peking opera, but changed her singing and acting style to play Granny Li. Traditional Peking opera's conversation is hard to understand because of its unique singing-like intonations. But I was very touched by Gao's telling of their family's story during Scene Five. She not only adjusted to spoken language but effectively used the exaggerated intonations of traditional Peking opera in her storytelling, thus grabbing the audience's attention. Her quavering voice recreated the tragic scene from seventeen years before. With her penetrating eyes, she encouraged Tiemei to uphold the red lantern left by her adoptive father, Li Yuhe, and fight the Japanese invaders to the bitter end.

Although model Peking operas were created with Jiang Qing's political agenda in mind, from an artistic point of view I believe that model Peking operas are worthwhile. They use the strengths of traditional Peking opera to portray contemporary heroes and characters. The major arias from *The Red Lantern* reflect the strong spirit of the era while preserving some of the best artistic features of traditional Peking opera. I came to realize how beautiful the art of Peking opera is and how rich its heritage.

My contribution to this field was not large. There was still much left to accomplish.

However, during the ten-year Cultural Revolution, Jiang Qing made her small number of model operas the only repertoire allowed on China's stages, and people later became tired of them.

CHAPTER 20

4701 Army Farm

Mao Zedong had given a directive on May 7, 1966, advocating that workers, peasants, PLA, schools, and cadres should each form their own "big school." There they should combine manual labor with studies of politics, acquiring military skills and literacy, and criticizing the bourgeoisie. Two years later, Mao wrote a specific instruction to send all cadres to work farms, later called May Seventh Cadre Schools. Cadres and intellectuals, "sent down" from cities, would experience manual labor and undertake re-education from the poor and lower-middle peasants.

During the Cultural Revolution, this became a favored method to remove potentially dissident cadres and intellectuals from the cities. Starting in late 1968, hundreds of thousands of cadres from the central government and lower-level government offices, along with their families, were sent to these May Seventh Cadre Schools set up all over the country for re-education. Deng Xiaoping was one of those cadres.

Meanwhile, Mao Zedong initiated the Up to the Mountains and Down to the Countryside Movement, targeting mainly high-school graduates, implemented in the late 1960s and early 1970s. I believe that Mao used the policy to eliminate the social disruption caused by the Red Guards, who had been authorized to wipe out the "four olds." Their actions had driven China into chaos. According to PRC sources, during the ten years of the Cultural Revolution more than sixteen million urban youths, mostly high-school graduates and even some college graduates, were sent to live and work in the countryside to be re-educated by the poor and lower-middle peasants.

Employees of the four model performing troupes in Beijing were told at the end of 1969 to respond to Mao's call to go to the May Seventh Cadre School. The model troupes were China National Peking Opera Company, Beijing Peking

Opera Troupe, Central Ballet Troupe, and Central Philharmonic Orchestra. My colleagues and I anxiously waited to hear who would be sent. I was among the first fifty to sixty people from the China National Peking Opera Company to go to the May Seventh Cadre School. Many of us were new graduates from CCOM, the Prep Music High School, the Central Academy of Drama, and the School of Chinese Theater Arts.

I was very worried about my injured arms. With the busy rehearsal schedule during the revision process of *The Red Lantern*, I often played piano accompaniment for a few hours without a break. The tendons in my arms and hands hurt more than before. Heavy physical labor would further injure my arms. I wanted to request an exemption from the May Seventh Cadre School until my arms recovered. Factory workers injured on the job were given time off to heal in socialist China. The injury had been caused by my work. However, my appeal would most likely be ignored. I decided to face the physical and mental challenges on the work farm, not knowing how severe they would be.

I cut off the two pigtails I had worn throughout my music-school years. In January 1970, carrying my bedding, I went with several hundred people from the four model performing troupes to the May Seventh Cadre School near Xiaotangshan (Little Tang Mountain), about two hours by bus from Beijing. The area, rich in natural hot springs, had large expanses of farmland, sparsely populated. We occupied a compound with rows of one-story dormitories. I shared a big dormitory room with more than ten female performers from the China National Peking Opera Company. We slept on bunk beds. The room was cold, with cracks between the window frames and the brick wall. I used strong paper to seal the cracks.

Every day we worked hard on the land for eight hours and only one hour of daily professional training was allowed. With few houses to block the wind, the north wind was stronger on the plains than in the city. Even in extreme weather we dug trenches and moved dirt to prepare for spring planting. Sometimes I carried two baskets full of dirt on a shoulder pole and walked across a narrow one-plank bridge. My back and legs were strong, but shoveling dirt made my hands hurt. Fortunately I was assigned the shoulder-pole job the next day, which allowed my hands to recover.

The manual labor soon showed its impact on my body. A female performer had once said to me, "Your facial skin looks so tender. If I pinch your cheek, I bet I could squeeze juice from you like from a pear." At the farm I tried to protect my face with a large scarf and a mask. But after three months of strong wind and blowing dirt, what I saw in a mirror shocked me: The skin around my eyes had turned dark and rough. I looked like an older peasant woman. At twenty-two, I felt as if a chunk of my life had been taken away from me.

Several men from the Central Philharmonic Orchestra were working in the field. I was surprised to hear their cheerful voices in an improvised rhythmic work chant. They enjoyed this camaraderie. Sheng Zhongguo, a well-known violin soloist with the orchestra, and several other men were pulling a heavy wooden frame with ropes tied to their shoulders, a tool used to smooth the surface of the bare field. Most people working in the May Seventh Cadre School expected to return to their performing troupe within a short time. Therefore I had not heard a lot of complaints yet.

However, practice for one hour a day will not keep performing artists in good technical shape. The Peking opera performers did their jumping and dancing exercises on the dirt outside, without a cushioned floor to protect their knees and feet. To keep themselves warm outdoors, they wore padded jackets and heavy pants, which limited their movements. The ballerinas from the Central Ballet Troupe could not practice with toe shoes on the dirt. The famous ballerina Bai Shuxiang was there. I remembered her beautiful slim figure, playing the role of the white swan in *Swan Lake*. Now in the May Seventh Cadre School, I hardly recognized her plump tanned face and full round figure. I found out that she had been branded a counterrevolutionary and was not allowed to dance or practice for four years.

In spite of the all-day-long heavy physical labor, I tried to keep up my music studies, expecting to continue my piano performance career when I returned to the city. There was a piano in the China National Peking Opera Company office, and I was allowed to practice between 7 a.m. and 8 a.m., but that was not enough time for professional training. To further my music studies, I decided to learn harmony, in my spare time, from a textbook I had brought. Harmony and other theory courses were part of the CCOM college-level curriculum, but the school had closed in 1966, so I planned to study these courses on my own. The harmony exercises in the textbook are usually done by playing the solutions on the piano first. But in my evenings, with no access to the piano, I tried to solve the problems by writing out the harmony solutions on staff paper. When I had difficulties, I sought help from a man in my group who had been a composition major in a music school. I was grateful for his timely help and patient explanations.

The meals were very plain. We had had much better quality food at the model troupe's canteen. But every other weekend, we were allowed to spend Sunday and Monday at home in the city of Beijing. The cadre school's shuttle buses transported all the people working there. During two days at home, we ate better food and I spent a lot of time listening to classical music records borrowed secretly from my friends.

On the farm I got to know some of the farm animals. My father was a well-known horse painter, and I was always fascinated with horses, but not familiar with real ones. I grew up with the idealized images of lean galloping horses in Father's Chinese ink brush paintings. But these farm horses were sturdy work horses for pulling carts. A beautiful white mare, big-boned and very muscular with large hooves, was pregnant, and at lunchtime I often watched her caretaker walking her in the yard. I was told that daily walking would ease the delivery. Holding my breath, I stood a few yards back to watch as the mare gave birth. She seemed to be in agony for about half an hour before the foal's thin legs showed. The caretaker gently pulled him out. Different from his mother, the foal was dark-colored and fragile-looking, his skin covered with mucus. After resting for a while, he tried to stand up. After a few tries, he was able to rise. He then stabilized himself and walked away from his mother. I was amazed.

One of the few things I really enjoyed at the May Seventh Cadre School was mingling with schoolmates from CCOM and the Prep Music High School. One pianist from the Beijing Peking Opera Troupe was Tao, a piano graduate from CCOM. She often advised me about how to take care of my hands. Shen, a violin graduate from CCOM, had worked in the orchestra of the Beijing Peking Opera Troupe and also suffered injury because of the long rehearsal hours in addition to individual daily practice. One evening she dropped by my dormitory.

"Hi, Fangfang."

"What a surprise. I am so glad to see you, Shen. Is this farm life okay with you?" I said.

"I am getting used to it. How about you? "

"The farm work was not too bad but the wind really wore me out. It was difficult to squeeze in an hour of piano in the morning. Have you practiced sometimes?"

"I have not been practicing my violin. I will wait and see if I can adapt to the farm work," Shen said.

"How do you like your dormitory?"

"I think I can live with it."

Shen seemed calm and did not complain. Looking at her fragile figure and thin arms, I wondered how she could endure the heavy physical labor. Being in a similar situation, I sympathized. Later I heard that she suffered depression because she had lost hope of recovering from the damage to her hands, and realized that she would never again be able to play the violin professionally. A few years later, I heard that she had committed suicide with an overdose of sleeping pills.

Like her, some schoolmates and I suffered irreversible career-related losses during the Cultural Revolution. Unfortunately, some did not survive their losses. Shen's round face and gentle voice are still vivid in my mind. I can imagine her unbearable pain. If only she had found the strength to live for her love of music!

• • •

After three months at the May Seventh Cadre School, I and all the new graduates from professional performing arts schools received orders from the cultural authority to join our schoolmates in the remote countryside. When I got my job with the China National Peking Opera Company, my unemployed schoolmates had been sent, by train and bus, to the 4701 Army Farm in Gegu. They had already been there for a year. The worker propaganda team in charge of the music school in 1968 determined who in the 1966 and 1967 graduating class at CCOM and the Prep Music High School should be sent to that farm.

Gegu is a small town near the port city Tanggu, close to the Bohai Bay in northern China. The notice I received to join my schoolmates at the 4701 Army Farm was a total surprise. I had thought that I could return to the China National Peking Opera Company possibly after a year, because working at the cadre school was on a rotation basis. But now I would be in the same boat as all my other schoolmates. They were never told how long they would be working at the army farm, nor when they would be assigned jobs as musicians.

I had no choice but to gather my strength for survival. I understood that working at the army farm for an extended period meant the end of my hope ever to perform as a professional pianist. There were no pianos on the farm and the heavy manual labor could further damage my hands and arms. But I thought I could still advance some of my music studies on my own. I packed my harmony textbook and some of my music scores, although unsure of how appropriate such studies on the farm would be. Having heard about the extreme weather and poor living conditions, I bought a thick pair of padded pants and had a fur jacket made. The fur jacket was long and baggy so that I could wear it on top of my padded jacket. I also bought a huge ugly pair of suede boots with thick fur lining. While trying them on, I looked like a giant from an imaginary kingdom. But I could not worry about my appearance because survival was the priority.

It was hard to say good-bye to Mom, who was not in good health.

With saddened eyes, Mom said, "Xiao Mei, I hate to see you go to the farm."

"Don't worry, Mom. I will be okay. I will write you as soon as I get there. Please take care of yourself. I worry about you when Qingping and I are both gone."

"When will I see you again? Probably not for a long time."

"Mom, we will share the same moon."

Walking towards the bus station, I looked back at our house. Mom's frail figure was still at the door, waving.

I traveled on the morning train for two hours to Tianjin. Only two buses daily went to Gegu from Tianjin. I got on the early-afternoon bus with a group of farmers. The bus chugged along for two hours, stopping at small towns along the way. As we pulled away from Tianjin, the fields looked more and more barren and my heart sank.

I had phoned the captain's office at the army farm, asking for someone to meet me at the long-distance-bus stop at Xincheng (New City). The 4701 Army Farm was twenty-two *li* or about seven miles from the Xincheng bus stop. I had to walk to the farm from there. I found Jin waiting for me, holding close to her a long bare shoulder pole. She had been a piano major in the 1966 graduating class of the Prep Music High School and was the student leader of the squad I would be with. I was happy to see her familiar face, with short hair, in this strange place. There was no sign of human habitation. Tall reeds encroached on the sides of the dirt road leading into the distance.

Walking seven miles carrying my fifty pounds of suitcase and bedding on that shoulder pole looked like a daunting task. That was my first challenge. Jin and I wrapped my bedding around my suitcase and then tied this big bundle to the middle of the shoulder pole. We each took one end of the shoulder pole. A thin woman, she must have built up her endurance from more than a year of farm work. I had to ask her to let me take breaks quite a few times along the way. By the time we got to the farm, it was dark.

The next morning I was shocked to see that my schoolmates and I were living in the middle of wilderness. On one side of the army farm, a large salt-water lake named Guanjiang (Pouring River) Lake stretched as far as one could see, surrounded by dense reeds as tall as a person. Few people lived in the Gegu area, and my schoolmates mentioned prison farms in the vicinity. The dirt path leading away from the army farm was lined with the same reeds, silently swaying in the wind, and nothing else. I realized that I had now become part of this hopeless, abandoned group.

Because Gegu is not too far from the Tanggu seaport, the area has saline-alkali soil with many cracks on its dry yellow surface. Our drinking water was hauled in from a nearby town via a cattle wagon. Our clothes faded after a few washings because the well water was full of caustic sodium. The People's Liberation Army unit 4701 had set up its farm to plant rice, using the salt water from Guanjiang Lake.

A total of about 600 new graduates from CCOM, the Prep Music High School, Beijing Dance School, and the School of Chinese Theater Arts had been sent to this farm to be re-educated. The ballet and Peking opera students lived near the farm's central office, close to the Xincheng bus stop. The roughly 200 music students formed the Eleventh Army Company, farther from the bus stop. We also shared our barracks with about one hundred Spanish-language majors from the Beijing Second Foreign Language Institute.

Our barracks were huts made from mud and bricks. The three parallel rows of huts formed two common areas used for army company meetings in the open air. Male students and female students lived in separate sections. There were no beds. Like peasants, five of us girls shared one *kang*, a masonry bed built with mud and bricks. In northern China's villages, exhaust from cooking fires is routed to a chamber under the *kang* and vented outside. This is how the *kang* is heated in winter. In our case the *kang* was not heated. But we were given a coal stove, which we could not keep fired all the time because our ration of coal was small. On winter nights we sometimes slept without heat. Our room was so cold that the wet towel hanging there froze. I was given a space on the *kang* next to the wall, barely enough to put my single mattress. Gaps between the bricks let the cold in, and soon my back hurt. The *kang* occupied sixty percent of the room, leaving little common space. Our furniture consisted of a short stool for each student, and a shared dining table with short legs, leaned against the wall after meals. On hot summer nights we used mosquito nets to fend off very aggressive mosquitoes from the nearby lake and marshes. Lying on the crowded *kang* we felt like five hams inside an oven.

Because we were being re-educated or brainwashed, enduring hardship was one of our tasks. Our meals, prepared by the student chef squad, were plain and lacked adequate nutrition. We were fed a single vegetable dish, primarily cabbage or turnips cooked in little or no oil, served with rice or *mantou*. I tried to eat as much rice or *mantou* as possible. But lacking protein and fat, my schoolmates and I felt hungry all the time, especially during the long hours of heavy physical labor in rice paddies. During the busy season, we ate our lunches in the fields. The food was already cold by the time it arrived at our work site. Eating cold *mantou* in the chilly wind caused me stomach trouble which lasted many years.

Each month my classmates and I received thirty-two *yuan* from the army farm's administrative officer, the salary given to graduates from professional schools even though we were not assigned professional work. There were few opportunities to use our money. The army farm store, open for a limited number of days per month, occasionally had cans of peanuts, but I was afraid to purchase them for fear of being criticized for a bourgeois lifestyle.

We supplemented our diet as best we could. Some boys caught and tried to cook a sea bird. The bird meat was so bitter that they had to throw it away. When one of the farm's pigs died of disease and was buried near the boys' latrine, that night several boys dug up the dead pig, cooked its meat in the privacy of the reeds, and ate it quickly, risking sickness. The best food source was the fish in the lake. But the fish belonged to the farm, and we were not allowed to take them. Some boys broke the ice on the lake in winter and secretly caught fish with a net. One summer morning, from my window I looked towards the pond near the boys' huts and saw a carp jump out of the water. It landed on the bank just as my good friend Xiaoling, a cello major, happened to be walking by. Xiaoling rushed to catch the wiggling carp with both hands and threw it in a bucket of water. That evening, hiding in the dense reeds by the lake, she and I built a reed fire and boiled the carp in my squad's aluminum meal basin. Although the smoke from the fire badly irritated my eyes, the boiled carp was a feast for us even without sauce or flavoring.

Near our barracks was a small natural stream ignored by the army farm. We could get away with fishing there. Once, in late fall, our student army company organized a fish-catching event in that stream. We built a dam to block the water, and when the water below the dam drained away, all the small fish in that section lay in the mud. The boys jumped into the mud and threw the fish onto the bank where we girls cut and cleaned them. That day, our whole army company enjoyed a treat of *liuyupian* (fish fillet cooked in sweet and sour sauce). I wished we could have such events more often. But that happened only once.

Farm work was the core of our re-education. We dug irrigation trenches in winter temperatures well below freezing. Very often the north wind cutting through my padded jacket was strong enough to blow me over unless I huddled close to the ground. None of the local peasants worked outdoors in such severe weather. The PLA officers simply wanted to put us through the hardship.

In early spring when the rice paddies were still covered with ice, we were there digging out rice-plant stubs left from the season before. Then we plowed deeply into the soil to prepare for planting rice seedlings. We worked in the fields every day from dawn until dark. I tried hard to catch up with my schoolmates who had developed endurance from more than a year of farm work. I was determined to get out of this "hell" alive. Father's example as a struggling young artist in Shanghai always encouraged me. I remembered his words, ". . .if a person at the end of his resources can still press on, then he is not a coward. . . ."[48] I thought if he could stand up to the challenges of life, so could I.

During the spring planting season, we stood barefooted all day in the almost knee-high rice paddy water. I found it hard to push seedlings into the compacted mud beneath the surface. We spent all summer weeding the rice paddies. We had no farm tools for a task called *naoyang*, meaning weeding rice paddies and loosening mud around rice seedling roots. This manual labor relied entirely on pressure concentrated in our fingers, really hurting our hands. At first I could not easily tell weeds and rice seedlings apart. But in a month, I could identify weeds by the shapes of their leaves. Leeches attached to our legs made my skin crawl. They could not be pulled off, but using my palm to hit my leg muscle nearest a leech shook it loose. During the busy harvest time, we cut rice plants with our sickles for more than ten days in a row, bent over all the while. When we woke up in the mornings, our fingers were so stiff and sore from holding sickles that we could hardly bend them.

Our music school had been singled out in the Cultural Revolution for its well-known "aristocratic" lifestyle. My schoolmates and I had once been very careful with our hands, but that was not the concern of our army farm leaders. Their job was to put us through this harsh life in order to purge our bourgeois thinking.

In addition to working in the rice paddies, we were required to grow our own vegetables so our army company would be self-sufficient. This was also for security reasons, to prepare for a possible war with the Soviets, a threat in the early 1970s. Each squad kept a vegetable patch tended in the evenings after the rice paddy work. We dug ditches leading to the vegetable patch and filled them with buckets of water scooped from the salt-water lake. Because of the water and soil, we grew only green onions, celery, and carrots. Some squads were able to grow white turnips, bell peppers, and kohlrabies.

The most repulsive work on the farm was composting our own waste in a large pit behind the latrines to make fertilizer for our vegetable patches. The squads rotated the job of cleaning the latrines and removing the waste. Our squad performed this three-hour task about every three weeks. We used a scoop with a long handle to dig out the latrine pits and carried the waste in a bucket to the open pit. Sometimes the content got on our hands and faces. It was so stinky that I felt like throwing up. Later we dug up our own composted human waste and carried it in two baskets on a shoulder pole to the vegetable patch about a quarter mile away.

The one reward for our hard work was enjoying the fresh vegetables. All the student vegetable fields together might have provided about half of the vegetables we consumed in summer. My favorite was kohlrabi: Its turnip-shaped stem tasted like cabbage. Having no fruit to eat on the farm, we called kohlrabies "earth apples." I liked kohlrabies so much that I once pulled one from a neighboring army unit's vegetable patch. I washed the dirt off in the river, bit off its light-green satin skin and enjoyed the crisp juicy stem as I sat on the riverbank, feeling like a devil. Years later, I found kohlrabies sold in grocery stores in the city. But they were small and dry, nothing like the fresh juicy kohlrabies on our farm.

After about a year, I adjusted to the hard physical labor. However, for most of us the worst part of the farm life was our lost career opportunities. My classmates and I were around age twenty-two in 1970. We should have been advancing our music studies, gaining technical skills at a crucial young age for reaching high performance standards. On the farm our fingers lost dexterity. Even worse, students were not allowed to practice their instruments at all in the first year, and in later years were given only limited time to practice. Most of us had studied music performance for more than ten years. This career setback was devastating to the majority of us. Uncertainty about our futures was probably harder on us than the physical stress.

During the second summer of my stay on the farm, about one hundred students, half of our army company, suddenly came down with dysentery. The origin of the disease was traced to the kitchen. I heard that our pigs from "Pig Island," just across from the boys' quarters, had one night raided the kitchen. After biting through the screened windows, they jumped onto the cutting boards and ransacked the kitchen for food. The student chefs saw the broken screens and pigs' footprints on the cutting boards.

My schoolmates, weak with dysentery, had to stay in bed and could not eat solid food for days. A short, bespectacled army doctor was sent over to treat the sick students. To my surprise, he did not prescribe any effective medication. Nor did he recommend any measures to prevent further spread of the disease. Instead, he applied acupuncture to the sick students and prescribed soup made from boiled purslane, a wild vegetable with small round leaves. Purslane was considered a weed, and was prevalent on the farm.

My healthy schoolmates and I were sent to collect purslane to make soup for the sick students. I spent all day squatting by the roadside, pulling purslane plants and sticking them into a large sack. It took a few weeks for many sick students to recover. Some were left with chronic conditions. We wondered whether the army doctor was trying to save money by not prescribing effective Western medicine. We ridiculed him as "Purslane Doctor" or "Wild Vegetable Doctor."

Sanitary conditions were very poor. Boiled drinking water was barely enough to brush our teeth, leaving little fresh water for cleaning ourselves. Bathing in a communal bathhouse was a once-a-month treat. About twenty girls shared a large indoor bathing pool. The unsanitary conditions and crowded living situation helped spread some contagions among the girls. Two girls contracted diseases in their uteri. By the time they were allowed to go to Beijing for treatment, it was already too late. I was told that they could never have children.

I took the only preventive action I could: trying to remain physically strong. I kept running on the farm's dirt path every morning, including cold winter days. I did not contract a contagious disease there.

• • •

Political indoctrination was a major theme for our re-education, led by PLA officers. Our student army company on the 4701 Army Farm was commanded by Captain Li from Henan Province. He was tall and thin with a long stern face. His slightly bulging eyes were located high on his face and shaded by the bill of his army cap. Commissar Wu was in charge of political work in the army company. He directed investigations into the radical actions taken by some students during the Cultural Revolution. Under the captain, a few platoon leaders took charge of the girls' and boys' platoons. Our platoon leader was from a village in Henan Province. He was friendly, and sometimes taught us how to do farm work. When he smiled, he showed rows of false teeth. He jokingly said, "You know how I eat? I rely on my stomach because my teeth hardly work."

The lowest unit in our student army company was the squad. Every squad had an army leader who directed our daily activities. Our squad leader Xiao Shen (Little Shen) was a young man from the countryside without much education. Sitting around our short dining table with five educated city girls, he was shy and hesitant. When he cautiously reached for the *mantou* on the dining table, one of the girls said, "Hey, Xiao Shen. Your hands move with the delicacy of a female traditional Peking opera performer." He blushed and smiled helplessly. However, after receiving an order from his superior, he immediately became very serious with us. Mustering some authority was difficult for him. So we followed his directive without much resistance.

In the morning, as soon as the wake-up whistle blew at 5, he knocked at our window in the dark, yelling with a Hubei accent: "Hurry up! Hurry up!" We dressed in a few minutes and gathered in the open space in a column. He led our morning drill, including running to his count. He also organized our political studies and discussions. In the morning, we had one hour to study works by Mao Zedong, Marx, and Engels. Xiao Shen held meetings at which all of us were expected to talk about ridding ourselves of our bourgeois thinking by studying Mao's works and doing manual labor. Self-criticism was encouraged. However, our self-criticisms were not all that sincere.

One student said, "After studying 'Serve the People' by Chairman Mao, I realized that I led a bourgeois lifestyle before. In the past I sought a pleasurable life. I liked eating good food and wearing stylish clothing. But Chairman Mao's article taught me to dedicate myself to the people's interests. I am determined to get rid of my bourgeois thinking and serve the people wholeheartedly." We said what the squad leader wanted to hear. Some of us were so bored at these meetings that we would have chosen instead to do our daily farm work.

Another military drill was movie watching. The captain, on some evenings, ordered all the students to march three miles to the army farm's central location to watch a movie in an open space, surrounded by barracks and the farm's main administrative office. Only a couple of Albanian movies were allowed on the farm, describing Albanian workers building socialism. We were required to watch them repeatedly. In winter, this was the most grueling test, sitting on our short stools outside for two hours in severe cold and strong freezing winds. I usually put my fur jacket on top of my padded coat, and wore my padded pants and fur-lined boots. Huddling down to my knees to keep my body heat, I could hardly open my eyes because the wind whipped dust into my face.

In warm weather, the soldiers gathering in the open space before the movie usually sang competitively, one military unit at a time. However, their singing was yelling in unison as if they were competing in loudness and enthusiasm. The soldier conductors each had a unique gesture. Some looked as if they were chopping wood vigorously. Others moved their arms horizontally as if pulling a heavy curtain open from the middle with both hands. The soldiers were emphasizing the spirit, not the music. They sang the "March of the Chinese People's Liberation Army": "Forward! Forward! Forward! Our troops face the sun. . ."

Another song favored by the soldiers depicts the success of soldiers' target shooting. The lyrics say:

The sun sets in the west.
Colorful clouds are flying.
The soldiers are returning to their barracks after target shooting.

Red flowers on their chests echo the colorful clouds.
Their happy songs are heard across the sky.
Mi-sol-la-mi-sol,
la-sol-mi-do-re.
Their happy songs are heard across the sky.

Such activities were our only entertainment.

The hopeless future, the heavy physical labor, the harsh living conditions, and the meaningless indoctrination became unbearable for many students. One of my classmates, Xiaoyan (Little Swallow), started showing signs of mental imbalance. She had come to the Prep Music High School in 1964 as an overseas Chinese from Indonesia. I imagine that the change from a well-to-do overseas Chinese family life to harsh farm life was too difficult an adjustment. I also heard that in the first year some students tried to escape. While on their seven-mile walk to the long-distance-bus stop, some were intercepted by the officers. Those who succeeded in running away usually returned to the farm after staying in Beijing for about two weeks. Upon their return, they had to criticize themselves publicly in front of their peers. These students returned mainly because they realized that the army farm would determine their eventual destiny, namely job assignment. Students could not find employment on their own. In China, everyone belonged to a unit. All job assignments or transfers had to go through the administrative office of the unit which kept one's personal files. The army farm leaders controlled the students' files. Everyone knew that good standing with the army farm leaders was important. Inevitably we had to submit to the life on the farm for as long as it might take.

Some students behaved defiantly. The captain had two dogs, one called A Hei (Blackie) and the other called A Huang (Yeller). I remember them following me on the dirt path leading to the long-distance-bus stop. They peed on the way so that they could trace their way back. I kept away from them. One winter day, a male student lured Blackie to a hut in which a few girls from Squad Ten smothered Blackie, butchered him, and cooked his meat in a soup. I dropped in on Squad Ten that day, unaware of what had happened. One girl offered me a spoonful of soup with meat.

"Can you guess what the meat is?" she asked.

I thought for a second and replied, "Perhaps beef."

She laughed and said, "You were eating Blackie, the captain's dog."

I heard the story and was shocked. Later, I realized that the girls in Squad Ten must have worried that I might be a snitch, so they had fed me the soup and tricked me into being their co-conspirator.

The next day the captain summoned all the students in the Eleventh Army Company and walked up and down restlessly in front of us. With his bulging eyes he stared fiercely at the girls in Squad Ten. He yelled, "I will bombard you with one hundred thousand tons of bombs!" I lowered my head, hoping no one would report that I had also tasted Blackie's meat. No one did.

In this authoritarian environment I pursued my music studies in whatever ways were possible. In late 1970, the army farm leaders finally allowed us to practice our instruments for one hour in the morning. I envied the violin students who were able to bring their instruments to the farm. They also practiced again in the evenings. I remember hearing the music from model Peking operas around our mud huts. I had no piano on the farm. I did have a violin in Beijing, acquired from a second-hand store. A schoolmate brought it to me after his home visit to Beijing. Zheng, a college-level student on the farm and a very good violinist, gave me violin lessons. I enjoyed playing excerpts of some classical violin pieces after a year of learning the basics. Although I could not expect to play the violin professionally, my learning helped me understand string instruments and better blend my piano playing with a chamber music ensemble.

Meanwhile, I decided to purchase an accordion, to be used to keep up my harmony studies. A few months after I came to the farm, I got permission to go to Tianjin to see a doctor. The captain allowed only two students from our army company to go to Tianjin on any particular day, so we could visit Tianjin once or twice a year at most. On that valuable trip to Tianjin, in a musical-instrument store I found a red accordion with 120 bass for 510 *yuan*, which I liked very much. It was the Parrot brand made in Tianjin. The demonstration model on display was the only one left and it was not for sale. I was told that more would be coming in a month. Then I went to visit my "little uncle," Xuezheng, a student at Tianjin University. I gave him 510 *yuan*, all my savings, and asked him to buy the accordion for me when it became available.

In a few weeks, Xuezheng came to my farm, carrying the accordion on his shoulder. He sat in my room for only ten minutes because he wanted to catch the long-distance bus back to Tianjin the same day. I thanked him for walking seven miles to bring my precious instrument.

Xu Fangfang playing the violin in front of a mud hut on the 4701 Army Farm, Gegu, 1971. There was no piano on the farm.

With the accordion, I was able to continue studying harmony from the textbook. I also started practicing the accompaniment for some well-known arias from *The Red Lantern* and other model Peking operas, the only politically correct pieces to play. Several students on the farm came to ask me to accompany them on the accordion while they sang the arias. A student sang Xiao Chang Bao (Little Chang Bao)'s aria about the murder of her family members by bandits, a story from the model Peking opera *Taking the Tiger Mountain by Strategy*. One of the army farm officers sang the aria of the People's Liberation Army hero Yang Zirong, in response to Xiao Chang Bao's tragic story. After some rehearsal, the three of us performed these arias for the soldiers, in the open air with the audience sitting on the dirt. I felt lucky to have had these performance opportunities.

To broaden my music studies, I secretly ventured into learning some Western operas. A CCOM opera student on the farm had hidden the opera piano score for Bizet's *Carmen*. One Sunday afternoon, a CCOM soprano student named

Mo and I went to an isolated spot surrounded by reeds, carrying my accordion and the *Carmen* score. It was the first time I had played the arias from *Carmen* on the accordion. Mo sang Micaela's aria, in which Micaela tries to convince Don Jose to return home to see his dying mother. As I played the introductory phrase on my accordion, Mo lifted her voice in the lyrical melody. At that moment, I forgot my hard life on the army farm. This touching aria carried me back to my passionate times in the music school when we dedicated ourselves to studying the Western classical music we loved.

I also tried to study English. This was not easy. We were closely watched by the army squad leader and other officers and I was not able to listen to the BBC or Voice of America on the farm. I had not brought my English textbooks, fearing being criticized for studying bourgeois literature. But I did have the English translations of some articles by Mao Zedong such as "Serve the People," "In Memory of Norman Bethune," and "The Foolish Old Man Who Removed the Mountains." I had also brought a few articles in English by Karl Marx and Friedrich Engels, plus *The Communist Manifesto*. During the one-hour political study time in the morning, I tried to read these articles in English. I had to look up many new words, especially in the articles written by Marx and Engels. But I was able to compare the English version with the Chinese version, which helped me understand the difficult text. Our army squad leader, Xiao Shen, left me alone, knowing that I was studying our great leaders' works.

During the long, tedious years on the farm, some of my schoolmates gave up their studying. Quite a few spent all their evenings and weekends making shoes or knitting sweaters. Perhaps they had given up the hope of ever being a musician. I was one of the few students who tried to study English there. I often thought about Father pursuing his career with such passion, painting in a German museum for hours, often without stopping to take food or water. His artistic dream for me was still hidden in my heart. Although I did not want to talk about his dream to anyone on the farm, I believed that someday my knowledge of music and English might be useful. How wonderful if I could read music literature in English! Perhaps I could do work requiring the knowledge of music and English. Perhaps someday I could go abroad to study Western classical music. These dreams seemed far-fetched when our stay on the farm was indefinite. But these beautiful dreams gave me the strength to face each day.

CHAPTER 21
Talents on the Farm

I was not the only person there with artistic dreams. In particular, I recall two talented classmates: Chang, a violin major, and Cui, a piano major. Chang entered the Prep Music Elementary School affiliated to the Central Conservatory of Music in Tianjin in 1957 after returning from Japan. He and I were in the same third-grade class and we shared many musical experiences growing up together. In sixth grade, he was one of the few students chosen from CCOM and its affiliated music schools privileged to study with a Hungarian violin expert.

In 1968, a student accused Chang of yelling a reactionary slogan, but there was no evidence or verification by any witness, and the alleged reactionary slogan was never disclosed. Chang's best friend, piano student Cui, said that he was pressured to expose Chang's other "crimes" while watching Chang being severely beaten by a mob of students. Cui suspected that Chang might have been forced to admit that he had accidentally reversed the meaning of a political slogan. I suspect that Chang, a top violin student, likely to be a first choice for the limited job assignments then available, was framed. This was common during the Cultural Revolution. In this situation no one dared to defend the accused.

Although Chang's political-slogan mishap was not verified, the worker propaganda team considered it a serious problem and he was branded a current counterrevolutionary. In September 1968, he was abused at a mass-criticism meeting on our music school campus. At mealtime, he was forced to his knees to eat from a plate of coarse grain on the ground, like a dog. I held back my tears as I saw this. Chang was like a brother to me, and it hurt me deeply to see him being mistreated.

At the army farm, Chang was assigned to the most consistently dirty work: stoking the boiler to boil hot water for our whole army company. His face and clothes were covered with coal dust and soot. But his hot water was always boiled to standard and on time. I heard that Chang had a girlfriend in Beijing. He never invited her to visit him on the farm where his humiliating situation would embarrass them both. He chose to visit her in Beijing during his home leave. When I went to the boiler room to fill my thermos with hot water, Chang and I talked briefly. I sensed that he preferred keeping to himself. Perhaps he was afraid of being nailed again for anything said improperly.

One night walking by the mud hut where he lived, I heard beautiful violin music coming from his room. It was *Melody* by Tchaikovsky, which Chang had played at the Prep Music High School. I could feel his same passion, sensitivity, and love of music as in the old days. I was elated that Chang kept his music, and perhaps some dream, or hope for a future music career.

Cui, the piano student, had been denied admission to our music school in 1961, because of his parents' supposed political problems. But he joined our second-year class the following year when the family background political check was relaxed for students with special talent. During the four years at the Prep Music High School, he developed his talent in composition by writing piano music on his own.

Unfortunately, Cui's composition and piano performance studies were interrupted by the Cultural Revolution. While on the army farm, he tried to learn composition skills without the piano. He borrowed from the composition students some orchestral scores such as the *New World Symphony* by Dvořák and *Concerto for Voice and Orchestra* by Glière. Through his exercise of reducing the orchestral score to a piano duet score, he learned the structure and orchestration of the symphonies by great Western composers. In the first year while doing heavy physical labor in the rice paddies, he sacrificed his nap time after lunch to read orchestral scores and write piano accompaniment for model Peking operas. Although he spent only his nap time to do this, he was still severely criticized publicly by the captain and the platoon leader for developing music skills, a crime during students' initial phase of re-education. At that time, students were not allowed to practice their instruments or pursue any music studies. The criticism did not deter Cui from continuing to develop his composition skills. He probably assumed that the situation could not get any worse because the army leaders already had a bad opinion of him.

In the third year on the farm, Cui was assigned to raise pigs on "Pig Island." I remember him as a quiet man always in dirty clothes. "Pig Island" was actually a long natural walkway separating the pond near the boys' huts from the big lake. I often saw a piglet and its mother swim across the pond to get to our vegetable patches, the piglet holding in its mouth the curly tail of its mother. The student on duty watching the vegetable patches immediately threw stones at the pigs who tried to eat our precious vegetables.

During two years as a pig herder, Cui observed and came to understand pigs. He once said, "Pigs are very smart. They respond to whatever you did for them. They could tell my footsteps from those of a hundred or so other people in our army company marching together. These pigs are like longtime acquaintances." Because the pigs required his attention frequently, especially when the piglets were delivered, Cui was excused from the boring political study sessions. Left alone most of the time, he had more flexibility to pursue his composition studies.

I admired Cui's talent, persistence, and resourcefulness which paid off in the end. His creative spark might have been buried among the pigs and reeds. Several years later, he finally got work as a composer and pianist with the Central Philharmonic Orchestra. He was able to compose piano accompaniment quickly without the piano as he traveled, and attributed the skill to his practice on the farm.

He performed one of his own works, *Piano Symphonic Rhapsody*, in May 2005, accompanied by the China National Symphony Orchestra, in Beijing National Library Concert Hall. Several classmates and I attended this concert. I was impressed with this work featuring a combination of Chinese folk music on the piano with Western orchestra. After the concert, I went backstage to congratulate him. He was very happy and surprised to see me and we took a photo together with our classmates.

During the farm years, I developed friendships with some schoolmates. These bonds helped strengthen each of us, and together we survived.

In winter 1971, the army farm authorities turned their attention to investigating the counterrevolutionary May Sixteenth conspirators, who had been active in 1967. Investigations against students' actions in previous years were also going on in other parts of the country. In this movement, some students were telling lies or betraying their friends and family members to save their own skins. Even so, there were still honest people who stood up for their principles. My classmate Ai'yi was one of them.

A piano major who had come to our music school in sixth grade from Shenyang, Ai'yi looked small, with two thin pigtails falling to her shoulders. She was shy but warm-hearted. In December 1966, she had joined Tian Sheng and other schoolmates from the Prep Music High School in their actions against Wang Shuxiao. In the winter of 1971, Ai'yi came to my dorm, whispering to me, "Can we take a walk outside? I have something important to tell you."

I followed her immediately. As we walked along the stream away from the barracks, she said in a quiet voice, "Two people from Beijing questioned me today in the captain's office. They were investigating our actions against Wang Shuxiao in December 1966. They looked stern-faced and a little threatening. But I did not tell them anything that could harm you or your mother."

I was very surprised and touched. "Thank you, Ai'yi," I said. "I will never forget your friendship."

I appreciated the information about the investigation and particularly her standing up for justice even under pressure. I immediately wrote to Mom to warn her. However, in the next few months, nothing happened to me or Mom concerning our actions against Wang Shuxiao. The officers on the farm did not even mention that investigation to me. To this day, I still remember Ai'yi's integrity and friendship. These were even more valuable during a time when everyone's political fate could be in jeopardy.

Another friend was my squad member Wu, a piano major, one year ahead of me in the Prep Music High School. One Sunday afternoon in early spring, she and I decided to walk to a farmer's small store several miles away to buy some eggs. We got permission to go there and return before dinnertime. It was a sunny day but very cold. Wu and I both wore boots and padded jackets. We bought a dozen eggs, planning to share them with our schoolmates.

On our way back in late afternoon as we walked along a small river, Wu said abruptly, "Let's cross the ice. We'd be back in no time."

"But the ice looks thin," I countered.

"I do not think so."

Bull-headedly, she walked onto the ice. I stayed on the riverbank. In a few minutes, came her yells: "Help! Help!"

Ignoring the danger to myself, I rushed over. The large sheet I walked on sank slightly, soaking my feet. Wu was in a hole, waist-deep in icy water. Luckily the river was not deep. I reached out and pulled her out of the water. The ice barely sustained our combined weight. All the life had been drained from her face, leaving only her terrified eyes. Her lips quivered and her teeth chattered. All the eggs in her bag were broken. I helped her carry her bag and we walked as quickly as we could. Icicles hung from her pants cuffs. As soon as she returned to our barracks, she dried herself off and got under her quilt. She remained chilled for a long time. I gave her some hot water to warm her up. Meanwhile I tried to boil the few remaining half-broken eggs on our coal stove before they were completely wasted. I was very relieved that she did not develop a fever.

In spite of the hard living conditions, schoolmates and I tried to have some fun. In summer, several of us girls swam in the small pond near the boys' huts. The boys shouted encouragement for our antics. In winter, when the pond froze over, we enjoyed skating on the ice. I asked Mom to send my skates to the farm. Early in the morning and on weekends, a few of us showed off our skating feats there. After all, we were performing students. I felt fresh and light-hearted when skating.

The salt-water lake formed a large natural rink. Students without skates made a simple wooden sleigh with metal runners. Three students could stand on the sleigh while one pushed with a pole. Several friends and I ventured out on that sleigh a couple of times on weekends. As we slid away from our barracks and beyond the reeds, miles into the large lake, our laughing and yelling cut across the ice in the cold winter air.

Xu Fangfang (front row, far right) and schoolmates on the 4701 Army Farm, Gegu, 1971.

Xu Fangfang (right) and schoolmates riding a sleigh on Guanjiang (Pouring River) Lake on the 4701 Army Farm, Gegu, 1971.

As months became years, we adapted to the isolated rural life and began feeling like country bumpkins. During our precious visits to Tianjin, we all managed to eat a good meal in Qishilin, Tianjin's only Western food restaurant. One day, a female voice student from our farm ordered ice cream there. When preparing her scoop of vanilla ice cream, the waitress poured onto it some hot fudge from a tall glass bottle with a slender neck. The student said, "Comrade, I do not want soy sauce on my ice cream." This anecdote spread to all the students on the farm, and beyond.

• • •

I missed Mom and Qingping very much. Fortunately, Qingping came to visit me during my first summer on the farm, traveling the whole day and walking the seven miles from the long-distance-bus stop. I was overjoyed to see him, wearing his old cotton Mao suit with his canvas school bag on his shoulder and his usual smiling eyes behind his thick glasses. He and his classmates at the Beijing Second Foreign Language Institute were about to move to a very poor village near Minggang in Henan Province, farther south from Beijing.

Uncertain about the length of their stay there, he had made the trip to the army farm to say good-bye to me. He brought me a delicious dish Mom had made and packed in a glass bottle. It was stir-fried pork cooked with eggs and wood-ear mushrooms, one of my favorite dishes. I was happy that Qingping brought Mom's love to me.

While he and I took a walk along the nearby stream, he told me about Mom's illness. She was sometimes too sick to leave her bed. Chinese herbal medicine did not seem to work and there was no diagnosis. Now that Qingping was leaving, Mom would be alone at home with seven-year-old Maomao, our little brother. We were both worried. Shenpo had recently moved in with her daughter-in-law to care for her young grandchildren. Uncle Huang had been sent to the May Seventh Cadre School with his work unit, the China Film Workers Association. He had asked Mom to request that he be allowed to remain in Beijing with the excuse of caring for her. But at the time the Party policy stated that only sick, disabled, or very old people were exempt. Mom refused to help Uncle Huang, saying, "I would look like a stinker if I were to make such a request." Qingping and I had followed the Party's directive without hesitating. We did not then know that some cities allowed each family to keep one of their high-school-graduate children from going to the countryside to receive re-education. At the time, neither Qingping's college nor my music school honored such a policy.

Qingping stayed in one of the boys' rooms that night and left early the following morning. I walked him to the dirt path leading away from the army farm. We encouraged each other to remain strong and optimistic. As he faded into the distance, I experienced sudden loneliness. The huge lake in front of me was so silent that the steamy heat from the water was all one could feel. There was nothing I could see but dense reeds on the far side of the lake, blending into the greyish sky. I felt that this salt-water lake trapped and separated me from my family and everything important to me.

Some CCOM students had been married before coming to the farm. Their spouses visited them briefly. But intimacy was not shown publicly. One of the piano graduate students, Lao Bao (Old Bao), now a student chef on the farm, was the wife of a world-champion ping-pong player. When he came to visit, he received no fanfare. I saw him carrying two buckets of water on a shoulder pole. He left the water in the kitchen where Lao Bao and other student chefs were preparing meals for our army company. Not knowing who Lao Bao's husband was, one of the officers criticized his stylish T-shirt and shorts. "Over here we do not wear those fancy outfits," the officer said.

The ping-pong champion retorted, "In my world, we do wear these outfits."

Lao Bao did not receive any special treatment during her husband's visit. But she was allowed to visit him in Beijing before each of his overseas trips for ping-pong tournaments.

Married students living on the farm were occasionally given brief conjugal time. I remember a married CCOM student couple staying in a mud hut by the roadside, with two rough-cut glassless openings for windows. Curious, I dropped by to visit them with a few other students. Their room had no furniture except for a bed. The interior was rough dry mud. I hoped that they enjoyed their few days together away from the noisy barracks.

Army officers were not allowed to date soldiers or students. However, I heard that a platoon leader named Dong broke the rule and dated one of the female students from our army company. They tried to see each other secretly in the middle of the night near our vegetable fields. After the affair was discovered, Dong was demoted and transferred to another army location. I heard he had treated the male students harshly, and they were happy to see him leave.

Home visit time was limited and very precious. Every student was allowed a fourteen-day home leave per year, including travel time. Some students begged the captain to cut their waiting time for home leave but to no avail. One opera student kept harassing the captain about this, scratching the captain's office windowpane with a piece of broken glass. Irritated by the grating noise, the captain yelled at her, "Devil! Devil! Leave me alone." It was not until the summer of 1971, more than a year after I came to the farm, that I was given home leave. Mom had scheduled an operation to remove a tumor. Her high blood pressure made the operation risky. Qingping and I both got permission to come home to take care of her.

Mom was very happy to see Qingping and me. She had always looked youthful, but during my home visit she appeared pale and weak. The day after my arrival, she went into the Union Hospital, then the best hospital in Beijing. Her operation took several hours. Qingping and I waited nervously in the hallway. Finally, Mom was wheeled out. To my relief, the doctor said that her tumor was benign, but her recovery would be slow. Mom, lying under a white sheet, looked weaker, but her weary face showed a faint smile.

I went to see Mom in the hospital every day. Her condition improved gradually. At home, I passionately pursued my music studies. I had not played the piano for more than a year, so could only ease into practicing. I borrowed classical music records from my friends in Beijing, including Western operas such as *Tosca* by Puccini. While listening to the records, I tried to read the English text on the record sleeves.

While in Beijing I caught up with two of my old girlfriends and classmates from the Prep Music High School, now working for the Beijing Peking Opera Troupe. Chunhua was a violin major from Harbin in northeastern China. Li Lu was a cello major whose father was Li Delun, principal conductor at the Central Philharmonic Orchestra. Before leaving for the army farm a year before, I had asked these two good friends to visit my mother sometimes, to keep her company. They gladly promised. Later while I worked on the farm, Mom moved to an apartment which happened to be opposite from my friends' work unit. They frequently visited Mom in the evenings after work. Mom and my two friends came to know each other quite well. Chunhua and Li Lu even confided in Mom about their dating experiences and asked for her advice.

In summer 1971, my two friends came to visit me and we shared music together. Looking at my tanned face, Li Lu said, "You look so strong. Look at me; I have grown double chins. The model troupe's rich meals really fattened me up."

"How lucky you are, still doing music work," I said.

Chunhua said, "Our lives are so different. I do not think I could survive that farm work. I admire you."

I played the piano accompaniment for an aria from the model Peking opera *The Red Lantern*. Surprisingly, my classmates commented that my hands were still in good shape. But I knew that I was out of practice. I said to Li Lu, "I wish to find a music job in Beijing. Could you keep your ears open for me?"

After thinking for a moment, Li Lu said, "Why don't you visit my home this weekend? My parents may have some suggestions for you."

I had never met Li Lu's mother, a violinist with the Central Opera Company in Beijing. But I had met Li Lu's father, Li Delun, a year before the Cultural Revolution broke out. He came to our class to talk about how he had changed: Formerly infatuated with Western classical music, he now devoted himself to the symphony *Shajiabang*. I remember enjoying the content he presented so freely and with occasional humor.

I found Li Lu's family members very friendly and her father, Li Delun, easy to talk with. His eighty-plus-year-old mother lived with him, and the family kept their Muslim tradition of not eating pork within the household. The three generations of family members seemed to have a close relationship. There was also a strong family resemblance between Li Lu and her father. They both talked openly and light-heartedly. I told Li Delun that I had enjoyed his concert of Beethoven *Symphony No. 5* with the Central Philharmonic Orchestra. Li Lu had told her father about my music background and that I could read English. I told him that I was keeping up my studies of English. Li Delun knew of no job openings. But he said he would keep me informed should there be any positions in which I could use my knowledge of music and English.

Unfortunately, the twelve days of my home leave flew past. I had set aside two whole days for traveling. Saying good-bye to Mom was difficult. She looked sad in her hospital bed. When I turned to look at her before walking out the door, her distressed eyes followed me. We both wished for more time together. As the train pulled out of Beijing, I watched the buildings, streets, and everything I loved quickly fall away.

• • •

A few months after returning to the farm, I heard about a big political event concerning Lin Biao, whose status had been second only to Chairman Mao's after 1968. At the Ninth CCP Congress in 1969, the new Party constitution was modified to officially designate Lin as Mao's successor. I remember seeing him on the Tiananmen gate tower, standing next to Mao while waving the little red book, *Quotations from Chairman Mao Zedong*. On many occasions, Chairman Mao's name was linked with Lin's, and they were referred to as "Chairman Mao and Vice Chairman Lin."

In October 1971, my schoolmates and I were shocked when Captain Li read to us an official report about Lin Biao and his supporters' plans to oust Mao Zedong in a military coup, including attempts to assassinate Chairman Mao. After their plans failed, Lin Biao, his wife Ye Qun, and their son, Lin Liguo, tried to escape on a tri-plane out of China. In September 1971, their plane crashed in Mongolia. Lin and all the people on board were killed.

My schoolmates and I, sitting on the dirt, listened to the announcement and could not believe it. For the first time, I asked myself, "How could Chairman

Mao name a successor, written into the Party constitution, who turned out to be his worst enemy?" I used to genuinely believe in Chairman Mao and the Party. But after Lin Biao's failed coup, I questioned the legitimacy of the Cultural Revolution and the motives of the authority directing it. I suspected that there was an intense power struggle within the CCP's top leadership, but kept these thoughts to myself because sharing them could cause me trouble.

During the next few years, political power shifts and policy changes did happen, affecting many people's lives, including ours. In 1973, Deng Xiaoping, who had been attacked at the beginning of the Cultural Revolution, was transferred back to Beijing. In 1974, Premier Zhou Enlai convinced Chairman Mao to nominate Deng as first vice premier, directing day-to-day government affairs.

Starting in early 1972, cadres and intellectuals, as well as their families, were allowed to return from May Seventh Cadre Schools to cities and resume their work. Quite a few artists from CAFA returned to Beijing from the countryside to paint oil paintings for hotels serving foreign guests. In the next few years, May Seventh Cadre Schools were gradually closed. In late 1971, both Mom and I had seen the possibility of music students coming back to cities to continue their music careers. Finding a job in Beijing was on our minds, yet while we were at the farm, job-search resources were limited.

During my second home leave, Mom told me that she had written a letter to Premier Zhou Enlai, explaining that Fangfang, her daughter with Beihong, had been working on an army farm for two years. She expressed her desire for Fangfang to study music composition with the famous pianist Yin Chengzong at the Central Philharmonic Orchestra. The secretary of Premier Zhou's office called her, telling her that Premier Zhou had read her letter, understood the situation, and that Fangfang would be transferred to Beijing soon.

I heard that Premier Zhou Enlai's office staff called one of the leaders at the Central Philharmonic Orchestra, possibly Li Delun, inquiring about a position for me. During that home leave in 1972, Li Delun contacted me about a position as a music researcher and translator in the orchestra's music research group. Its mission was studying contemporary Soviet and Western music and translating articles about contemporary Western music from foreign journals. The group's reports on these subjects were submitted to Jiang Qing and cultural leaders. Li Delun arranged for me to take music theory and composition lessons from Yanqiao, one of the composers with the orchestra. I was very grateful to Li Delun.

I was thrilled that I could use my knowledge of music and English. Information concerning contemporary Western music was blocked to the people in China. To look into the music world outside was a privilege. Best of all, I could further my music and English studies.

Premier Zhou Enlai's concern for me was touching. Father had died nineteen years before, yet Premier Zhou still honored their friendship. Premier Zhou was like a guardian angel to us. He opened the door for me to work with the Central Philharmonic Orchestra. Without his help, my immediate family might not have survived the devastation of the Cultural Revolution intact. Many of our artist friends did not.

At the end of my home leave, I told Mom that I had accepted the job offer. Mom looked relieved when I left for the farm this time because I would soon be back. The paperwork might take some time, but I felt confident about returning to Beijing.

Soon after my return to the farm, the captain announced the names of the first few students with job assignments in Beijing. Award-winning pianist Lao Bao would now become a performing pianist with the Central Philharmonic Orchestra. The other students were assigned teaching jobs at the new Central May Seventh College of Arts, established by Jiang Qing, in the suburbs of Beijing.

Some of my schoolmates held a small party for the departing students. Those left behind were envious; one girl even cried. I remained calm, knowing that my turn would come.

A month later, the captain announced my name in the second group of students to return to Beijing. I was overjoyed. For a farewell dinner, I shared with my squad members a few preserved eggs brought back from my home leave. I thanked them and several good friends for their friendship and support and hoped that they would leave the farm soon. Later I heard that the remaining music students were all assigned jobs in cities within the year.

My army squad leader, Xiao Shen, helped me wrap all my belongings in my bedding. He cinched my big bundle tightly with his strong hands, showing a genuine smile on his young face as we shook hands at parting. I carried my red Parrot accordion in its case. My faithful instrument had given me joy and helped me learn many new pieces of music. I would now take it home.

The army farm arranged for a truck to take the few of us to the Tianjin train station. Usually only high-ranking officers did not have to walk the seven miles to the long-distance-bus stop. I had been fortunate, once, to hitch a ride on a tractor.

As our truck pulled away from the barracks, the dried reed stalks around the big salt-water lake quivered in the light snowfall. I felt sad. There I had lost two years of my professional music career, a very untimely loss for a young musician. Yet many schoolmates and I had continued our music studies, each in his or her own limited way. Surviving the army farm gave us confidence and willpower we might not have acquired otherwise. More importantly, I developed empathy. Before the Cultural Revolution, I had lived a well-to-do life with some privileges reserved for well-known artists and intellectuals. At the farm I learned to appreciate common people as well as my friends. I treasured my friendships with Ai'yi and many other schoolmates. I had survived emotionally only with their support.

CHAPTER 22

Qingping's Resolve

Qingping in 1969 was sent with some of his classmates from the Beijing Second Foreign Language Institute to the East-Is-Red Oil Refinery in Beijing's rural suburbs. They helped install electric wires and oil transmission pipes, but without proper safety measures: The workers were installing electric wires before the oil tanks were completely drained. Fire broke out four times that year and one of the master workers burned to death. At the factory's request, Qingping painted a posthumous portrait of that master worker.

In summer 1970, Qingping and his classmates working at the refinery were ordered to move to their May Seventh Cadre School, a work farm near Minggang in Henan Province. They worked there until 1971, doing heavy physical labor. The peasants in the nearby villages had nothing but sweet potato roots to eat all year round, and only dry weeds for fuel.

Qingping and his classmates were hungry all the time, fed rationed watered-down rice, and cabbage cooked with no oil. Many students contracted hepatitis, a disease common in that area. Students were paid a college-graduate salary of forty-six *yuan* monthly and had a day off every other week. Some students on their days off went to a restaurant in a nearby small town. To their surprise, the bowls and plates were not washed after each use. Seeing the students' worried faces, a waitress said, "I wiped the bowls and dishes with a rag only for you special Beijing students." The farm Party leaders said students who ate nutritious snacks were pursuing a bourgeois lifestyle. One day, feeling that he was about to get sick, Qingping secretly bought two turtles from a peasant, cooked them using the same dry weeds for fuel, and quickly ate them. Qingping believed eating the turtles strengthened him and helped him avoid hepatitis.

While there, Qingping continued his studies of art and the French language under very difficult conditions. He secretly carried a pocket version, in French, of *Apollo*, a book of the history of art throughout the ages, not available in China. It had survived the Red Guards' home raids. Mom had bought that book from one of Father's friends who had brought it back from France. Qingping often studied *Apollo* while hiding himself among the grave mounds in a nearby cemetery during work breaks. In the first few years of the Cultural Revolution when all universities were closed, he studied French on his own. By the early 1970s he was already able to read Balzac's novels while many classmates were still struggling with basic French grammar. He also continued painting in his spare time, dreaming of studying art in France someday, like Father. At the beginning of the Cultural Revolution, at the request of his college he painted large oil portraits of Mao Zedong. After moving to Minggang, he was invited by the local railroad station to paint several large-scale propaganda paintings on outdoor billboards there. The paintings were to glorify the PLA soldiers fighting during the Sino-Soviet border conflict in 1969, near Zhenbao (Damansky) Island in northeastern China. He heard that large numbers of PLA soldiers were to pass through this railroad station soon, so completing those propaganda paintings was an urgent matter. It took him a couple of months to finish. During that period, his schoolmates were engaged in the movement to seize May Sixteenth conspirators. Qingping knew that some innocent schoolmates, then isolated for investigation, were being accused of counterrevolutionary activities. Working on the propaganda paintings, he deliberately left early in the morning and returned after bedtime, so he was able to avoid participating in this finger-pointing.

In late 1971, Qingping and his classmates were allowed to return to their college. Because universities closed since 1966 had produced no graduates, there was a shortage of young diplomats fluent in foreign languages. With Premier Zhou's permission, students who had entered the Beijing Foreign Languages Institute and the Beijing Second Foreign Language Institute in 1965 were told to return to their studies. The graduates could then fill the vacancies at the Ministry of Foreign Affairs.

Qingping and his classmates took a comprehensive French-language exam for graduation in summer 1972. He achieved full scores, the highest in his class. Mom and I were very proud of him, expecting him to get a position at the Ministry of Foreign Affairs.

However, when the job assignments were announced, Qingping was assigned to a tailor's shop in Beijing, to help with foreign customers. Qingping was surprised and Mom was so greatly disappointed that she could not eat or sleep for days. Qingping inquired about the reason for his assignment, and the answer was that our third uncle, Liao Ping, was jailed for counterrevolutionary crimes, i.e., defending Liu Shaoqi, the biggest capitalist roader inside the CCP. A person with close relatives jailed or executed could not pass the political check required to become a diplomat. Even Father's status as an accomplished artist, politically supported at the time by top leaders in China, could not help.

I remember the summer day back in 1967 when a visibly shaken Third Uncle Liao Ping had come to our house in Haibo Hutong. Not the lively, joyful uncle I had last seen a year before, he leaned against a column on our porch, trembling as he sobbed. Before the Cultural Revolution broke out, he had had what seemed to have been a lasting relationship with a young female student at the Beijing Film Academy. College students in the 1960s were not allowed to marry, so they had to wait until she graduated. When the Cultural Revolution broke out, he came under attack and was assigned to do heavy, dirty labor in the factory's foundry shop. After a few months, his girlfriend refused to see him. Third Uncle was heartbroken. Mom tried to console him, offering hospitality and sharing our household essentials. He often took a bath in our house after work.

Third Uncle Liao Ping disappeared in 1968. Later, I heard the following:

Liao Ping had written a long letter, more than ten thousand words, to the Central Committee of the CCP in the winter of 1967. In his letter he defended Peng Zhen, mayor of Beijing and first secretary of the Beijing Municipal Party Committee of the CCP. More importantly, his letter defended Liu Shaoqi, the major target of the Cultural Revolution. Liao Ping quoted many passages from Mao Zedong's works to support his viewpoints. He argued that the charges which the CCP brought against Liu Shaoqi were not well-founded.

The leading group in charge of the Cultural Revolution in Beijing No. 1 Machine Tool Plant could not successfully counter Liao Ping's arguments. But defending Liu Shaoqi was a serious counterrevolutionary crime. Although Liao Ping was not officially convicted, the leading group felt justified in sending him, in 1968, to the Beijing Municipal Public Security Bureau to be locked up. We did not know where he was jailed.

Qingping remained silent about his disappointing job assignment but did not give up. He found out from a Beijing municipal government department covering personnel affairs that Beijing Language Institute badly needed French teachers. Actually the teachers there were anxious to have Qingping, a top student in his class, teach in their school. Over the next month, Qingping, the employment office at the Beijing Second Foreign Language Institute, and the recruiters at Beijing Language Institute had many discussions. Finally, Qingping was offered a French-language teaching job at Beijing Language Institute. However, the political problem tied to Third Uncle Liao Ping remained. Qingping became the only teacher in his department not given any opportunities to travel abroad.

Qingping had dreamt of going to France to study art, like Father, and becoming a painter, fulfilling Father's wish. Although frustrated, he persisted in studying both painting and French on the work farm and later while teaching.

Soon after he started working at Beijing Language Institute, Qingping was sent to another May Seventh Cadre School, but in the rural suburbs of Beijing. He and five other teachers shared one *kang* in an unheated horse stable. One of the teachers found a coal stove without a chimney, the only thing available to heat their room. One night, its fumes might have suffocated them all except that the leaky windows, made from broken paper, provided some fresh air. Fortunately one of the teachers woke up in the middle of the night and aired the room by opening the door.

During his three months at the May Seventh Cadre School, Qingping got up early every morning to sketch the horses. Living in the stable, he made friends with old horses, young stallions, mares, and their foals. He could feel their breathing, read the expressions in their eyes, and sense their moods: happiness, sadness, and anger. The tenderness between the mare and her foal impressed him in particular. His careful observations are apparent in his lively Chinese ink brush paintings of horses.

Qingping, the only painter among Father's four children, was finally able to go to Paris in 1981, after the Cultural Revolution. He had competed in examinations and obtained a UNESCO translator's position. He worked for UNESCO as its highest-level French-Chinese translator from 1981 to 1985. Qingping cut into his sleeping time to study at Paris-Sorbonne University at night, where he earned his Ph.D. in art history. In 1987, two years after returning to China, he transferred from Beijing Language Institute to the Central Academy of Fine Arts to teach Western art history. Father had been the academy's first president. I was happy for Qingping and impressed with his

Chinese ink brush paintings of Notre Dame and other Paris sites, done in his spare time. Father had hoped one of his children would study painting. This part of Father's dream finally came true.

CHAPTER 23
Window to the West

The music research group at the Central Philharmonic Orchestra was initiated by Jiang Qing in 1969 after she was informed that the theme music for a new documentary, *Nanjing Yangtze River Bridge*, had been copied from a Soviet song, "Lenin's Mountains," a song well known in China. This lyrical song expressing love for Moscow was composed in the late 1940s by Yuriy Milyutin with lyrics by Evgeniy Dolmatovskiy. Jiang Qing was very angry about the use of the "Soviet revisionist music." She instructed conductor Li Delun to form a music research group to collect information about Soviet revisionist music and composers for the purpose of criticizing them and their influence in China.

One of the research group's missions in 1972 was to publish internally-circulated articles about contemporary Western and Soviet music. These were to be submitted to Jiang Qing and the cultural leaders supporting her. For this purpose, three musicology teachers from CCOM became researchers. Teacher Huang, who had studied in the Soviet Union, was fluent in Russian. He specialized in foreign music research and teaching Western music history with a focus on Russian composers. The other two musicology teachers had never studied abroad. Their English level was about the same as mine when I first joined the group. As the youngest member of the group, I became one of the English translators. I was the only pianist there who had the skills to play ensemble scores on the piano for our music research.

Wu Zuqiang, the head of our group, did not do actual research work but gave us overall direction and communicated with Li Delun for further direction. Wu was a composer from CCOM who had graduated from the Tchaikovsky Moscow State Conservatory in the 1950s. He had collaborated with another CCOM composition faculty member, Du Mingxin, in writing the music for the ballet *The Red Detachment of Women*, which had debuted in 1964.

Conductor Li Delun was our big boss and one of the Party leaders at the Central Philharmonic Orchestra. Returning from the Tchaikovsky Moscow State Conservatory where he had studied in the 1950s, Li Delun had become conductor of the Central Philharmonic Orchestra, established in 1956. Besides leading the Central Philharmonic on international tours, Li guest-conducted international orchestras and performed with soloists such as David Oistrakh, Isaac Stern, Yehudi Menuhin, Yo-Yo Ma, Fou Ts'ong, Liu Shikun, and Yin Chengzong. In the 1960s, Li worked with the Central Philharmonic Orchestra to develop the symphony *Shajiabang*, a model performing work, under Jiang Qing's guidance.

Through an unusual arrangement made by the Central Philharmonic Orchestra, our office was in the building of *Guangming Daily*, a comprehensive national CCP newspaper, influential in the fields of science, technology, education, and culture. We could use its library and other facilities. In return, our group members, upon request, wrote critiques of music and dance performances. CCOM was only twenty minutes away by bus, allowing us to have frequent discussions with CCOM Western music history faculty, and, in addition, our office was only a few minutes' walk from my home.

The Central Philharmonic Orchestra was the national orchestra and also the best symphony orchestra in China. We went there frequently for meetings and performance activities, including rehearsals of new music such as the *pipa* concerto *Little Sisters of the Grassland* by Wu Zuqiang and two other musicians. The wit and creative passion of these first-rate composers and musicians resonated with me.

Coming to the Central Philharmonic Orchestra was like finally arriving at an oasis after crossing a parched desert. To make my contribution, I worked hard to improve my English. For my first assignment, I was to translate an article on pop music and rock and roll. Published in a U.S. music journal, released to our group for research only, this article was not available to the public. I was unfamiliar with the subjects because China had been cut off from the Western world for twenty years. The colloquial expressions baffled me. I sought help from knowledgeable friends in Xinhua News Agency. Wu Zuqiang showed my final Chinese translation to Li Delun, who had good comprehension of English. Li made a few minor revisions but was satisfied overall.

Even so, the rock-and-roll article still left me puzzled. The music features described in the article did not exist anywhere in the music I was familiar with. I assumed that everyone in the West loved rock and roll and wondered why. There were no examples to listen to.

Next, I translated an article by Leonard Bernstein, a contemporary American composer and conductor. This article dealt with works by himself and other contemporary American composers. Later in 1972, my translation of that article and a couple of other articles on Western music translated by our group were submitted as a special publication to Jiang Qing and cultural leaders. Our group started to translate *Music and Musical Life in Soviet Russia, 1917-1970* by Boris Schwarz, a two hundred thousand-word book written in English. Jiang Qing and her associates who authorized our research projects probably wanted to be able to criticize the music's political content. I felt that my English was far from being adequate to do my part in translating the two hundred thousand-word Soviet Russian history.

Through Wu Zuoren's wife, painter Xiao Shufang, I met Joan, a fifty-eight-year-old daughter of a British mother and a Chinese father. Her husband had worked for the United Nations in Geneva, their family's home for many years. Joan and her family moved to Beijing right before the Cultural Revolution. She was then one of the few people in Beijing who spoke perfect English. All the foreign teachers at universities had left China in 1966. I took a forty-five-minute bike ride to Joan's home in the west part of Beijing once a week for my English lessons, which continued for several years. Joan helped me with speaking, reading comprehension, and writing. But each lesson lasted only a couple of hours, not enough time to practice my oral English. In order to speak like an English person, I tried to train myself to think in English.

I enjoyed visiting Joan's spacious apartment. She described their life in Switzerland and other European countries. They kept some Western customs in their household: In their well-heated home, her daughter wore a woolen skirt. Skirts were seldom seen in Beijing in winter. In the 1970s when milk was rationed, no butter or cheese was available for average residents in Beijing. But I learned from Joan how to make cream cheese, adding its rich taste when I spread it on my *mantou*.

Joan had access to modern English publications and some contemporary Western music not available in China. I borrowed from her the book *Red*

Star over China by Edgar Snow, an American journalist, who had visited Yan'an, a communist-controlled area, in 1936. This latest English edition was not available in China in the 1970s. Although this was my first reading of an original English book, I could not put the book down, finding the biographies of Communist leaders, including Jiang Qing's earlier life, fascinating.

Amazingly, Joan had been able to bring their large phonograph record collection when her family moved to Beijing. I remember listening to Bob Dylan's anti-war songs, and liked the musical *West Side Story* so much that she lent me the record for a couple of weeks. The cold war had left us with no concept of American music or culture. Joan's records helped me understand the articles about contemporary Western music I was translating. Hearing her family's experiences enlightened me on what freedom meant in Western countries, where people had access to all kinds of music, literature, and political information. How wonderful if I could experience living in a Western country and enjoy its freedom! But it was an impossible dream.

I used my spare time to continue my music studies. Li Delun had arranged for me to take music theory and composition lessons from Yanqiao, a talented composer with the Central Philharmonic Orchestra. Form and composition analysis, harmony, and orchestration were required courses for music composition majors at CCOM. I appreciated Yanqiao's emphasis on the practical applications of these courses. In harmony studies, instead of working out harmony exercise solutions on paper only, he gave me many strenuous keyboard harmony exercises from a Russian harmony book. In the evening, when I practiced on the piano the complicated harmony sequences at a fast tempo, my brain had to move so quickly that I got dizzy. Yanqiao's teaching method, although unconventional for China, gave me very useful keyboard harmony skills rarely taught in the music schools in the 1960s. These skills allowed me to sight read a full ensemble score and play it swiftly on the piano, bringing out essential features. I was also able to change keys rapidly when improvising piano accompaniment.

For orchestration, Yanqiao required me to condense a full orchestral score to a four-part score. This helped me understand how composers structured and interconnected different instruments in orchestral music. I also watched the Central Philharmonic Orchestra's rehearsals, trying to discern what the composer had envisioned while writing the music for each instrument.

These studies gave me more in-depth understanding and more enjoyment of orchestral music. It was like uncovering the elaborate interior roof structure of the imperial-style Temple of Heaven in Beijing. Yanqiao assigned me to interview the players of different instruments. He said, "You will gain first-hand information. You will probably remember that better than reading from a textbook." During the rehearsal break, I spoke with a few wind instrument players and the harpist. They gladly explained the sound range of their instruments through the scales and demonstrated the tone qualities in different regions. These conversations left a deep impression on me.

After work, I practiced piano for two hours in the evening, playing Chopin's etudes and many other classical piano pieces I loved. Even though I could not become a full-time concert pianist, piano skills were still very important for my work. I was required on short notice to play ensemble scores from foreign musicians' proposed repertoire so my group could evaluate them.

My first two years at the Central Philharmonic Orchestra were my happiest since the Cultural Revolution had broken out. I was finally beginning to live my father's dream that I become a well-educated person, and perhaps an accomplished musician. Trying to make up for my lost time on the farm, I worked extremely hard. My boss and the teachers in my group supported my desire to learn, allowing me to take my English lessons and music theory and composition lessons during work hours as long as I finished my assignments on time. My knowledge of music and English was truly enriched. I felt proud to contribute to influential cultural leaders my growing understanding of Western music, not knowing the political ramifications.

• • •

Western classical music, banned since 1966, returned to the stage on several special occasions in 1973 because of diplomatic initiatives between China and Western countries. I had been on the army farm when U.S. president Richard Nixon had visited China in 1972. His meeting with Chairman Mao and Premier Zhou led to normalized relations between the two countries, ending twenty-two years of diplomatic isolation and hostile opposition. The Central Philharmonic Orchestra performed Beethoven's *Symphony No. 6,"Pastoral"* in a closed-door session for National Security Advisor Henry Kissinger during his visit to Beijing in 1973. The musicians were enthusiastic about performing a major Western symphony again.

President Nixon's visit resulted in cultural exchanges and the establishment of Liaison Offices in Beijing and Washington, D.C. In spring 1972, Pete Seeger, a well-known American folk singer, visited Beijing with his wife and teenage daughter. The Central Philharmonic Orchestra hosted them, and our research group members held discussions with Pete Seeger about American folk music and his own songs. Unfortunately, at the time my English was not good enough to follow all the conversation. I attended the banquet in the Beijing Hotel given by the Central Philharmonic Orchestra in his honor. Pete Seeger performed in the large banquet hall after the meal. This was the first time I had ever attended an American singer's performance. I found his singing very engaging. He sang his own folk songs in an informal style while playing the banjo, sometimes pausing between songs to explain the lyrics and the capabilities of the banjo. All the Central Philharmonic Orchestra musicians, including myself, applauded him warmly.

As a friendly gesture, our *pipa* soloist, Liu Dehai, performed "Liuyang River," a song from Hunan Province in southern China. I knew that Liu was not a trained singer and had never performed singing before. But that night, he mimicked Seeger's style, singing "Liuyang River" like a folk singer accompanied by his own plucking instrument, *pipa*. Pete Seeger was thrilled, praising Liu's performance as the best he had seen in China. I was very moved by this friendly exchange. I felt that as musicians, we could communicate through the common language of music, transcending cultural, language, and political barriers.

In March 1973, the London Philharmonic Orchestra became the first Western orchestra visiting China since 1949. My CCOM schoolmates and teachers back from the farm, and the classical-music lovers in the audience, cheered the British musicians. It was the first time since the middle of the 1960s that we had heard Beethoven, Brahms, Dvořák, Haydn, and English composer Edward Elgar's orchestral music performed in Beijing. The Vienna Philharmonic Orchestra visited China the same year, playing in the large Capital Stadium. Their light music including Strauss waltzes sent thousands of Beijing music lovers into a frenzy.

The highlight of 1973 was the Philadelphia Orchestra's visit to China. Under the direction of maestro Eugene Ormandy, it became the first American orchestra to travel to the People's Republic of China. During their two-week visit to Beijing and Shanghai they gave six concerts. Three of the programs included a performance of the *Yellow River Piano Concerto*, played by Yin Chengzong, the Central Philharmonic Orchestra pianist. This was a new piano concerto written by a group of composers from the Central Philharmonic Orchestra and approved by Jiang Qing. Other pieces performed ranged from Mozart to Respighi's *The Pines of Rome* and Beethoven's *Symphony No. 6, "Pastoral."*

I went to several Philadelphia Orchestra rehearsals, for the first time watching a world-class orchestra at close range. I was impressed with maestro Eugene Ormandy and liked his interpretation of *The Pines of Rome*. He was able to bring out this illustrative piece's required full range of colors.

At the Philadelphia Orchestra's first performance in September 1973, Beijing National Palace Theater near downtown was packed. Tickets had been distributed by the cultural authorities throughout the music circles in Beijing. Members of the Central Philharmonic Orchestra were in the audience. Selected workers, peasants, and soldiers also received tickets. Those without tickets crowded the entranceway. Most had not seen American musicians perform, and I believed everyone in the audience was curious. Maestro Eugene Ormandy said that he had never encountered such an attentive audience. They warmly applauded the Beethoven symphony and the *Yellow River Piano Concerto* at that Philadelphia Orchestra performance.

The highlight was the opportunity for informal conversation between the musicians. The Philadelphia Orchestra was invited to hear the Central Philharmonic Orchestra in our rehearsal hall at Hepingli. Our Central Philharmonic Chorus sang "America the Beautiful" in English. They had rehearsed for days. Their enthusiastic performance moved some of the Americans to tears.

After conductor Li Delun rehearsed the first movement of Beethoven's *Symphony No. 5*, he asked Ormandy to conduct. Ormandy took the baton, smiled at the Chinese players, and worked through the symphony's second movement with them. Ormandy connected well with our orchestra musicians. After the rehearsal, players of both orchestras mingled and talked.

My conversation with a Philadelphia Orchestra violinist was my first opportunity to speak with a musician from the United States. Containing my nervousness, I said casually, "How do you like your visit to China?"

He smiled. "I like it very much so far. I am looking forward to visiting the Great Wall." At that get-together, some of my colleagues from the orchestra and chorus spoke English directly with their counterparts from the Philadelphia Orchestra. I could hear the chatting blended with laughter, common among musicians during a normal rehearsal break. Musicians from both orchestras discussed their instruments and even hugged. Philadelphia Orchestra members gave our orchestra some instruments, recordings, and original scores including American composers' works, not available in China. Our musicians gave them traditional Chinese instruments.

That event opened the door to long-lasting exchanges. Players from the Philadelphia Orchestra sent letters, magazines, and scores to Chinese colleagues for years after the tour. Months after the concert, we were still talking about the Philadelphia Orchestra's visit, and their musicians' capability and virtuosity. My violinist friends from our orchestra joyfully tried the original scores given by the Philadelphia Orchestra musicians. This eye-opening exchange experience aroused my curiosity about the music world in America. I even imagined that future music students might study in each other's countries and further understand each other's cultures. I hoped that this dream could come true for me.

Jiang Qing was against inviting President Nixon to visit China, but had been overruled. Having no power over diplomacy, she made her first diplomatic appearance in February 1972 at the performance of *The Red Detachment of Women*, a model ballet created under her guidance. President and Mrs. Nixon attended the show. While there, Jiang Qing asked President Nixon sharply pointed questions. Did the President share her enthusiasm for John Steinbeck? And, "Why," she challenged him, "did you not come to China before now?"

During the Philadelphia Orchestra's visit, Jiang Qing made herself visible at all major events, and was photographed among American musicians. But on important occasions she and her supporters had challenged the proposed Western music repertoire. Originally Premier Zhou had suggested performing a Beethoven symphony for Henry Kissinger. Li Delun recommended that the Central Philharmonic Orchestra perform Beethoven's *Symphony No. 5*. However, Yu Huiyong, a member of the Cultural Group under the State Council, told Jiang Qing that Beethoven's *Symphony No. 5* promoted fatalism. As a result, Jiang Qing forced the Central Philharmonic Orchestra to change its repertoire to Beethoven's *Symphony No. 6, "Pastoral."*

To prepare for the Philadelphia Orchestra's performance in China, our music research group wrote descriptions of all of the pieces on their three proposed concert programs. These descriptions were submitted to the top leaders via Li Delun. The programs had been negotiated by both sides and approved by the top leaders in China. However, two days before their arrival, Jiang Qing requested that the Philadelphia Orchestra change the planned program. She wanted to force the Philadelphia Orchestra to perform a series of pieces proposed by her, including *El Salon Mexico, Carmen Suite, Invitation to the Dance* by Weber, *Scheherazade, In the Steppes of Central Asia* by Borodin, and Beethoven's *Symphony No. 6, "Pastoral."* Concerning Jiang's request, Premier Zhou responded, "Do not impose on others. The program cannot be changed." However, to save face for Jiang Qing, Premier Zhou asked the liaison people to hint to the Americans about adding Beethoven's *Symphony No. 6, "Pastoral"* to the program. The Americans agreed.

While attending one of the Philadelphia Orchestra's concerts in Beijing, Jiang Qing complained about *The Pines of Rome*. According to Li Delun, she said in a puzzled voice while listening to the last movement, "How those pines can make such a loud sound!"[49] Actually she did not understand the music, and neither did she read our group's description of this work, which she was holding in her hand during the concert. The last movement portrays an ancient Roman army approaching from far away. Marching down one of the most famous avenues in Rome, these soldiers form a magnificent procession energized by brass, bass drums, and timpani. Jiang Qing did not understand any of that. I suspected that Jiang Qing's criticism of the Western classical music performers' repertoire was targeting Premier Zhou Enlai. This foreshadowed Jiang Qing's launch of an even larger campaign against Western classical music months later. This time the campaign was directed towards diplomatic policies implemented by Premier Zhou. Jiang Qing had hoped to extend her influence into foreign policy making.

CHAPTER 24
Reopening the Museum

In mid-1973, seeing the relatively favorable political situation following Lin Biao's disappearance, Mom wrote a letter to Chairman Mao. She told me the content of her letter: "During the Cultural Revolution, Xu Beihong was branded a reactionary authority. I was beaten up to the point of unconsciousness a couple of times and afterward resuscitated. The Xu Beihong Memorial Museum was demolished and his tombstone smashed. Now I ask that the Xu Beihong Memorial Museum be reinstated."

A little more than a month after Mom sent the letter, Chairman Mao approved the reinstatement of the Xu Beihong Memorial Museum. The day after Mao's approval, Premier Zhou sent Wu Qingtong to see Mom with Premier Zhou's letter to her:

> Comrade Liao Jingwen:
>
> Your letter to Chairman Mao was received. The chairman on July 15 responded with a written instruction, asking me to see about reinstating [the Xu Beihong Memorial Museum] after verification. I first inform you and will ask Comrade Wu Qingtong from the State Council Office to discuss this matter with you.
>
> Zhou Enlai
> July 16, 1973

Wu Qingtong was director of the State Council Office. I remember him coming to our Hufang Road apartment in summer 1973. Sitting on our couch, he spoke to Mom in a friendly, modest manner, saying, "If you have any specific requests, please let me know." After seeing Premier Zhou's letter, Mom said,

"The total area of the museum should be equivalent to that in the former one. It cannot be too small. The location should not be in a remote place."

As I watched Wu Qingtong talking with Mom, once again Premier Zhou's concern touched my heart. During the chaotic Cultural Revolution, Premier Zhou had consistently given support to Father, his family, and his artworks. At that time I was very excited about the possibility of reopening the Xu Beihong Memorial Museum, and I knew how important this was to Mom.

Working through the bureaucratic process to complete the new Xu Beihong Memorial Museum building took ten years. It was not opened until 1983. Back around 1975, when Premier Zhou was hospitalized for his terminal illness, Mom heard about his asking whether the Xu Beihong Memorial Museum had been reinstated.[50] Premier Zhou indicated that he had not been aware of the plan to demolish the Xu Beihong Memorial Museum, saying that the subway construction path could have been altered.[51] Mom realized that her letter to Premier Zhou in 1965 concerning preserving the Xu Beihong Memorial Museum had never been forwarded to him. She had misjudged and trusted an acquaintance in the government to deliver the letter to Premier Zhou.

In 1973, the Beijing Municipal Bureau of Culture set up a preparatory group headed by my mother to reopen the Xu Beihong Memorial Museum. But for many years, this group did not even have an office. Mom worked out of her home, talking to her staff in our living room. But she spent most of her time wading through various government bureaucracies.

After selecting a location in Xinjiekou in Beijing's West City District, her next move was to persuade the head of the Beijing Municipal Housing Bureau to provide apartments for the more than thirty families living in the museum's chosen location. Because private property ownership had been eliminated, everyone lived in government-owned and subsidized houses or apartments allocated by government housing authorities. The shortage of available housing had Beijing residents living in very crowded situations. Relocation caused by government construction projects presented an opportunity for residents to demand better housing. The families living in the museum's chosen site refused to move unless they were given desirable apartments.

For several years, Mom became a familiar figure at the entrance of the Beijing Municipal Housing Bureau. Every day she waited there early in the morning to catch and talk to the director of the bureau. It took her more than five years and much effort to relocate all the families.

In the late 1970s she also had to initiate the new museum construction project through the National Capital Construction Commission, the central government construction authority. The head of the Commission was a ministerial official, even harder to access than the head of the Beijing Municipal Housing Bureau. Mom persisted in building the *guanxi* necessary to get the new museum construction project into the government plan.

The final step was acquiring building materials, in short supply in the late 1970s. The new museum construction project was then one of a dozen approved projects in Beijing without building materials. Mom did not know how long she would have to wait.

The Xu Beihong Memorial Museum's construction project was assigned to the Beijing Housing Construction and Maintenance Company in the late 1970s. Manager Feng, in his mid-forties, was in charge of the project. He turned out to be sympathetic and honorable. Mom took Manager Feng, plus the department head, and the section chief from the Beijing Housing Construction and Maintenance Company to the storage room in the huge Forbidden City complex, under guard during the Cultural Revolution. Artworks by Xu Beihong and those in his personal collection had been stored there since the summer of 1966. This was how Xu Beihong's artworks and those in his personal collection had escaped the Red Guard raids. The storage room was in a leaky, drafty old building. Seeing the mildewed and deteriorating paintings, Manager Feng said, "We cannot wait anymore. Our company will provide our own building materials in advance to get the construction started. After the Beijing municipal government obtains the building materials, they can return them to our company." A year later, the Beijing municipal government approved the building materials and Mom authorized the materials to be given to the Beijing Housing Construction and Maintenance Company as repayment. Amazingly, Feng's commitment was not contingent on *guanxi*. With his timely help, the Xu Beihong Memorial Museum's construction was able to start a year earlier.

Some special materials were not available in Beijing. For example, steel window frames had to be ordered from Shanghai. Obtaining them also required Mom's building *guanxi* with the National Capital Construction Commission.

I admired Mom's perseverance. She had lived for her love and commitment to Beihong all those years, determined to reopen the Xu Beihong Memorial Museum for him, whatever it might take. The Xu family appreciated the support from many of our friends, art lovers, and sympathetic cadres like Manager Feng who helped make my parents' dream come true.

The new and larger Xu Beihong Memorial Museum opened its doors to visitors in 1983 on one of the busy streets in Xinjiekou. Mom was reinstated as director of the museum. The more than 1200 artworks by Xu Beihong and those in his personal collection were being properly displayed in the new exhibition space on a rotating basis. In the new political climate and with an expanded professional staff, the museum would soon hold exhibitions of Xu Beihong's works across China and abroad.[52] Mom, Qingping, and I felt as if Father were with us again. Mom once told me, "Having this museum here is like your father being alive."

• • •

Mom's marriage with Uncle Huang ended in 1973. They had distanced themselves from each other since the beginning of the Cultural Revolution, and Mom had not shown any affection for Uncle Huang for several years. But the trigger of the divorce was the political problem of my jailed third uncle, Liao Ping. Seeing how Third Uncle's problem prevented Qingping from getting a diplomatic job, Uncle Huang was afraid for his own political future. In 1972 when I returned from the farm, Uncle Huang had already moved out of our apartment. Later that year he filed for divorce, which was finalized in 1973, and Mom took full financial responsibility for raising Maomao. Mom and Maomao shared a caring relationship until the end of her life.

Mom seemed to feel better after Uncle Huang moved out of her life. She devoted herself to reopening the Xu Beihong Memorial Museum and writing a biography of Xu Beihong. I told her that Qingping and I would take care of her in her old age.

In 1971, our family had moved from the quadrangle house in Haibo Hutong because underground tunnels destroyed our sewage system, forcing Mom and Maomao to share the public latrines on the street. These tunnels had been dug all over Beijing to prepare for a possible war with the Soviets. Mom managed to exchange our rooms for a three-bedroom apartment on Hufang Road. Although in this move we lost our yard and had less room, we had a gas stove and radiator heat. Our gas was supplied via pipes available only in limited areas of Beijing.

In 1973 Qingping married and moved to an assigned room in the employee housing of his wife's Beijing work unit. Mom, Maomao, then age ten, and I remained in our Hufang Road apartment. Mom did most of the cooking while I cleaned the rooms and washed Maomao's clothes by hand; washing machines were not available then in Chinese households. I gave Maomao piano lessons and later supervised his violin practice for four years. I hoped that Maomao would learn some music skills so that he could find a job in Beijing when he grew up.

I stayed with Mom from the time I was twenty-four until I was twenty-nine. We often took walks together in the evenings around Taoranting (Happy Pavilion) Park in our neighborhood. I treasured the time we shared. She told me about the difficulties of overseeing the Xu Beihong Memorial Museum construction and how she missed my father. I became a sympathetic listener.

CHAPTER 25

Where Is Third Uncle?

The desire to find her brother and my third uncle, Liao Ping, must have weighed heavily on Mom's mind. But trying to track down a jailed political prisoner would have been very risky for our family. We had lost touch with him in 1968 and had no idea where he was jailed or even whether he was still alive.

In 1972, Mom thought that the political situation had eased enough for her to search for Liao Ping. She decided that it would be less risky for my "little uncle," Xuezheng, to start the search. A young man, he would be less likely to attract political attention. Xuezheng had delivered my accordion to the army farm two years before. After graduating from Tianjin University in radio engineering, he was assigned a factory job in Fushun, in northeastern China. During his visit to Beijing on business in 1972, Mom asked him to inquire about Liao Ping's whereabouts.

Xuezheng first tried to meet with Zhu, director of the revolutionary committee at Beijing No. 1 Machine Tool Plant. But Zhu refused to see him. Xuezheng then talked with Li, director of the political department at the factory, expressing his desire to see Liao Ping in order to persuade him to recognize his mistakes.

Li wrote an official letter addressed to the Beijing Municipal Public Security Bureau, saying that Liao Ping's younger brother, Liao Xuezheng, wanted to see him. With this official letter, Xuezheng went to the reception center of the Beijing Municipal Public Security Bureau. After many inquiries, he was referred to the pretrial department, because Liao Ping had been held for four years without trial or conviction. Finally a person in plainclothes, named Yue, came out to talk to Xuezheng. Yue, a sympathetic person, said Liao Ping was jailed in Houma Special District in Shanxi Province where he could not receive any visitors without an appropriate leader's approval. Liao Ping's case had dragged on for a long time. Yue considered his problem to be simply incorrect thoughts. Yue recognized that Liao Ping had done much good work for the Party. But Liao Ping refused to change his viewpoint regarding Liu Shaoqi. Yue's recommendation was, "Liao Ping's sister is Xu Beihong's widow. Why doesn't she use that to her advantage to write a letter to higher authorities?"

After much discussion with us, Mom wrote a letter to Wu De, Party secretary of the Beijing Municipal Party Committee of the CCP. It said, "I have not heard from my younger brother, Liao Ping, for more than four years. I request permission to see him. If his problem is serious, I will draw a line between him and myself. If his mistakes were incorrect thoughts, I will try to persuade him to recognize his mistakes."

Through many connections, Mom's letter finally reached Wu De. In 1973, Wu gave his approval for an intermediate-people's-court judge to accompany a family member to see Liao Ping. The courts appointed Judge Liu to go with Mom to the city of Jishan in Shanxi Province where Liao Ping was jailed. Judge Liu would try Liao Ping's case there. Like many political prisoners, Liao Ping had no lawyer. Mom would be allowed to attend the trial as a family member but was told not to speak.

Before Mom wrote the letter to Wu De, the court had asked Wu for instruction concerning Liao Ping's case. Wu's answer was to deal severely with the case. Perhaps he was trying to demonstrate a strong leftist hand so as not to be accused of association with a counterrevolutionary. Some judges considered Liao Ping a current counterrevolutionary. Others believed that he had had incorrect thoughts and could be persuaded to recognize his mistakes. Still other judges argued that according to the Party constitution, Party members had the right to present their views to Party organizations at higher levels, even up to the Central Committee. The judges had not been able to agree. That was why Liao Ping had not been tried.

Right before Judge Liu and Mom went to Shanxi for Liao Ping's trial, Mom was told that if Liao Ping recognized his mistakes, his case could be dealt with as thought problems. If he insisted on his viewpoint concerning Liu Shaoqi, he would be convicted of counterrevolutionary crime.

I helped Mom prepare a big bag of food to take to Third Uncle. I boiled dozens of cured goose eggs and bought about fifty meat dumplings and a variety of breads wrapped in waxed paper. Neither Mom nor I knew what to expect, and I worried whether Mom could stand the psychological stress of seeing Third Uncle.

Yue told Mom that Liao Ping had been wearing the same clothes since 1968. In winter, he had neither padded jacket nor socks. As a result, he had developed chronic bronchitis. He cut the cuffs off his cotton sweater to wrap around his feet. His cotton shoes were so worn through that they looked like straw sandals. Mom was allowed to send clothes to him through the court system before their meeting.

During the long train ride from Beijing to Jishan in Shanxi Province, my mother and Judge Liu shared much conversation. She told him stories from ancient Chinese history in which a lady suffered a great deal when she was wrongly convicted. Judge Liu gradually began to show some sympathy toward Liao Ping.

Mom finally met Liao Ping in prison, in the prison office with its dirt floor. Thin with a shaven head and yellowed face, a sign of malnutrition, he and the other prisoners were fed two meals of watery grain porridge per day. Liao Ping had picked up turnip peelings left in the prison yard to stuff his empty stomach. I heard that he and other prisoners had been transported from Beijing in sealed train cars in 1969, and that Liao Ping had once been handcuffed behind his back, day and night, for two months, even though he had not been tried and convicted. When encountering a prison official, he had to bow.

Mom gave him a loaf of sweet bread she had brought from Beijing. He devoured it and even ate the crumbs which had dropped to the floor. Then in the presence of Judge Liu and the chief prison guard, Mom handed Liao Ping a basket and a travel bag of food. When she saw him the next day and asked him about the food, he said, "All gone. I shared with other inmates. But I ate a little more than they did. They never received visitors."

Judge Liu held a trial. Court stenographer Zhou was the only court staff present besides Liu. Mom was allowed to observe. First, Judge Liu asked Liao Ping to read an official newspaper article denouncing Liu Shaoqi as a scab and traitor.

Liao Ping responded in a monotone, "All this evidence was fabricated by the Kuomintang."

Mom interrupted, saying, "Please do not talk like that!" But Judge Liu told her not to interrupt.

Later during her visit, Mom tried to persuade Liao Ping to recognize his mistake.

"Third Brother, if you write a criticism of your mistakes, you could go back to Beijing."

He replied without looking at her, "I have heard of this before. Why don't you go back home and mind your own business?"

Mom wept and pleaded. "I came such a long way to see you. Why don't you think about what I said? You really disappointed me."

Mom met with her brother three times during her visit and each time she cried in his presence. But he remained unresponsive. In fact, he looked emotionally blank all the time. Mom felt so hopeless about helping him that she could not eat or sleep for three days. Even sleeping pills did not help. One night she passed out in the restroom. She felt sure that Liao Ping would be convicted.

However, after analyzing his abnormal behavior, Mom suspected that he was mentally imbalanced. Coincidentally, a health conference was being held in Jishan, and a newspaper reporter from *Shanxi Daily* shared the same hostel with Mom. The reporter mentioned that she had met a psychiatrist at the conference. With the reporter's referral and Judge Liu's permission, Mom took Liao Ping to see the psychiatrist. He said he suspected that Liao Ping was mentally ill. Perhaps not wanting the responsibility of giving a final diagnosis for a political prisoner, the psychiatrist recommended that Liao Ping be sent to a higher mental institution for further diagnosis.

Surprisingly, Judge Liu acted speedily to bring Liao Ping to a Beijing mental hospital. He had developed enough sympathy for Liao Ping to want to help him. The Beijing mental hospital's psychiatrist confirmed that Liao Ping was mentally ill.

A few months later, in January 1974, Liao Ping was released from prison based on the diagnosis of his mental illness. Mom decided to have him live with us. When I finally met him one cold winter day in our apartment, my heart ached for him. The handsome, joyful Third Uncle I remembered from my childhood was gone. Now he looked old and his face dull. He signed a paper handed to him by a policeman for his release. Wearing a new blue padded jacket and pants Mom had made for him, he sat down to his first dinner with us and ate two big bowls of rice.

Liao Ping had been a healthy and lively person. But when the Cultural Revolution broke out, as acting Party secretary of Beijing No. 1 Machine Tool

Plant he was attacked severely. His girlfriend, a Beijing Film Academy student, then broke up with him, traumatizing him further. In 1974 when he first lived with our family after his release, he remained quiet and kept to himself. But after undertaking medical treatment for a couple of months, his head started to clear and he regained much of his original personality.

When he felt better, Liao Ping started doing four hours a day of manual labor at Beijing No. 1 Machine Tool Plant. Later he resumed full-time work there and was able to perform a self-criticism publicly in his factory. I do not think that his belief concerning Liu Shaoqi ever wavered. However, he realized that he had to bend with the prevailing wind. After fulfilling the requirement of admitting his "mistakes," he was allowed to renew his CCP membership and became assistant director of Beijing Second Automobile Factory. Later he was appointed director of Beijing Gear Wheel Factory. Beijing No. 1 Machine Tool Plant compensated him with back pay for the time he was incarcerated. He wanted to give all that money to the Party as membership dues. But Mom persuaded him to keep part of the amount for his future family, should he marry.

I felt sad; Third Uncle Liao Ping had lost six years in prison and might have died there. But now I felt very relieved for both Mom and Third Uncle, who had a second chance at life. Judge Liu, the psychiatrists, and other people in the judicial system were able to act out of sympathy, which was rare during the Cultural Revolution. In 1980, Third Uncle married and formed his own family. Later in the 1980s, he was promoted to vice director of the Beijing Municipal Commission of Economics with responsibility for all the factories in Beijing.

After the Cultural Revolution ended in 1976, Liu Shaoqi's reputation was restored posthumously. Another Communist Party leader, whom Liao Ping had defended, was also rehabilitated: Peng Zhen, former mayor of Beijing and former first secretary of the Beijing Municipal Party Committee of the CCP. In the late 1970s, *Beijing Daily*, a CCP newspaper, highly praised Liao Ping for upholding the truth even when threatened by force and persecuted in jail. He was described as a model Communist Party member made of special materials.

Liao Ping seldom talked about his experience in prison. I suspect that his experience as a political prisoner must have left deep scars in his heart that even the lapse of time could not heal.

CHAPTER 26

The "Absolute Music" Controversy

One of our music research group's projects in 1973 led to a significant political event that shook China's arts fields. The event originated with a proposed visit by a Turkish violinist and a pianist. Teacher Huang of our music research group wrote the controversial paragraph describing their proposed repertoire.

The scores for their repertoire were forwarded to our music research group via the Chinese People's Association for Friendship with Foreign Countries (the Association). To evaluate the repertoire, in early October 1973 our music research group met in a CCOM studio in Building No. 2. Li Delun came to that meeting. Because no recordings were available, I demonstrated on the piano some of their proposed repertoire, combining both the violin and piano scores while sight reading. After some discussion with our group, Li Delun approved the repertoire offered by the Turkish musicians.

Then the Association called our group on October 7, 1973, requesting written descriptions of the Turkish musicians' proposed repertoire. Teacher Huang wrote the following descriptive paragraph:

> The music works played by the two performers together belong to classical music repertoire frequently performed at concerts for solo instrumental music in Europe. Most of these works do not contain profound social content, nor do they have specific plots or titles but merely express certain emotional changes and contrasts of the composers. Generally speaking, the music is relatively robust and cheerful.[53]

I remember reading the descriptive paragraph Teacher Huang had written before its submission. I felt the same way about the music. However, this very descriptive paragraph was later criticized by Jiang Qing and her supporters.

Premier Zhou, Hua Guofeng, and other Politburo members in Beijing all read the Association's report without expressing any objection. Jiang Qing, Yao Wenyuan, and Zhang Chunqiao circled their names to confirm that they had read the report. However, on the pages of that report, they all wrote notes concerning the descriptive paragraph Teacher Huang had written. They selected phrases out of context to criticize Huang's supposed view that all absolute music merely expresses certain emotional changes and contrasts without any social content.

Examples of absolute music include sonatas and symphonies named only with numerals, such as Mozart's *Piano Sonata No. 10 in C Major, K. 330* and Beethoven's *Symphony No. 7 in A Major, Op. 92*. The absence of any descriptive title gives listeners flexibility to imagine what the music is about.

To fit his political agenda, Yao Wenyuan altered certain phrases Teacher Huang had written. In his note, Yao left out the word "profound" from the original phrase "profound social content." Jiang Qing added a note: "I agree with Comrade Wenyuan's opinion. Schumann's and particularly Brahms' music seem puzzling and sound hysterical. We cannot talk about anything having no profound social content while ignoring class standpoint."[54]

In another note, Jiang Qing wrote: "P.S. As for the music with titles, they can play wildly, deviating from the descriptive title as in *The Pines of Rome* performed by the Philadelphia Orchestra. Comrade Li Delun should provide the Central Committee with accurate information for reference to avoid our being fooled."[55]

Jiang Qing, in a note, also told Chinese musicians what type of Chinese music should be performed for foreign visitors: "Perform Chinese music, preferably revolutionary music. If classical or folk music is to be introduced, the repertoire should be submitted for approval. Do not introduce *The Moon Reflected on the Second Spring* anymore."[56]

Jiang Qing's definition of revolutionary music included model works such as modern Peking operas, ballets, and the symphony *Shajiabang* created under her guidance. These model works were the only ones permitted on Chinese stages during the Cultural Revolution. By 1973, music lovers and musicians including myself had grown tired of her model works.

Because of the comments made by Jiang, Yao, and Zhang, the Association made an additional report, submitted through the proper channel to the Central Committee of the CCP. In response, Premier Zhou instructed that discussions be undertaken with the Turkish musicians to see if they wanted to visit in November 1973 because the prolonged approval process had delayed the concert, scheduled for the fiftieth Turkish National Day. Premier Zhou's handling of the Turkish musicians' visit showed his efforts to demonstrate China's goodwill towards the Turkish people. At the same time, he made sure that Jiang Qing and the other important leaders reviewed all the documents concerning this diplomatic activity, which could be politically sensitive.

The Association discussed the issue with the Turkish musicians. They still wanted to come and perform. They also confirmed the dates of their visit. The Association then submitted the report for the third time through the proper channel to the Central Committee. This time Premier Zhou's written instruction stated that the brief descriptions of the repertoire had been sent to Zhang Chunqiao, Jiang Qing, and Yao Wenyuan for review, and directed that his tentatively approved report be sent for verification to six top leaders, including Zhang, Jiang, and Yao.

The leaders on the circulation list, including Jiang Qing, all confirmed that they had reviewed the document. However, Jiang Qing wrote the following additional note: "I suggest that we receive fewer or no arts groups from capitalist countries. The consequences could be severe! This is for your reference whether or not my above opinion is appropriate."[57]

Premier Zhou's written response to Jiang Qing's note was as follows:

> In the future, we should try to receive fewer or selected [groups].
> Not receiving any [groups] is nearly impossible. But I can investigate beforehand to avoid inviting arts groups which we cannot receive or have no crucial information about. The Association should pay special attention to this issue.
> Please ask Comrade Jiang Qing to read it again.
>
> Zhou Enlai
> November 19, 1973[58]

I could see that Premier Zhou disagreed with Jiang Qing, who wanted to close the door to arts groups from capitalist countries.

Immediately after he received them, our boss, Li Delun, relayed to us verbally these notes, comments, and instructions from top leaders. The Association filed all the original notes, comments, and instructions. I was worried about the political implications of the argument on absolute music. I thought that our group definitely could provide better information about the meaning of the music proposed by future foreign musicians. But I sensed that Jiang Qing's comments might lead to trouble for future public performances of the Western classical music I loved so much.

The two Turkish musicians came to China on a later date but kept the same repertoire. Unfortunately, their performance was not publicized through the media, which was completely controlled by Jiang Qing and her supporters. I was glad that their planned performance came through, yet the events that followed confirmed my worries. After the Turkish musicians' performance, Jiang Qing and her supporters launched a campaign called "discussion about absolute music," attacking Western classical music recently performed in China and the people who had approved the performances. The real target of the campaign was Premier Zhou, who had approved the foreign musicians' visits.

Jiang Qing, Yao Wenyuan, and Zhang Chunqiao launched organized propaganda attacks. The Cultural Group directed the campaign, relaying Jiang's, Zhang's, and Yao's instructions to organizations in Beijing and Shanghai to plan on "combating the resurgence of the black line." They released a report calling the issue "the new signal of the class struggle" and "class enemies attempting to reverse the verdicts of the Cultural Revolution."

The Cultural Group held a mass rally on December 7, 1973. Representatives from Beijing's arts circle were required to attend this criticism event in Beijing National Palace Theater. Yu Huiyong spoke at the rally, attacking the viewpoint expressed in Teacher Huang's descriptive paragraph: ". . .We must expose the essence and purpose of this viewpoint. . .The purpose [of the person holding this viewpoint] is not to claim that music has no social content. He wants to import lots of this material without criticizing it so that he can enjoy it freely in his own world."[59]

At a conference held in Tianjin in December 1973, the Cultural Group gave instructions to attendees from all the provinces and major cities in China as to how to carry out the campaign. Jiang Qing and Yao Wenyuan wrote comments on a report by the Cultural Group concerning this conference. Yao Wenyuan wrote on January 24, 1974:

> I agree with Comrade Jiang Qing's opinion. This is an issue concerning a struggle between the proletariat and the bourgeoisie and between Marxism and revisionism in music fields. The issue exists in the creation and performance of absolute music and music with titles. Some works by Debussy have titles. The problem lies in their position, viewpoint, and method.[60]

Here Jiang and Yao were trying to label all Western music works as having political implications. They fabricated accusations against not only absolute music but all Western music. This sounded just like the accusation against bourgeois classical music at the beginning of the Cultural Revolution when all Western classical music was banned.

Meanwhile, the more intense "Criticize Lin Biao, Criticize Confucius" campaign mobilized the entire country and the "discussion about absolute music" had been clearly coordinated with it. The real target of this campaign was Premier Zhou Enlai. I believe that the main objective of Jiang Qing and her supporters was to gain power at the top, particularly in Premier Zhou's sphere of influence.

In 1974, the Central Philharmonic Orchestra held its own mass-criticism meetings. The speakers at the meetings exaggerated the political implications of the "discussion about absolute music" in order to fabricate more accusations.

One excerpt from the speeches says, "Both Lin Biao and Confucius utilized literature and art to restore an old order. Some people said that bourgeois classical music has no social content. This agrees with the imperialist...viewpoint. Written in the report, it is a poisonous arrow...targeting the Central Committee of the Party and striving for landowners and bourgeoisie to restore their dictatorship."[61]

Between December 1973 and April 1974, newspapers and magazines all over China published more than 120 articles, including one in *People's Daily*. Its punitive criticism echoed Yao Wenyuan's tone, calling the issue a struggle between the proletariat and the bourgeoisie.

My music research group attended the first criticism meeting held at the Central Philharmonic Orchestra's rehearsal hall. The atmosphere was very intense. I could imagine the pressure on Teacher Huang, who must have felt humiliated.

At this first criticism meeting, I came across Yanqiao, my composer teacher, from whom I had been taking music theory and composition lessons for more than a year. He whispered to me, "We have to stop your lessons on composition analysis." He referred to the Western classical music works we had been studying. I nodded reluctantly, disappointed by what was happening. I tried to picture the happy gathering of musicians from the Philadelphia Orchestra and our orchestra in this very rehearsal hall a few months before. I could still hear Beethoven's *Symphony No. 5* played by our orchestra under Eugene Ormandy's baton. In such a short time, our musicians and I were returning to the dark ages. This campaign ended my opportunity, and that of many other music students, to pursue a music career with Western classical music training. For most of the Chinese people, the campaign about "absolute music" signaled the end of a brief period in 1973 when Western classical music was allowed on Chinese stages. Now the Central Philharmonic Orchestra played only Jiang Qing-approved revolutionary repertoire: the symphony *Shajiabang* and the newly composed *Yellow River Piano Concerto.*

CHAPTER 27

A Brilliant Artist's "Black Paintings"

In order to attack other targets in the arts for the "Criticize Lin Biao, Criticize Confucius" campaign, certain fine art painters were singled out in 1974 and branded "black artists." This initiative was known as the "Criticizing Black Painting" campaign.

The real target of the movement was Premier Zhou, who in 1971 had directed that Chinese ink brush paintings be hung in hotels serving foreign visitors. Premier Zhou stated that the interior arrangements there should be simple, in good taste, and reflect China's long cultural history and artistic standards. The paintings should be in Chinese contemporary styles. Based on Premier Zhou's directive, a government department organized artists, including CAFA faculty members, to paint apolitical subjects such as flowers and landscapes in Chinese ink brush style. These paintings were soon hung in hotels and in the International Club serving foreign guests. Jiang Qing saw these activities handled by Premier Zhou as a challenge to her authority over arts fields.

Through the command of Yao Wenyuan, more than 200 of these apolitical works, many done under Premier Zhou's direction, were gathered from hotels, art galleries, and art academies in Beijing and other cities and displayed in "black painting" exhibitions in Beijing where they were publicly criticized. In 1974 I visited such an exhibition, which featured works by well-known Chinese ink brush painters including quite a few of my father's former students. Most of the paintings there did not suggest to me any political theme. Labeling them "black paintings" was unjust. However, the arts leaders publicly denounced these works as "poisonous weeds viciously attacking the socialist system," calling them "a resurgence of the black line in visual arts, an attempt at restoring the old order."

One of my father's students, Li Kuchan, had in 1972 painted a Chinese ink brush painting of eight withering lotus flowers for the International Club. The painting was now interpreted as a criticism of Jiang Qing's eight model performing works, which had become unpopular among the people. Zong Qixiang, one of Father's best students and head of the Chinese landscape painting specialty at CAFA, painted for a hotel in 1973 a Chinese ink brush painting of three tigers named *Lively Tigers*. This painting became a major "black painting," construed as defending Lin Biao because the Chinese character "biao" has three strokes attached to the character "tiger." Hence Zong's three tigers supposedly suggested Lin's name, Biao. Another "black painter," Li Hu,[62] a faculty member of the Chinese painting department at CAFA, in 1973 painted several Chinese ink brush paintings for decorating the Beijing Hotel. *Family on the Water* portrays life on the Yangtze River, depicting a weathered wooden boat highlighted with hints of colored clothing strung above the deck. The painting was criticized as an attack on the socialist system, showing people with no homes.

Li Hu's ink brush painting *Night Navigation through the Three Gorges* (Fig. 9) was hung in another "black painting" exhibition at the Great Hall of the People. In 1971, Li Hu and two other well-known Chinese ink brush painters were transferred from a re-education farm to Beijing to make paintings for the Minzu Hotel, in case President Nixon visited. Li Hu created *Night Navigation through the Three Gorges*, displayed in the main restaurant on the ground floor of that hotel, which received Kissinger later that year. This painting became popular. In 1972 at the Ministry of Foreign Affairs' request, Li Hu painted a similar painting, hung in the office of the Permanent Mission of the People's Republic of China to the United Nations, in New York. This painting creates an atmosphere of moonlight and shadow on the water, seldom done in traditional Chinese painting. The steamers shown in the distance are dwarfed by the dark towering cliffs through which they can now navigate. During the same year, China's Central Newsreel and Documentary Film Studio made a documentary film, *China Today*, featuring Li Hu painting this landscape painting. The documentary was made for overseas distribution only.

Li Hu had meant to portray an accomplishment. Socialist construction projects had dredged the Three Gorges region of the Yangtze River so it could be navigated at night. However, in 1974 Jiang Qing's agents branded it a "black painting" because of the extensive use of dark ink in the night landscape.

According to Li Hu's son, Li Fan, someone from the Cultural Group questioned He Jianguo, an artist staff member at the film studio, about the intentions of the documentary that featured Li Hu's painting. He Jianguo responded, "The documentary showed that night navigation through the Three Gorges region was now possible, a socialist accomplishment."

Li Hu was an accomplished artist and a close friend of my family. Born into a poor family in Sichuan Province in 1919, Li Hu loved painting, even in his childhood. In 1942, he was admitted to the art department of National Central University in Chongqing and became one of Father's best students.

Li Hu developed new means of expressions in Chinese ink brush landscape and figure painting. Carrying forward my father's legacy, he painted Chinese figures and landscapes from life with a Chinese ink brush. He and Zong Qixiang, another student of Father's, were the most successful Chinese ink brush painters of night landscapes. Their use of light and shadow combined with traditional ink and brush work captured the wonders of Chinese nighttime landscapes, which traditional Chinese painters had not been able to render. While at Central University, Father admired Li Hu's groundbreaking accomplishment and wrote the following calligraphy to help Li Hu gain recognition and raise funds for his first painting exhibition in 1946: "After the art department of Central University moved to Sichuan, the method of working from life with Chinese ink and paper, using Western painting technique, was created. Younger brother Li Hu is the most successful in this approach."[63]

Li Hu's ink brush figure paintings were exceptionally insightful. His Chinese ink brush *Portrait of an Indian Woman* and *Portrait of a Policewoman* are currently in the collection of the National Art Museum of China. An image from another of Li Hu's important Chinese ink brush paintings, *Guan Hanqing* (Fig. 10), was used on stamps issued in 1958 by China and the Soviet Union to honor thirteenth-century Yuan-dynasty playwright Guan Hanqing. This painting was acquired by the National Museum of Chinese History, now the National Museum of China.

Like my father, Li Hu was a good teacher. In 1948, Father invited him to move from Sichuan Province to Beiping. With my father's recommendation, he first taught in the architecture department of Tsinghua University. In 1951 he transferred to CAFA where he was known for his excellent drawing skills. His pencil drawing of a plaster bust was displayed in the hallway at

Figure 9. Li Hu (1919-1975), *Night Navigation through the Three Gorges*, 1971, 125 x 175 cm, ink and color on paper, collection of Li Hu's family

Figure 10. Li Hu (1919-1975), *Guan Hanqing*, 1962, 85 x 60 cm, ink and color on paper, collection of Li Hu's family

CAFA as a benchmark example for students in the mid-1950s, when Soviet artists' drawings were most admired. As head of the figure painting specialty in the academy's Chinese painting department, Li Hu developed many capable artists, encouraging them to explore new techniques to portray the people of the new era.

I had known Li Hu since my childhood. I remember him as a short man, wearing a beret. I liked his kind smile and the humor that came out through the distinctively melodic tone of his Sichuan dialect. During my early teens, he often came to our house to give drawing lessons to Qingping. I remember Qingping drawing a plaster bust of a Greek lady during a lesson with Li Hu. Li's teaching and his corrections to Qingping's drawing that day impressed me. Qingping said, "Mr. Li taught me to capture the essence of the subject."

During the Cultural Revolution, Li Hu underwent re-education, as did all Chinese intellectuals. Despite cirrhosis of the liver, which he had suffered since the 1950s, he went, together with the other CAFA faculty, to a re-education farm to do hard physical labor. When I came back to Beijing from the army farm in 1972, I heard that he had also returned to Beijing. One evening in the spring of 1973, I was delighted to see Li Hu visiting us again as in the old days, but this time in our small Hufang Road apartment, a modest environment compared with our spacious house before the Cultural Revolution. He seemed high-spirited, talking about his recently completed *Night Navigation through the Three Gorges*.

Mom said to me, "Xiao Mei, why don't you play a piano piece for Mr. Li?"

In the past I had not been always willing to show off my piano performance skills for Mom's guests. But for this dear friend I gladly accepted the invitation. I played *Nocturne in E-flat Major, Op. 9, No. 2* by Chopin. This romantic piece was one of my favorites and I played it from my heart, expressing the dream-like beauty as well as the passion near the end. Through my music, I showed him my happiness in renewing our friendship and my dream for a better future for all of us in the arts. After my performance, Li Hu thanked me sincerely with his usual kind smile which always warmed me.

However, our hopes were dashed by the political swing in 1974. Accompanied by his son, Li Hu visited the "black painting" exhibition at the National Art Museum of China, showing his *Family on the Water*. Li Hu felt that the accusation against his painting was unjustified. According to his son, Li Fan, Li Hu said he saw beauty along the riverside. Yet he was not allowed to defend himself. At the "black painting" exhibition a few "black artists" were forced to read confessions publicly. Big-character posters hanging on art academy campuses criticized the "black artists." *Beijing Daily* and other newspapers published articles denouncing "black paintings," such as Zong Qixiang's *Lively Tigers*, for "venting hatred towards the Party and socialism." Li Hu and other "black artists" were required to attend criticism meetings at CAFA where they were forced to perform self-criticism. Mass rallies were also held there to publicly humiliate these artists. Although exempt from the humiliation at mass rallies because of his poor health, Li Hu was upset about the false accusation. When Mom, Qingping, and I visited him in winter 1974 he was bedridden from his hepatic illness, which had worsened under the political pressure, but he expressed the hope that Chinese herbal medicine might help.

One sunny spring afternoon a few months later, I was alone in our Hufang Road apartment when I heard a gentle knock. To my surprise, Li Hu stood at our door. He looked tired, having climbed the stairs to the second floor. His face, although slightly swollen, still carried the gentle smile. "I came to see Xu Shimu (Master Xu's wife)," he said softly.

I shook his hand immediately and asked him to stay for a visit even though Mom was not home.

He said, "I am sorry I cannot stay because a cab is waiting outside to take me home before my caretaker returns from her errands. Here are two jars of honey for Xu Shimu."

I realized that he had hired a cab for this brief visit to show his appreciation of his teacher's family. I walked him downstairs. It hurt me to see his notably weakened condition and the effort it took to step into the tiny three-wheel cab with its canvas top. That was the last time I saw him. A few months after that visit he died at age fifty-six.

I will never forget his last visit and the warmth he brought us at the end of his life. I regret that he did not live to see the downfall of the Gang of Four, namely, Jiang Qing and her supporters, a year later, in 1976. I will always remember Li Hu as a warm friend, an encouraging teacher, and a brilliant artist.

CHAPTER 28
A Surge of Hope

The sky was grey with large dark clouds. The wind wailed through the streets of Beijing. When twilight fell upon Tiananmen Square and the nearby Chang'an Avenue, a solemn silence hung over this central area of the city. It was January 11, 1976, three days after Premier Zhou Enlai had passed away. My mother and I were among the thousands gathering along Chang'an Avenue, waiting for our beloved premier's hearse to pass by on its way to the Babaoshan Revolutionary Cemetery.

Strangely, Jiang Qing and her associates disallowed any public display of mourning for Premier Zhou, as if they wanted the premier to disappear from the people's memory as soon as possible. Yet nothing could hold back the people's feelings for Premier Zhou, a brilliant government leader who had dedicated his whole life to the liberation and progress of his people. During the devastation of the Cultural Revolution, he was the only top leader who, in spite of possible dangers, was able to repeatedly resist Jiang Qing and her associates in his efforts to prevent innocent people's persecution.

After the sad news had spread over China, Tiananmen Square became the center of mourning for Premier Zhou. Crowds laid homemade paper wreaths in front of the Monument to the People's Heroes. It was their way of commemorating Premier Zhou, who did not have a monument of his own. As a result, the pine trees near that monument were covered by numerous white paper flowers which looked like snow scattered on the green leaves. The grey cityscape of Beijing in winter took on a new look.

Around Tiananmen Square and along Chang'an Avenue, hundreds of thousands of people from all walks of life, from all over China, assembled and waited for hours to pay their last respects to their beloved premier. In spite of the sharp wind, the huge crowds were growing every minute. Mom and I had been waiting there since that morning, without eating. At last came the moment. The hearse that had started out from the nearby Beijing Hospital moved slowly along Chang'an Avenue. Although lacking ceremony, this single black hearse decorated with a few black ribbons was more memorable to me than any funeral procession. The immense crowd stirred. People around me jostled and nudged each other. I looked at the sea of tearful faces among the white paper flowers held by the mourners. Thousands of eyes full of sorrow and desperation followed the hearse intensely, as if trying to engrave this significant moment upon memory forever.

Tears blurred my vision, but in my mind's eye, I saw Premier Zhou talking intimately with some workers at a work site. I saw him working twenty hours a day in his sparsely furnished office, directing government affairs, helping China establish diplomatic relations with Western countries and orchestrate U.S. president Nixon's visit to China. The historic meeting between President Nixon and Chairman Mao opened the door to the normalization of Sino-American relations. I also saw Premier Zhou talking with Father in the early 1950s, showing his concern for Father's work and well-being. After Father died, at every critical moment and during the Cultural Revolution, Mom had appealed to Premier Zhou, trusting him to find a solution to avert disaster for our family. Each time he responded to her request as a trusted friend. I heard that he had also protected many senior cadres, scientists, academics, and artists from the abuses of the Cultural Revolution. However, I also saw Premier Zhou attacked by Jiang Qing and her associates, who considered him Jiang's major rival for future control of the country.

My most recent and also most memorable impression of Premier Zhou was his speech at the Fourth National People's Congress in 1975, a year before his death. His speech filled us with hope for China's future in those dark years, inspiring us to work for the Four Modernizations of our motherland in the fields of agriculture, industry, national defense, and science and technology.

But now Premier Zhou had left us. The hope of the Chinese people was gone. "What is the future holding for us?" I wondered. The people in the crowd were sobbing and whispering their last words to Premier Zhou. However, in their choked sadness I sensed a smoldering anger. It was hatred for the totalitarian rule of Jiang Qing's clique, who had persecuted and brought death to so many good, capable leaders.

The people's anger fermented as they formed a huge procession following Premier Zhou's remains for several miles along Chang'an Avenue. It was the first time that the people had defied the authority of Jiang Qing and her associates with such a large-scale action, organizing themselves of their own will. While Mom and I were marching hand in hand with thousands in the funeral procession, I felt a growing strength hidden in the silence of mourning, a strength that had accumulated through the ten years of oppression, and that would show itself sooner or later.

In the next few months, the momentum of protests continued to grow. In late March 1976, crowds gathered spontaneously at Tiananmen Square to continue to mourn Premier Zhou. But now, messages implicitly criticizing Jiang Qing and her associates appeared on the posters attached to the wreaths. An example was a poem indirectly criticizing Jiang Qing's ambition by making an analogy with Wu Zetian, a seventh-century Tang-dynasty empress who built her power base, planning to take her husband's position when he passed away. Jiang Qing through her controlled media tried to stifle the public expression of grief for Premier Zhou. They discouraged people from going to Tiananmen Square. The more they tried to suppress the people's mourning for Premier Zhou, the more the people's anger swelled. In the days leading up to April 5, 1976, more than one million people gathered around Tiananmen Square. The white paper wreaths they placed formed an ocean of white flowers. Starting from the Monument to the People's Heroes, these white flowers overflowed to the rows of pine trees surrounding Tiananmen Square. The outpouring of love and grief was unprecedented.

I was then dating Yu, an English teacher at a military academy in Nanjing. We shared love for Premier Zhou and hatred for Jiang Qing and her associates. We went to Tiananmen Square every day between late March and early April 1976. I had to keep this secret from my colleagues at the Central Philharmonic Orchestra.

We put our white paper wreath anonymously at the foot of the Monument to the People's Heroes. The scene there was like a show with new exhibits added every day. I had never seen such a large-scale open display of political expression against Jiang Qing's clique. People were reciting poems that they had written for Premier Zhou. Speakers were protesting publicly. As I walked around reading the poems and posters among the thousands of wreaths, I was moved by their content and creativity. The following became a famous poem, written by a young man named Wang Lishan:

In my grief I hear demons shriek;
I weep while wolves laugh.
Though tears I shed to mourn a hero,
Head raised high, I draw my sword.

Messages appeared supporting Deng Xiaoping, close comrade of Premier Zhou. After his re-emergence in 1973, Deng focused on rebuilding the country's economy, damaged by the Cultural Revolution. His accomplishments won the people's support. During the Tiananmen Square protests, I saw a little glass bottle hanging on the branch of a pine tree, a symbol for Deng's first name, Xiaoping, which has the same pronunciation as "little bottle" in Chinese. I marveled at this subtle, creative protest.

One morning I spotted a small wreath the size of a headband placed on the railing of the Monument to the People's Heroes. The words on the attached wide paper ribbons read: "Dedicated to our beloved Premier Zhou from two comrades of the Beijing Peking Opera Troupe." Later I learned that the two comrades were fellow CCOM alumnae, Zhao and Duan, now in the orchestra of the Beijing Peking Opera Troupe, another model performing troupe under Jiang Qing's control.

According to Zhao, the same day their wreath appeared at Tiananmen Square, the Party secretary of their troupe received an evening phone call from Yu Huiyong, now minister of the Ministry of Culture. Yu requested an investigation. Immediately, the Party secretary talked to Zhao and Duan individually, questioning their reason for using the name of Beijing Peking Opera Troupe on their wreath and asking them to admit their mistake publicly. But Zhao said, "My mother made the wreath, and Duan and I displayed it at the Monument to the People's Heroes to mourn Premier Zhou. We represented ourselves as individuals working with the Beijing Peking Opera Troupe. We did not do anything wrong."

The next morning, Yu Huiyong harangued the leaders of the Beijing Peking Opera Troupe, yelling at the top of his raspy voice, "Look what you have allowed to happen! I told you early on to develop your employees' dedication to our top leader. The public display of a wreath by model troupe members is a disgrace to her. You must investigate why they chose to write the name of Beijing Peking Opera Troupe on the wreath."

The troupe's leaders investigated Zhao and Duan's backgrounds but did not find any connection with political forces high up. Although no disciplinary actions were taken, the two musicians continued to feel political pressure, primarily from some of the Peking opera acrobatic actors who closely followed Jiang Qing.

Years later I asked Zhao, "Why did you choose to disclose your affiliation with the Beijing Peking Opera Troupe? Did you think about the possible consequences?" Zhao said, "At the time, some of us in the model troupe did not think much of Jiang Qing. Duan and I felt resentful for not being allowed to mourn Premier Zhou at Tiananmen Square. We respected our premier so much. In a fit of anger, we went to Tiananmen Square and identified our affiliation purposely, to show our defiance."

After Premier Zhou's death, like many Chinese people, I could not foresee any positive change in China's political future. However, hope surged in my heart as I stood among the thousands of people mourning Premier Zhou and protesting for change. This spontaneous mass protest movement was so powerful and uplifting that I wanted to be there every day to be part of this emerging force. The people there gave me hope for China.

As the people's protest was escalating, Jiang Qing's suppression forces were also mounting. I saw plainclothes police snapping photos of the people giving protest speeches. April 4, 1976 was the Qingming Festival. During that night, the police hauled away all the wreaths, poems, and posters placed on Tiananmen Square and also arrested many mourners who refused to leave. On April 5, tens of thousands of people in Beijing returning to Tiananmen Square were blocked and turned away by public security personnel guarding the Monument to the People's Heroes. The crowd in the square became outraged and vocal. They demanded the return of the wreaths and the release of their comrades. Physical conflict broke out between the protesters and some police and militiamen.

I had been to Tiananmen Square on the cold morning of April 5. The sky was filled with large heavy clouds pressing down from all sides, as if to suffocate us. Having a premonition that something bad might happen, I decided to stay home for the rest of the day.

In the early evening, as Mom and I were eating dinner, we heard a string of rapid knocks on the door. Two strong men in military postures were at the door. They wore leather belts tied around the waists of their cotton overcoats. Their red armbands showed that they were worker militiamen from Beijing Gear Wheel Factory, where Third Uncle Liao Ping worked. The taller man said, "We are here to fetch Liao Ping's overcoat for him. He needs it for tonight's action."

Mom paused and responded in a gentle voice, "I am Liao Ping's sister. You know Liao Ping is not in good health. Could you please let him come home tonight?"

The man replied, "I will report to my superior and you should know the answer soon."

Later I learned that the Central Committee of the CCP had ordered large numbers of worker militiamen and police to crack down on the protesters remaining on Tiananmen Square the night of April 5. Third Uncle had shared his disapproval of Jiang Qing with us and told us that he wanted no part of the crackdown on the protesters at Tiananmen Square. After the militiamen left, Mom and I waited anxiously. Third Uncle returned home within the hour, much to our relief.

During that evening, when the majority of the large crowds left, the police and militiamen used batons and nightsticks to drive away the few thousand remaining mourners. Blood covered Tiananmen Square. I heard that about 4000 people were arrested in or near the square.

A couple of days later, *People's Daily*, under Yao Wenyuan's direction, published an article that declared the Tiananmen Square protests to be "counterrevolutionary," and framed Deng Xiaoping as the mastermind behind the protests. Based on Chairman Mao's recommendations, the Political Bureau of the CCP Central Committee removed Deng Xiaoping from all leading positions and approved Hua Guofeng to be premier and first vice chairman of the Party.

This mass protest against Jiang Qing and her associates' repression became known as the April Fifth Movement or Tiananmen Incident. After the crackdown, Tiananmen Square was under surveillance for days. Passing by the square on a bus, I saw the deserted expanse of the square now cordoned off by public security forces, and felt a painful loss. Only the five-star national flag in the middle of the empty square flew solitary in the cold wind.

The people's movement had been violently suppressed. The brief period of free political expression ended in bloodshed. Police searches and arrests continued for months. I heard that CCOM schoolmates active in the protests were detained for investigation. Sources of all rumors about Jiang Qing were traced. In the Central Philharmonic Orchestra, we were summoned to meetings for the purpose of writing reports about our own activities as well as "criminal" activities we were aware of during the Tiananmen Square protests. We were required to write the reports on the spot silently with no possibility of coordinating our stories. I did not report anything. Luckily, no one in my family got into trouble.

The months following the April Fifth Movement were very depressing. Jiang Qing's clique regained power. I saw no hope for change in the near future. However, more upheavals awaited us. On July 28, a big earthquake shook Beijing and damaged some of the houses. The epicenter was near Tangshan, about one hundred miles from Beijing. Tangshan was an industrial city with more than one million residents. The earthquake's death toll is estimated to be in the hundreds of thousands, the worst in the twentieth century. This natural disaster disturbed all the Beijing residents. Most, including my family, built sheds and camped on the streets for a month. The unstable situation prevented many people, including myself, from going to work. Instead we stayed in parks or other open spaces, away from tall buildings.

The earthquake seemed to be a precursor of earth-shaking political events involving the Chinese Communist Party. On September 9, 1976, Chairman Mao died. For the following weeks, the whole nation was in mourning. Public performances and all entertainment were prohibited nationwide. I could not even play my piano at home. All day long, the radio broadcast funeral music. I did not feel that much grief. Like many Chinese people, I was anxious about the power shift at the top. It would decide our fate.

The swiftness of the change was unexpected. On October 14, our Central Philharmonic Orchestra received astounding news, officially relayed to us. The Gang of Four had been smashed by the CCP Central Committee headed by Hua Guofeng. Jiang Qing and her three associates, Zhang Chunqiao, Yao Wenyuan, and Wang Hongwen, denounced as the Gang of Four, had been arrested on October 6, 1976. This event marked the end of the Cultural Revolution. All of Beijing went into a frenzied celebration for days.

I joined the parade of the Central Philharmonic Orchestra. We marched for hours from Hepingli in the northern part of Beijing to Tiananmen Square, where all the parading groups converged to a mass of more than a million people, spontaneously celebrating. I was happy to see in the parade some of the well-known artists, writers, and musicians who had been persecuted during the Cultural Revolution. We now had real hope for a better future.

CHAPTER 29

A Practical Choice

After the Gang of Four was crushed, the leadership in Jiang Qing's model performing troupes changed. Some of her favorite performers in the model performing works were under investigation. In the Central Philharmonic Orchestra, the famous pianist Yin Chengzong, one of the composers of the *Yellow River Piano Concerto*, was kept in isolation for investigation.

Hua Guofeng now became chairman of the Party and maintained the direction Mao Zedong had set for the country. Despite our expectations from the sudden political change, most people's daily lives remained the same for months in 1977. However, I made a life-changing personal decision that year. In 1976, my boyfriend, Yu, left the military academy in Nanjing where he had been an English teacher. At the end of 1976, he landed a job in Beijing as an English interpreter for a research institute. With this secure job, we decided to marry in January 1977.

Yu was not the ideal man that I had expected and my mother did not like him. But at age twenty-nine, I was looking forward to settling into my own home for an independent life.

In the 1970s, dating was difficult for many because of political background concerns and gossip about dating behavior. And as a dutiful daughter, I followed my mother's advice: She did not allow me to date until I was twenty-four. She expected me to achieve my career goals before shouldering family responsibilities. She regretted having dropped out of college and given up her career in science because she had been in love and married young. She also wanted to make sure that I remained a virgin before marriage. That was the social norm in the 1960s and 1970s. A young woman who had premarital sex would certainly have a bad reputation, making her undesirable to many eligible men.

However, during my teenage years, in spite of my mother's expectations, I fantasized about falling in love with a young man just like the characters in nineteenth-century European romantic novels. In summer 1967, at nineteen, I met Li, a college student at Beijing Institute of Machinery, a place I visited for building revolutionary ties in the Cultural Revolution. A quiet man dressed casually in a blue sweater with an open collar, he was very friendly. Soon after we met, he invited me to a student performance in his school in the evening. I got permission from Mom to go with him. We both had a good time. But I did not consider our friendship to be intimate. Then he started coming by for short visits to our quadrangle house in Haibo Hutong. One aspect of his behavior puzzled me. I tried to share my love of music with him during his visit. But when I started playing the piano, sometimes a mazurka or nocturne by Chopin, he would get up and leave with an excuse. I thought that perhaps he did not like my piano music.

In summer 1968, I moved to one of the practice rooms in the Prep Music High School, away from my mother's control. I made other male acquaintances among college students. Chen, from Beijing University of Technology, expressed an interest in a relationship with me in a letter. But we did not have common interests. One evening I visited Li in his dormitory at Beijing Institute of Machinery. During our conversation, I showed him the letter from Chen and asked for his advice as to how to handle that. Li blushed, looking away from me as he said, "You trust me so much with this secret. You probably know how I feel about you. I have had the feelings for a long time." He looked embarrassed, struggling with his head down. Although he never said "I love you," I could sense his passion for me.

That evening, he walked with me for two hours from Beijing Institute of Machinery in the eastern suburbs to the Prep Music High School in the western part of the city. Late-night buses stopped running. We basked in the stillness of the wide Beijing streets, just the two of us, something I had never experienced in this bustling city. We stopped at the top of the arched Beihai Bridge, looking out across the lake. The distant details were obscured by the darkness, arousing our imaginations. We talked about the romantic stories in nineteenth-century Russian literature, which we both loved. Surprisingly for a technical major, Li was well-read in Western and Chinese classical literature, and a capable reporter for his Red Guard group's newspaper. Gazing at the moon's vague reflection on the water surface, we shared our thoughts about the future and the uncertainty about the career prospects of music students and college students.

Later Li asked me out to Yuyuantan (Deep Jade Pool) Park at night. Although cautious, I was curious about his affection for me. We sat by the water surrounded by dense woods. A few frogs softly croaked from the water, keeping us company. In the darkness, Li's face was lit only by the moonlight as he turned to me and told me the following story:

In a southern town by a lake lived a beautiful young soprano. She often practiced singing with her window open. Her sweet, lyrical voice filled the night air. One day she was singing a classical aria while accompanying herself on the piano. A young man knocked at her door, stating that he was so drawn to the emotions in her voice that he had to introduce himself. They started spending time together. During one of his visits to her home, it started to rain. He had no umbrella, so she gave him her white scarf. While he was leaving, he invited her to visit his home the next day.

When the soprano came to her friend's house, no one was there. To her surprise, she saw a large photo of the young man she was dating hanging in the living room. It was a posthumous photo with black silk strips draped around the frame. She started wondering what had happened to him when she spotted a note on the table by the young man, which read: "I came into your life to reveal my identical twin brother's love for you. He had come every night for almost a year to watch you and listen to your singing from the shadows outside your window. But he was unable to express his love for you before he recently died. Please visit his grave in the west suburbs cemetery to comfort his soul."

The soprano rushed out. When she arrived at the cemetery, she found her own white scarf flying from a branch near the twin brother's tombstone. In this deserted place, the white scarf was the only sign of remembrance for the dead. Autumn wind rustled through the branches, stirring fallen leaves that gradually drifted away from the cemetery.

I reached out and held Li's hand in mine. I understood the meaning of his story, which explained his disturbed response to my classical piano playing during his visits. The night shrouded us as we sat close to each other in silence. His scholarly hands were not big for a man, yet I felt their warmth throughout my body. The nearby Telegraph Tower bell struck 10, rudely breaking our silent fantasies. I had to return to the Prep Music High School before its gate was locked.

On my way back to the music school, I realized gossip could arise from my date with Li, and my mother's reprimand awaited me. I must have broken his heart when I told him, "I am not sure if I am ready for a relationship with you. I want to pursue a piano performance career, which is very important for me now."

Li said, "With your talent, I am sure that someday I will hear you perform over the radio."

We hugged each other outside my school gate. I could sense Li's passion before he reluctantly walked away.

Later I shared my dating story with Mom and showed her Li's letters to me. She asked me to stop seeing him. Then Li came to my house once again and gave me a thin white scarf as a farewell gift.

My date with Li at Yuyuantan Park was my first real date. My memory of his quiet passion and tenderness stayed with me for many years. I remember the romantic moments and youthful fantasies, which ceased when I became a mature woman. In the 1970s, I heard that Li had been assigned a job in a factory in Beijing and had married. After I returned to Beijing from the army farm, although I thought about him, I chose not to contact him. I only wanted to remember his shy innocence as we were holding hands in the quiet summer night by the lake at Yuyuantan Park.

My mother expected my future husband to be an honest, loving man with education, and from a family similar to ours. None of my boyfriends met her high expectations. During the Cultural Revolution, a very important consideration for a relationship was the political background of one's prospective spouse and family. Marrying into a problematic family meant political trouble for a person's future.

To make things more difficult for me, I decided not to date any artists or my music schoolmates. From my observation, young men in artistic circles had little interest in developing knowledge beyond their major studies. I was also cautious because they might be after my father's reputation. In arts circles, I was known as Xu Beihong's daughter. A young artist who married into our family would share our family's celebrity social status and reputation in the arts. I preferred a man with expertise in science or technology, who also enjoyed arts and literature. These qualities were intellectually more stimulating to me. Men in technical fields also had relatively better job security and were less susceptible to political swings than those in arts and education in the early 1970s. All these considerations made eligible men scarce for me.

In 1972, right after I had come back to Beijing from the army farm, my mother introduced to me my first boyfriend, Xiao Zhang (Little Zhang), a six-foot-tall, good-looking young man. He had gone to Tsinghua University, majoring in architectural history and theory. As a Communist Party member from a working-class family, he was employed by Tsinghua University to do political work for the Party. My mother was happy with his political background and his appearance. I was allowed to date him.

Xiao Zhang and I fell in love quickly. He often rode his bike for more than an hour to see me in my Hufang Road apartment. We enjoyed going swimming and hiking in the Western Hills. He was an honest, loving man, and proposed to me a year after we started dating. But I was hesitant. At twenty-five, I wanted to pursue my career before committing myself to a marriage. I hoped to go to college overseas to study music and other useful subjects to fulfill my artistic dream, following my father's example. Xiao Zhang's college education had been cut short because of the Cultural Revolution. I thought that his one year of study at Tsinghua would not qualify him for an academic position at that university. That was a big disappointment for me because my family and I expected my future husband to be accomplished in his academic or technical field. I encouraged him to learn English and educate himself in his spare time. He followed my advice. However, his boss criticized him for pursuing a bourgeois intellectual path instead of devoting himself to the Party's political work. He was sent to a May Seventh Cadre School to do manual labor for a year in order to reform his bourgeois thoughts, as his boss put it. This created tension in our relationship. We started arguing with each other. In 1973, we finally broke up.

I felt lonely and went for a time without a boyfriend. In artistic circles I would have had plenty of opportunities. But I refused to consider anyone there. In 1975 a family friend introduced Yu to me. His English ability, intelligence, and love of music attracted me although he was seven years older than I and not good-looking. The first time we met, his army uniform earned some of my respect because I held a high opinion of the People's Liberation Army. But when we started dating, my mother disapproved. His family's status did not match mine.

Yu and I were both quick-tempered, leading to frequent arguments. However, at the time women were pressured to marry before age thirty. At twenty-nine, I was afraid of becoming an old maid "whom no one wanted." I believe that both thirty-six-year-old Yu and I were making a practical choice when we married.

I asked the Central Philharmonic Orchestra for permission to marry Yu. Our human resources staff investigated Yu and his family's political background. After he passed the political check I was given a letter of permission with our orchestra's official seal. With that letter and a similar letter from Yu's work unit, we were able to register at a government office for our marriage license.

Our wedding in January 1977 was not romantic in the way I had imagined during my teenage years. I lived with my new husband in a small one-bedroom apartment in the eastern suburbs of Beijing. But I was satisfied. During the housing shortage when many young couples could not obtain housing, I was fortunate to be allocated this apartment. This might have been compensation to my mother for giving up her big quadrangle house at the beginning of the Cultural Revolution.

We visited my mother once a week. At that point, Mom accepted Yu and expected me to give her a grandchild as soon as possible. I still had my dream of going to college. But in the beginning of 1977, there was no news indicating that universities would reopen. To fulfill my mother's wish, I became pregnant soon after our wedding. I nicknamed my son "Pangpang," which means chubby; he was a chubby baby. As an adult, he is known as James Xu.

CHAPTER 30

The Door Opens

While I was delivering my baby boy at the end of October 1977, exciting news came: Deng Xiaoping, who had been restored to power in July, had chosen as one of his earliest major political changes the reinstatement of the national college entrance examination system. The long-awaited examinations were to resume in December. But I was not able to take the exams then. I was disappointed at losing the educational opportunity I had dreamed about for ten years. I had no concept of the joy my son and my grandchildren would give me in the future.

In early 1978, I heard about the millions who had applied for college in 1977, potential students accumulated over the past ten years when universities had been closed. Only about five percent were admitted, based mainly on college-entrance examination scores. My Prep Music High School classmates told me that CCOM accepted only applicants born after January 1, 1949. This unfairly forced my classmates and me into the lost generation, unable to pursue a music performance career.

In spring 1978, after recovering from childbirth, I discussed with Yu my desire to apply to college. The only possibility for me was applying to a university's English program. Perhaps with my knowledge of English I could later go abroad to further my education. To my surprise, Yu supported my plan. My English tutor, Joan, also encouraged me. She said, "Don't let the baby stop you. Your English is good and you should be able to get into a good college."

My oral English ability did in fact give me an advantage over many applicants for placement in a university's English department. From winter 1974 through 1975, I had attended the English refresher courses offered by Beijing Language Institute, where I had learned to speak English fluently by practicing with some foreign students learning Chinese there. Although without degree programs, the school allowed Chinese students to speak with foreign students on campus during a time when everywhere else Chinese people were not permitted to speak freely with foreigners. However, my classmates had criticized me for taking every opportunity to speak with foreign students.

In 1978 Yu wanted to apply to the Graduate School of Chinese Academy of Social Sciences. We considered leaving our Pangpang with a babysitter during the week if we both went to school.

The 1978 national college entrance examination was to be held in the beginning of July. There were just as many applicants, ranging in age from eighteen to their early thirties, and the chance of admission was as slim as the year before. Although I had a solid foundation in English and Chinese, I still needed to catch up with regular high-school students in other examination subjects such as politics, history, and geography.

I had never been afraid of examinations in the music school. But as a thirty-year-old working mother, I was under a lot of pressure and could not concentrate on studies. Having no experience raising a child, I made many mistakes and Pangpang was often sick. During my entrance examination preparation, I still had to wake up every four hours at night to give Pangpang medicine for his cough and cold. Not having enough sleep and working full-time left me little energy. Fortunately, three weeks before the exam date, my boss at the Central Philharmonic Orchestra approved time off for me. Locking myself in an empty office in the orchestra building, I tried to cram all the necessary knowledge into my head. I followed Yu's advice to study *Xu Guozhang English* containing basic English grammar, which turned out to be very useful. The office was hot and stuffy, but I was motivated to seize every minute, fearing that I might never get this opportunity again.

By early July, before the three-day exams, I felt ready. In the previous few months I had lost thirty pounds. The national college entrance examination was to be held on the same three days all over China. These were known later as the "three dark days," when the fates of all applicants would be determined. The schedules included morning and afternoon exams on different subjects with a short lunch break in between.

My exam location was in a primary school in my neighborhood. When I walked into the classroom for my English exam, serious faces surrounded me; some looked much younger than mine. In the unbearable heat, I could hear my heart beat quickly. Water had been sprinkled on the bare wooden floor to make it feel somewhat cooler. The two-and-a-half-hour English exam was most important because I planned to apply to the English teacher training department at the Beijing Institute of Aeronautics. The English department of this university might consider applicants older than twenty-five, while foreign-language institutes would not.

The proctor announced that we could begin. I glanced through the exam paper. The reading comprehension section consisted of multiple-choice questions, which I had never seen before. My hands trembled, and for a moment I felt confused. I decided to complete the other sections first and come back to the reading section. After concentrating on the other sections, I calmed down and was able to figure out the tricky multiple-choice answers. I completed the exam in about an hour and a half, leaving plenty of time to check my answers. I turned in my paper before the exam ended and felt confident that I had done well.

Two weeks later, the Central Philharmonic Orchestra notified me about taking my oral English exam. I was then sharing a two-bedroom apartment in my work unit's employee housing, close to work. The night before my oral exam, my roommate played loud music all night. I was not able to sleep and felt dizzy the next morning. But luckily, the oral English exam turned out to be easy. We were asked only to answer a few questions about a short story that we had to read on the spot. I believed that I did well.

In two weeks, I was notified that I had passed the college entrance examination and could go to Jiuxianqiao (Nine Fairy Bridge) Hospital for the physical examination, a requirement for college entrance, in addition to the political check. High-spirited, I rode my bike for more than an hour to this rural hospital in the suburbs of Beijing. While there, I saw several other student applicants with worried faces waiting in the hallway for a second chance to test their blood pressure, which had shot up because they were so nervous. I passed the physical exam.

My English examination score of 95.5 out of 100 could qualify me for admission to an English program in a good university. I went to the College Student Recruitment Office in Beijing to state the universities of my choice. While there, I found a few newly-listed universities. The English teacher training department at Renmin University of China caught my attention. It was one of China's top liberal arts universities. With my artistic background I much preferred Renmin University of China to the Beijing Institute of Aeronautics, a technical university. I selected the English teacher training department at Renmin University of China as my first choice, and the same department at the Beijing Institute of Aeronautics as my second choice.

In spite of my examination scores, obstacles still existed. In 1978, most universities' English departments would not consider applicants older than twenty-five. But there was a shortage of English teachers at several universities and at the newly reopened Renmin University of China in particular. In August, the English department heads of Renmin University of China interviewed me.

The department head said, "I understand you have a newborn. College student life has a lot of pressure. Can you handle the heavy workload?"

"Yes, I can. I have hired a babysitter," I said.

Later I heard that my English examination score ranked the highest among their applicants. In the middle of August, I received my expected admissions letter.

Several young people from the Central Philharmonic Orchestra had also applied to college that year, but I was the only one admitted to a college. Yu was admitted to the Graduate School of Chinese Academy of Social Sciences, majoring in philosophy.

In my excitement, I thought about Qingping's experience of applying to the Beijing Foreign Languages Institute thirteen years before. His pain and struggle were still fresh in my memory. But in 1978, hundreds of thousands of qualified college applicants including myself were admitted to college based on our competitive college-entrance examination scores, an accomplishment for our generation and hope for China's future. After the Cultural Revolution, the political check focused on an applicant's political behavior. An applicant's family background was no longer a consideration.

I felt fortunate. Although I had missed out by not dating or actively participating in the Cultural Revolution, I had secretly studied on my own. Those efforts were finally paying off. No longer did I need to hide in my mother's closet to listen to the BBC or Voice of America or endure hard physical labor which took energy and time away from my studies. I finally realized my dream of being educated at one of China's top universities.

• • •

Deng Xiaoping in 1978 rejected Mao Zedong's policy of "taking class struggle as the key link" and shifted the Party's focus toward socialist modernization. Under the new direction, the Central Committee of the CCP rehabilitated former rightists branded in 1957. Unbelievably, the Party reversed Mao's verdict on Liu Shaoqi, the top target of the Cultural Revolution. To our relief, the Cultural Revolution was officially condemned. The endless political movements that had exhausted us during the past decades finally ended. By 1981, Deng had consolidated his political power and ousted Hua Guofeng, Mao's appointed successor, from his top leadership position.

Deng's leadership started a new era of economic reforms. Contrary to Mao's policy of self-reliance and hard struggle, Deng's vision was to build a wealthy, modern, powerful socialist China. He encouraged the creation of a socialist market economy. He encouraged the creation of a socialist market economy and opened the door to foreign capital and technology. His famous saying from the 1960s was once again popular: "It doesn't matter whether a cat is black or white. A cat that catches mice is a good cat."

Great changes also took place in arts and education. One of the most important was the restoration of the national college entrance examination system. In 1978, Deng initiated the removal of the sending-down-to-the-countryside policy for high-school graduates. That process was completed by 1981. For many intellectuals and artists around me, Deng Xiaoping's abolition of the class background system was like a second liberation. This policy change allowed many knowledgeable scholars, professors, prominent artists, and musicians to return to educational institutions and performing groups. Their talents and knowledge were once again put to use and appreciated by all of us.

Artists resumed visiting Mom on weekends when I was also visiting. Huang Zhou, a well-known Chinese ink brush painter, drew a portrait of me in pencil and gave it to me. Father had discovered his talent and remained his advocate in the artistic circle. I often visited Father's students, such as Wu Zuoren, who was Joan's neighbor. I enjoyed seeing their recent paintings demonstrating their creative talents.

Our English teacher training department at Renmin University of China benefited from the policy change. We were assigned knowledgeable professors who had been recently rehabilitated. Professor Xu, an English professor in his seventies, had been jailed for his supposed political crimes. Renmin University brought him from the shack where he and his family had lived to a new spacious campus apartment. I learned from his lectures advanced English grammar and the proper use of prepositions. His lectures were always filled, and students from other university departments crowded into the back and at the entrances of the lecture hall. He kept a sense of humor. Once during his lecture, he caught me off guard by saying, "I met Fangfang's father in Malaysia where I worked as a diplomat. Now he sent his daughter for me to teach." Everyone laughed, but I was embarrassed.

Knowledge was no longer considered a threat to the regime but potentially useful. An American teacher gave our department some Western literature in original English text, among them adventure and mystery novels which would have been considered corruptive elements during the Cultural Revolution. My classmates and I were so absorbed in the adventure stories that we could not put the books down.

The thirty-six students in our class came from diverse backgrounds. Among them were high-school teachers, workers, and fresh high-school graduates. I was the only musician. The ages of my classmates ranged from eighteen to thirty. Although a small department in the university, we were envied by other university students because of our English-language skills and our opportunity to learn English professionally. A case in point was our student demonstration that took place in the fall of 1979.

After all universities had been closed, our university campus was occupied by the Second Artillery Corps (SAC) of the PLA. At the beginning of my freshman year in 1978, the SAC still occupied much of the campus. Our English classes were held in the open air, all the students sitting on the grass around the teacher. By September 1979, our university did not have enough dormitories, classrooms, and dining halls for the more than 2500 students from the classes of 1977, 1978, and 1979.

Negotiations with the SAC did not yield the needed facilities. Some Renmin University students organized a campus-wide strike in order to regain some classrooms and dormitories. Classes were suspended for a few days, and our classmates and English teachers also joined the strike. One sunny day in early October 1979, we held an orderly demonstration against the SAC's occupation of our campus. The authorities, including the police, had been informed of the demonstration and did not obstruct it.

We marched with banners that read "Return our classrooms, dormitories, and dining halls!" I proudly walked with my classmates along the west part of Chang'an Avenue, close to Tiananmen Square. The more than 2000 students formed a magnificent mile-long procession. Our destination was Xinhuamen, the main gate to Zhongnanhai, where we would deliver our petition to the CCP leaders.

When we arrived at Tiananmen Square, several foreign journalists and many spectators approached and surrounded us. Soon our class was inundated with questions, because we were the only students there able to communicate fluently in English. Talking to Western journalists could mean trouble because certain information was not supposed to be shared with the outside world; therefore I excused myself from the crowd. The next day, I heard that Western news sources had reported on our demonstration, identifying some of my classmates by name. Luckily, they did not get into trouble. Our strike and demonstration seemed fruitful. When classes resumed in a few days, our class was allocated two classrooms.

Even more exciting for me was studying with the first American teacher I had ever met, Mr. Dekker, who came to teach us in September 1979. A tall man in his forties with a broad smile and easygoing manner, he soon blended in with the Chinese teachers and students. He wore bell-bottom jeans and a new blue cotton Mao jacket with his red school badge pinned to it, as did the Chinese teachers. My classmates and I sometimes visited him and his eleven-year-old son in the nearby Beijing Friendship Hotel where they lived. In a short time, he made many friends among the students, who often accompanied him to places he wanted to visit in Beijing.

Mr. Dekker's lectures were our window to America. He gave a lecture about America to approximately 1000 Renmin University students in the largest lecture hall on campus. He spoke very slowly and wrote his key points on the blackboard so that non-English-major students could follow. In addition to general information about the United States, he also explained some unfamiliar economic concepts such as the gold standard, the American stock market, and the Dow Jones Industrial Average. Nothing similar had been established in China. Mr. Dekker's life in America and particularly the universities he had attended fascinated me. From him I first heard about the University of California, Berkeley, where Mr. Dekker had received his bachelor's degree. To introduce us to some American culture, Mr. Dekker taught us disco dancing.

One day after our class ended, we pushed all the desks and chairs aside to make a dance floor. Forming a circle around Mr. Dekker, my classmates and I mimicked his movements to the upbeat music from *Saturday Night Fever*. Although very different from my experience of ballroom dancing to classical music, Mr. Dekker's version of disco dancing felt free and fun.

The English majors often saw American movies not shown to the Chinese public. I had mixed feelings about those movies, including *Roots* and *In the Heat of the Night*. I did not like the racial discrimination portrayed in the movies, and wondered how prevalent it was in the United States. Chinese newspapers published stories about discrimination against Taiwanese students in capitalist America, and about old American ladies living lonely lives without anyone caring for them. How I wished to see America with my own eyes. I longed to learn from UC Berkeley professors and become a knowledgeable person like Mr. Dekker.

China and the United States established diplomatic relations in 1979. Everyone in my class eagerly anticipated their prospects after this breakthrough in Sino-American relations. Deng Xiaoping was already allowing students who had their own funds to study abroad. A music-school classmate was on his way to study in San Francisco, sponsored by his godfather who lived there.

In winter 1979, I sat in my apartment, looking out of my window. The north wind roared, stirring up dust and blowing it through the bleak grey streets. I looked into my future, which promised nothing more than a job teaching English for the rest of my life at Renmin University. I had asked permission from the university to apply to graduate school, but my request was denied. Then I asked permission to apply for a United Nations' interpreter training program in Beijing. This request was also denied. The reason was that the university needed me as an English teacher.

I would have preferred to pursue an advanced educational opportunity in Beijing to stay close to my little Pangpang. But Renmin University blocked all of these opportunities. Going abroad to study meant leaving my family for an extended period. Yu had left his graduate school before finishing the program. He found a good interpreter's job with a new joint venture between a Chinese and an American company. He would definitely stay in China.

It was a hard decision for me to leave Pangpang behind. I knew that at age three, he needed his mother. But I chose to take this window of opportunity to go to the U.S., the only path for my career advancement beyond Renmin

University. In America I could probably provide a better future for my son. More importantly, I might be able to realize Father's dream of holding his solo exhibition in the U.S. I had learned to think independently during the Cultural Revolution, and to seize any momentary opportunity before a policy change could close the door.

In 1980, when Pangpang was almost three, I asked Mr. Dekker, going home for summer vacation, to get an application form for me from UC Berkeley. I talked with my mother and Yu about my plan to study at UC Berkeley for two years to earn my bachelor's degree. I expressed willingness to work on campus to help pay for that. In the end, I won their support. Privately I worried about surviving UC Berkeley and the unfamiliar American life. But I was determined to go, believing that nothing would be harder than what I had endured on the army farm eight years before.

My other American teacher, Mr. Tumposky, introduced me to Dr. Frederic Wakeman, well-known professor of Chinese history from UC Berkeley, who was teaching at Peking University. I visited him in his apartment at the Beijing Friendship Hotel. Professor Wakeman, a sturdy, bearded man, seemed interested in learning about my background. I explained my hard life as a musician during the Cultural Revolution and my plans to go to UC Berkeley in 1981. I must have impressed him with my fluent English, rare among Chinese students at the time. Professor Wakeman was very easy to talk with despite his status. He patiently answered all my questions about UC Berkeley's major programs in liberal arts. He even wrote letters of introduction to his colleagues in music, Chinese art history, and Chinese literature. He described my father, Xu Beihong, as a major Chinese artist and asked his colleagues to assist me with my studies. I was touched by Professor Wakeman's efforts to help me at our first meeting. His introductions would open doors for me. My meeting with him gave me confidence because he made me feel that I could talk with a professor and get the needed help.

UC Berkeley was the only American university I applied to and I thought my chance of admission was slim, particularly as a PRC student. At the end of 1980, I received my I-20 from UC Berkeley, a document needed for getting my student visa to the U.S. I was elated.

When I informed the English department director of my application to UC Berkeley, he was not surprised. A classmate had already gone to Boston University in late 1980, and several others were also applying to U.S. universities. In a few weeks, I received my passport. Getting my student visa was the last possible barrier between myself and America. On a cold morning in January 1981, I arrived at the U.S. Embassy in Beijing at about 5:30, expecting to avoid a crowd. When the visa office opened, I was the second in line among a dozen applicants to be interviewed. After a short conversation in English, the American visa officer granted me a student visa.

I felt relieved that I was finally able to go to America, the land that I had seen only in my imagination.

With a month and a half before my planned departure, Yu, Pangpang, and I enjoyed a brief vacation together during Renmin University's winter break. We had a family picture taken in a photo studio. Pangpang showed a sweet smile. It was the last Chinese New Year we spent together, and the warm feeling stayed fresh in my memory throughout my student years in the U.S.

Mom and I spent several days shopping for a few nice outfits that I could take to the U.S. This was a rare time that we shared talking about our expectations of what I should accomplish in the U.S. Mom said, "I feel better about your leaving this time than when you left for the army farm."

She paid for my plane ticket to San Francisco. I realized that it was a large chunk of her savings. The remainder of my funding was left for me to figure out.

The government tightly controlled foreign exchange and allowed students to exchange from Chinese currency into U.S. dollars only the equivalent of the student's air fare. I exchanged from my savings the equivalent of 510 dollars, which was all the money I had with me when I left China.

Yu and I discussed our future over lunch the day of my departure. We left our plans open. I might possibly return to China to find a better job after finishing my bachelor's degree at UC Berkeley. Alternatively, we could all live in the U.S. for a while.

The hardest thing was saying good-bye to my three-year-old Pangpang. On the morning of my departure, I went to his pre-school, where he stayed on weekdays. His teacher brought him to me and we spent a few minutes in the office. In his red jacket he looked small and shy. I told him to be a good boy and listen to his teachers. Then he rejoined his little friends. They were doing a children's dance, "Pulling Up a Turnip," in which the kids lined up in single file, each holding the back of the jacket belonging to the child ahead, and tugged rhythmically to piano music.

Pangpang was in synch with the other little kids in his group. I held back my tears when I waved good-bye. This last image of him was to stay with me for all the years I was to be away. I felt sad about leaving him behind, uncertain about when I might see him again. But I hoped that perhaps I could make a better life for him if I could establish myself in the U.S.

Yu was the only person seeing me off at the airport. We parted quietly. I walked towards the departure gate and did not look back.

As the plane took off, I looked at the blue sky ahead of me. It had no boundaries. My heart was filled with great expectations of finally living my dream and my father's dream.

EPILOGUE

On a Saturday afternoon in mid-January of 2012, the Anshultz Gallery in the Denver Art Museum was bustling with visitors. Thirty-three Asian-American art students from age five into their teens, all from California, gathered with drawing pads in front of the artworks by Xu Beihong. They were copying in pencil Xu Beihong's horse paintings and his drawing of a self-portrait. Their teacher, who had studied with one of Xu Beihong's students, taught them Xu Beihong's methods.

The students had prepared themselves for several months for this day. They had imitated Xu Beihong's self-portraits from prints and learned about the spirit and morality expressed in his artworks. Two students leading a procession carried a large flower basket and ceremoniously placed it beneath Xu Beihong's life-sized figure photo. Next to it was the exhibition's wall-sized title panel, *Xu Beihong: Pioneer of Modern Chinese Painting*,[64] the words in prominent white and red type against a black background. Floor-to-ceiling prints of Xu Beihong's ink brush painting *Six Galloping Horses* made for a dynamic entrance to the show. This first comprehensive solo U.S. exhibition of my father's work displayed sixty-one of his best works from the Xu Beihong Memorial Museum.

My son, James, his wife Diane Sun, their children Joshua Xu and Victor Xu, and I were in the crowd among curious American visitors and the scores of parents accompanying and observing the young artists as they worked to capture the spirit of Xu Beihong's artworks. Their drawings showed considerable skill, obviously the result of training.

One student wrote in the visitors' notebook: "When I am drawing Master Xu's galloping horses, I feel like I am running, too, because I am also a horse," and another wrote, "I have always wanted to make a difference in the world. Now because of Xu Beihong, I know that art can help me with it."

Other American visitors were also enthusiastic. A lady who brought her two young daughters to the show told me how my father's work touched their hearts. She wrote in the visitors' notebook:

> Such mesmerizing elegance and profound feelings in artistic realms.
> This man devoted his life to pursuits of which most know very little—the essence of nature, subtle and vibrant, dormant and alive, somber and robust.
> Xu Beihong—thank you for your legacy and gift.

Why were American audiences so interested in the art of Xu Beihong more than fifty years after his passing? Xu Beihong is widely spoken of as the father of modern Chinese painting. Throughout Asia, his iconic ink brush paintings of horses eloquently express the determination of the Chinese people in their struggles to master their own destiny. The human feelings and Chinese esthetics in his art have moved the hearts of many viewers throughout Asia, Europe, and recently in the United States. During his lifetime, he introduced his new style of painting to the world. With the knowledge he gained in Europe, he successfully integrated Western painting methods and techniques with traditional Chinese painting in order to develop Chinese painting. His creative work and extensive teaching offered a new direction for Chinese artists and art educators. At present, dealing with the relationship between Chinese culture and other cultures continues to be a challenge. Xu Beihong's artistic practice and advocacy remain an example of how to retain the best traditions of Chinese culture while integrating useful elements of other cultures.

Many visitors came to thank me for bringing my father's wonderful works to Denver. Tears welled in my eyes. I sensed that Father was there, interacting with the audience through his artworks. Elated to have been able to help initiate and bring this exhibition to the U.S., a dream that my father was not able to bring to fruition in 1941, seventy years before, I felt the joy that he might have felt at seeing his legacy and spirit being carried on by young artists in America.

Art students and their parents from California visiting the *Xu Beihong: Pioneer of Modern Chinese Painting* exhibition in the Denver Art Museum, Denver, January 2012. Xu Fangfang is directly beneath the Xu Beihong photo and Ronald Y. Otsuka, the museum's curator of Asian art, is to the right of her.

TIMELINE

Xu Beihong, Xu Fangfang, and Mao Zedong's Arts Policy

1895 Xu Beihong born.

1901 Xu Beihong begins learning Chinese classics from his father.

1904 Xu Beihong begins learning traditional Chinese painting from his father.

1911 Fall of the Qing dynasty.

1912 Republic of China founded by Sun Yat-sen.

1918 Xu Beihong writes "Improvement Methods for Chinese Painting." This article outlines methods for his later efforts to develop Chinese painting.

1919-1927 Xu Beihong studies in Europe. He enters the École Nationale Supérieure des Beaux Arts in Paris. His teachers include Flameng and Dagnan-Bouveret.

1921 The Chinese Communist Party established.

1927 Chiang Kai-shek becomes leader of the Kuomintang government.

1928 Xu Beihong accepts professorship of fine art at National Central University in Nanjing, where he introduces the high-standard Western practice of sketching from life, and modernizes China's art education. He pioneers innovation in Chinese painting in order to develop Chinese painting. He starts a major oil painting, *Tian Heng and His Five Hundred Warriors.*

1931 Japan invades northeastern China. Xu Beihong completes a large Chinese brush painting, *Jiufang Gao, Horse Judge* and works on another large oil painting, *Awaiting the Deliverer.*

1933-1934 Xu Beihong organizes and holds the first influential exhibition of contemporary Chinese paintings in Europe.

1934 The CCP's Red Army begins the Long March.

1935 Mao Zedong established as leader of the CCP.

1937-1945 War of Resistance against Japan.

1939, 1941 Xu Beihong holds benefit exhibitions of his paintings in Singapore and Malaysia to help China's War of Resistance.

1939-1940 At the invitation of the Indian poet Rabindranath Tagore, Xu Beihong holds exhibitions in India. Xu Beihong creates two oils and a Chinese brush painting, *The Foolish Old Man Who Removed the Mountains*, to encourage the Chinese people to persevere to the final victory in the War of Resistance.

1942 Mao Zedong sets guiding principles for arts in his "Talks at the Yan'an Forum on Literature and Art": Arts should serve workers, peasants, and soldiers, and the political goals of the Party.

1946 Xu Beihong and Liao Jingwen marry.

1946-1949 Chinese civil war. Xu Beihong becomes president of the National Beiping Arts College. Against strong opposition, he persists with his innovation in art education and Chinese painting.

1947 Xu Fangfang born.

1949 Founding of the People's Republic of China. The CCP takes control of all arts institutions, requiring artists to create works serving workers, peasants, soldiers, and the Party's policies. Xu Beihong appointed president of the Central Academy of Fine Arts and elected chairman of the All-China Art Workers Association. He creates a large oil painting, *Chairman Mao among the People.*

1951 Xu Beihong travels to a water control construction site in Shandong where he lives with the workers and sketches them as preparation for a large oil painting reflecting China's reconstruction.

1951-1952 "Three-anti" and "five-anti" campaigns against corruption.

1953 Xu Beihong dies.

1954 The Xu Beihong Memorial Museum established.

Mid-1950s-1959 Soviet arts professors invited to teach in China's leading arts institutions.

1957 Anti-Rightist campaign. Some intellectuals and artists who speak against the Party leaders in their work units are labeled rightists and removed from their positions. Liao Jingwen appointed director of the Xu Beihong Memorial Museum.

1957-1968 Xu Fangfang studies piano performance at the Prep Music Elementary School and Prep Music High School affiliated to the Central Conservatory of Music.

1958 Great Leap Forward led by Mao Zedong. The Great Leap Forward's failure leads to severe hardship and famine from 1959 to 1961.

1959-1963 Mao Zedong resigns as the state chairman in 1959. Liu Shaoqi rises to power. Liu emphasizes economic incentives to accelerate economic recovery. His agricultural policies allow private plots and set an output quota for each household, freeing peasants to make some profit beyond their quotas. Mao considers this to be capitalism. Chinese and European bourgeois arts are allowed to flourish. Some intellectuals take advantage of this atmosphere of greater freedom to engage in subtle, sophisticated sniping at leaders and policies they hold responsible for the famine. Wu Han writes the Peking opera *Hairui Dismissed from Office.*

1962 To counter Liu Shaoqi's policy, Mao Zedong warns the Party: "Never forget the class struggle." He insists that class struggle and the danger of capitalist restoration exist during the entire socialist period.

1963 Mao Zedong writes comments criticizing arts leaders who allow feudal and bourgeois arts to become dominant, contrary to his arts ideology.

1964 Mao Zedong and Jiang Qing are convinced that they must obtain supremacy in the arts. Mao wants to use model works to gain the upper hand ideologically over political opponents. Backed by Mao, Jiang Qing initiates her attack against the cultural leadership, whose high-level advocate is Liu Shaoqi. She denounces most of China's theater for portraying feudal and bourgeois content. Jiang Qing starts the revolution in Peking opera to establish herself as the standard-bearer for the revolution in proletarian literature and art. At the Festival of Peking Opera on Contemporary Themes in Beijing, Jiang Qing launches several politically correct Peking operas that later become models. New directions are given to performing arts groups to revolutionize their repertoire. Arts schools are told to revolutionize their curricula.

1963-1966 In 1963, the CCP initiates the Socialist Education Movement or the "Four Clean-ups" campaign, intending to cleanse the bureaucracy of new bourgeoisie in the political, economic, ideological, and organizational fields, to prevent capitalist restoration. In 1965, the target of the Socialist Education Movement is redefined by Mao Zedong to be Party persons in power taking the capitalist road, portending the Cultural Revolution. This new target is included in the twenty-three-article document "Some Current Problems Raised in the Socialist Education Movement in the Rural Areas," approved by the Central Committee of the CCP. Leaving their paintbrushes and instruments behind, CAFA, CCOM, and some performing arts groups, such as the Central Philharmonic Orchestra, participate in the Socialist Education Movement in the countryside during 1965 and 1966. The Preparatory Art High School affiliated to the Central Academy of Fine Arts conducts the Socialist Education Movement inside their school from 1964 to 1965.

1965 In response to Mao Zedong's criticism in 1963 and 1964, a rectification movement starts in the Ministry of Culture, the All-China Federation of Literary and Arts Circles, and arts associations. The movement criticizes the cultural authorities, some of whom are then removed from their positions. CAFA stops student recruitment in 1965, one year before the Cultural Revolution when all universities and professional arts schools are closed. Mao stresses the necessity of criticizing reactionary bourgeois ideology and Wu Han's *Hairui Dismissed from Office* in particular. Decision made to demolish the Xu Beihong Memorial Museum.

1966 In February Lin Biao entrusts Jiang Qing with the forum on literature and art in the armed forces. The Forum Summary contains the first open attack by Jiang Qing on the cultural leadership, a portent of the coming Cultural Revolution. One of its objectives is to seize power from cultural authorities. Xu Beihong Memorial Museum closed and demolished.

1966-1976 The Cultural Revolution, targeting capitalist roaders within the Party headed by Liu Shaoqi.

1967-1970 Eight model performing works are created under Jiang Qing's guidance. These and a few more created in the early 1970s are the only pieces allowed to be performed during the Cultural Revolution. These model works serve to strengthen Mao Zedong's leadership, his political line, and his control over the arts. To establish her authority over the arts, Jiang Qing designates her art theory for creating model operas as the only way of applying Mao's ideology to the arts. She bans all works in the arts that do not follow her rules. Western classical music and traditional Peking operas are banned.

1968-1969 Xu Fangfang graduates from the Prep Music High School and works as a piano accompanist for the China National Peking Opera Company, Jiang Qing's model troupe.

1968-early 1970s	Based on Mao Zedong's May Seventh Directive, government cadres, artists, and intellectuals are sent to May Seventh Cadre Schools in rural areas for manual labor and learning from the poor and lower-middle peasants. During the ten years of the Cultural Revolution, Mao's Down to the Countryside Movement sends a cumulative total of more than sixteen million urban youths, mostly high-school graduates and some college graduates, to live and work in the countryside for re-education.
1970-1972	Xu Fangfang re-educated on the 4701 Army Farm in Gegu.
1972	President Nixon visits China.
1972-1978	Xu Fangfang works with the Central Philharmonic Orchestra.
1973	The Philadelphia Orchestra performs in China.
1973-1974	The "discussion about absolute music" campaign.
1974	The "Criticize Lin Biao, Criticize Confucius" campaign. The "Criticizing Black Painting" campaign.
1976	Premier Zhou Enlai dies. Mao Zedong dies. The Gang of Four including Jiang Qing are arrested.
1978	Xu Fangfang commences B.A. in English in Renmin University of China.
1979	China and the United States establish diplomatic relations.
1981	Xu Fangfang moves to the U.S., earning a B.A. in history from the University of California, Berkeley in 1983 and an M.B.A. from Stanford Graduate School of Business in 1985.
1983	The new Xu Beihong Memorial Museum opens in its current location.
2011	*Xu Beihong: Pioneer of Modern Chinese Painting* exhibition held in the Denver Art Museum from October 2011 to January 2012.

ABBREVIATIONS

CAFA	Central Academy of Fine Arts
CCOM	Central Conservatory of Music
CCP	Chinese Communist Party
CYL	Communist Youth League of China
The Association	Chinese People's Association for Friendship with Foreign Countries
Fighting Regiment	Mao Zedong Thought Fighting Regiment
PLA	People's Liberation Army
Prep Art High School	Preparatory Art High School affiliated to the Central Academy of Fine Arts
Prep Music Elementary School	Preparatory Music Elementary School affiliated to the Central Conservatory of Music
Prep Music High School	Preparatory Music High School affiliated to the Central Conservatory of Music
PRC	People's Republic of China
Worker propaganda team	Worker Mao Zedong Thought propaganda team

SUGGESTED READING

Andrews, Julia F. *Painters and Politics in the People's Republic of China, 1949-1979.* Berkeley and Los Angeles, California: University of California Press; London, England: University of California Press, Ltd., 1994.

Ronald Y. Otsuka and Fangfang Xu, eds., *Xu Beihong: Pioneer of Modern Chinese Painting.* Denver, Colorado: Denver Art Museum, 2011. The book was published in conjunction with the exhibition *Xu Beihong: Pioneer of Modern Chinese Painting* presented at the Denver Art Museum from October 30, 2011 to January 29, 2012.

School History Project Group. *Zhongyang yinyue xueyuan jianshi gao, 1940-2010* (Brief History of the Central Conservatory of Music, 1940-2010). Beijing: Zhongyang yinyue xueyuan xuebaoshe, 2010.

Wang Zhen. *Xu Beihong nianpu changbian* (A Chronological Biography of Xu Beihong). Shanghai: Shanghai huabao chubanshe, December 2006.

Wang Zhen and Xu Boyang, eds., *Xu Beihong yishu wenji* (A Collection of Xu Beihong's Articles on Art), first ed. Yinchuan: Ningxia renmin chubanshe, December 1994.

Xu Beihong Memorial Museum. *Zhongguo yitan jujiang—Xu Beihong 1895-1953* (A Great Master of China—Xu Beihong 1895-1953), first ed. Beijing: Beijing chubanshe chubanjituan, Beijing meishu sheying chubanshe, September 2005.

ABOUT THE AUTHOR

Born and raised in Beijing, China, Xu Fangfang graduated in piano performance from Beijing's Preparatory Music High School affiliated to the Central Conservatory of Music. She moved to the U.S. in 1981 and earned a B.A. in history from the University of California, Berkeley, and an M.B.A. from Stanford University. In 2000, she became the founding director of the music department at Renmin University of China. She helped initiate and facilitate the first comprehensive solo U.S. exhibition of her father Xu Beihong's work, presented by the Denver Art Museum, Oct. 2011-Jan. 2012. She has published several articles on Xu Beihong and his art, including "Xu Beihong, Pioneer of Modern Chinese Painting" in *Arts of Asia* 42, no. 1 (2012), and "Xu Beihong's Life and Art" in *Xu Beihong: Pioneer of Modern Chinese Painting*, Denver Art Museum, 2011.

AUTHOR'S NOTE

Galloping Horses: Artist Xu Beihong and His Family in Mao's China is a work of nonfiction. Some individuals' names have been altered to protect their privacy. My research included interviews with family members, relatives, schoolmates, colleagues, and my father's former students; and notes kept by myself and family members. Some of the events described are my personal experiences and others are from my mother's recollections. These episodes were recorded to the best of our memories.

Xu Fangfang

June 2016

NOTES

1. Guo Weiqu (1908-1971), Chinese ink brush painter and a professional staff member at the Xu Beihong Memorial Museum (1956-1959). He was transferred to the Central Academy of Fine Arts to teach in 1960 and headed their bird-and-flower painting section in 1962.

2. Some descriptions of the Red Guard actions in chapters 1 and 2 came from interviews with Liao Jingwen and from her notes.

3. The three Guangxi Nationalist leaders portrayed in Xu Beihong's oil painting are Huang Xuchu, governor of Guangxi Province, and two army generals, Li Zongren and Bai Chongxi.

4. Liao Jingwen, *Xu Beihong yisheng—wode huiyi* (Life of Xu Beihong—My Recollections), first ed., Beijing: Zhongguo qingnian chubanshe, August 1982, 237-238.
廖靜文:《徐悲鴻一生—我的回憶》,北京:中國青年出版社,1982年8月第1版,237-238頁。

5. Some content in Chapter 2 was drawn from Fangfang Xu, "Xu Beihong's Life and Art," in Ronald Y. Otsuka and Fangfang Xu, ed., *Xu Beihong: Pioneer of Modern Chinese Painting*, Denver, Colorado: Denver Art Museum, 2011.

6. Xu Beihong, "Beihong zishu" (Beihong Telling His Own Stories), in *Liangyou* (*The Young Companion*), nos. 46, 47, Shanghai: April 1930, 119.
徐悲鴻:《悲鴻自述》,載《良友》第46、47期,上海:1930年4月,119页。

7. Traditional Chinese ink and wash painting mostly in freehand style is done with a brush and black ink, sometimes incorporating limited use of colors on Xuan paper. Another style called fine-brush painting uses many colors.

8. Xu Beihong, "Beihong zishu" (Beihong Telling His Own Stories), in *Liangyou* (*The Young Companion*), nos. 46, 47, Shanghai: April 1930, 122.
徐悲鴻:《悲鴻自述》,載《良友》第46、47期,上海:1930年4月,122页。

9. Xu Beihong, "Zhongguohua gailiang zhi fangfa" (Improvement Methods for Chinese Painting), in *Beijing Daxue ri kan* (Peking University Daily), Beijing, May 23-25, 1918, in Wang Zhen and Xu Boyang, ed., *Xu Beihong yishu wenji* (A Collection of Xu Beihong's Articles on Art), first ed., Yinchuan: Ningxia renmin chubanshe, December 1994, 11-12.
徐悲鴻:《中國畫改良之方法》, 載《北京大學日刊》, 北京, 1918年5月23-25日, 王震和徐伯陽編:《徐悲鴻藝術文集》, 銀川: 寧夏人民出版社, 1994年12月第1版, 11-12頁。

10. The name Beijing (Northern Capital) was changed to Beiping (Northern Peace) in 1928 when the Nationalists moved the capital to Nanjing. The name reverted to Beijing after the city became the capital of the PRC in 1949.

11. Liao Jingwen, *Xu Beihong yisheng—wode huiyi* (Life of Xu Beihong—My Recollections), first ed., Beijing: Zhongguo qingnian chubanshe, August 1982, 409.
廖靜文:《徐悲鴻一生—我的回憶》, 北京: 中國青年出版社, 1982年8月第1版, 409頁。

12. Ibid., 413.

13. Some content in Chapter 3 was drawn from Fangfang Xu, "Xu Beihong's Life and Art," in Ronald Y. Otsuka and Fangfang Xu, ed., *Xu Beihong: Pioneer of Modern Chinese Painting*, Denver, Colorado: Denver Art Museum, 2011.

14. Xu Beihong's French name was Ju Péon, which he used in Europe in the 1920s and later overseas.

15. Xu Beihong, "Beihong zishu" (Beihong Telling His Own Stories), in *Liangyou* (*The Young Companion*), nos. 46, 47, Shanghai: April 1930, 129.
徐悲鴻:《悲鴻自述》, 載《良友》第46、47期, 上海: 1930年4月, 129页。

16. Ibid.

17. Ibid.

18. Ibid., 119.

19. Xu Beihong emphasized drawing from memory. After he completed an important drawing from life he would draw the same subject from memory to discover weaknesses or deficiencies in his own observation, understanding, and memory. Then he would revise the memory drawing by comparing it with his original drawing from life. He felt that the benefit he received from a single study of this sort was equal to three studies without such drawing from memory. Xu Beihong graded students on their memory drawings instead of their original drawings from life.

20. Xu Beihong, "Zai quan'ou xuanchuan Zhongguomeishu zhi jingguo" (The Process of Promoting Chinese Art in Europe), in Wang Zhen and Xu Boyang, ed., *Xu Beihong yishu wenji* (A Collection of Xu Beihong's Articles on Art), first ed., Yinchuan: Ningxia renmin chubanshe, December 1994, 253.
徐悲鴻:《在全歐宣傳中國美術之經過》, 王震和徐伯陽編:《徐悲鴻藝術文集》, 銀川: 寧夏人民出版社, 1994年12月第1版, 253頁。

21. "Weishenmo yao xie Xu Beihong" (Why we should write about Xu Beihong), in *United Evening Paper*, Feature Article section, Singapore: Singapore Press Holdings, September 16, 1985.
《為什麼要寫徐悲鴻》, 載《聯合晚報》大特寫, 新加坡: 新加坡報業控股 (SPH) 公司, 1985年9月16日。

22. Liao Jingwen, *Xu Beihong yisheng—wode huiyi* (Life of Xu Beihong—My Recollections), first ed., Beijing: Zhongguo qingnian chubanshe, August 1982, 308.
廖靜文:《徐悲鴻一生—我的回憶》, 北京: 中國青年出版社, 1982年8月第1版, 308頁。

23. Ibid., 327.

24. Some graduates from the National Beiping Arts College later became well-known professors in the Central Conservatory of Music and other major conservatories, including violin professors Sui Keqiang and Wang Zhilong, vocalist and voice professor Guo Shuzhen, and piano professors Chen Huisu and Chen Wen.

25. In the National Beiping Arts College Xu Beihong recruited accomplished artists and capable art teachers in all disciplines, including Qi Baishi, Huang Binhong, Li Kuchan, Li Keran, Tian Shiguang, Ye Qianyu, and Jiang Zhaohe, who demonstrated creativity in their traditional Chinese painting specialty areas such as landscapes, birds-and-flowers, and human figures.

26. Xu Beihong, "Jieshao laojiefangqu meishu zuopin yiban" (Introducing Some Artworks from Old Liberated Areas), in *Jinbu ribao* (Progress Daily), Tianjin, April 3, 1949, in Wang Zhen and Xu Boyang, ed., *Xu Beihong yishu wenji* (A Collection of Xu Beihong's Articles on Art), first ed., Yinchuan: Ningxia renmin chubanshe, December 1994, 539.
徐悲鴻:《介紹老解放區美術作品一斑》, 載《進步日報》, 天津, 1949年4月3日, 王震和徐伯陽編:《徐悲鴻藝術文集》, 銀川: 寧夏人民出版社, 1994年12月第1版, 539頁。

27. In 1950 the central government of the PRC announced the Land Reform Law of the PRC which abolished landownership by landlords and introduced peasant landownership.

28. Dai Ze in Beijing told about CAFA teachers' criticism of Xu Beihong's oil painting *Chairman Mao among the People* in a telephone interview with the author on December 9, 2013.

29. In an interview with the author in Beijing on February 27, 2014, Dai Ze described Xu Beihong's defense of Xu's oil painting *Chairman Mao among the People*.

30. Liao Jingwen, *Xu Beihong yisheng—wode huiyi* (Life of Xu Beihong—My Recollections), first ed., Beijing: Zhongguo qingnian chubanshe, August 1982, 412.
廖靜文:《徐悲鴻一生—我的回憶》, 北京: 中國青年出版社, 1982年8月第1版, 412頁。

31. Ibid.

32. Xu Beihong's own calligraphy is based on the powerful structure of Northern Wei stone monument rubbings.

33. Chen Sanyuan (1853-1937), Chinese poet.

34. Hou Yimin described Jiang Feng's remark in an interview with the author in Beijing on March 6, 2014.

35. Hou Yimin recalled Qian Junrui's speech in an interview with the author in Beijing on March 6, 2014.

36. The excerpt of Liao Jingwen's speech came from her notes.

37. Premier Zhou's remark was recorded in Liao Jingwen's notes.

38. Xu Beihong, "Zhi Li Hongmo" (Letter to Li Hongmo), January 2, 1950, in Professor Xu Jingfei (Xu Lili)'s collection, in Wang Zhen and Xu Boyang, ed., *Xu Beihong yishu wenji* (A Collection of Xu Beihong's Articles on Art), first ed., Yinchuan: Ningxia renmin chubanshe, December 1994, 746.
徐悲鴻:《致黎鴻模》, 1950年1月2日, 徐靜斐教授（徐麗麗）收藏, 王震和徐伯陽編:《徐悲鴻藝術文集》, 銀川: 寧夏人民出版社, 1994年12月第1版, 746頁。

39. Liao Jingwen, *Xu Beihong yisheng—wode huiyi* (Life of Xu Beihong—My Recollections), first ed., Beijing: Zhongguo qingnian chubanshe, August 1982, 208.
廖靜文:《徐悲鴻一生—我的回憶》, 北京: 中國青年出版社, 1982年8月第1版, 208頁。

40. Premier Zhou's remark was recorded in Liao Jingwen's notes.

41. The Zhejiang Academy of Fine Arts was originally National Hangzhou Arts Academy, founded in 1928 in the city of Hangzhou. The name was changed to East China campus of CAFA in 1950, when Jiang Feng was its key administrator. In 1958 the school was renamed Zhejiang Academy of Fine Arts and placed under direct supervision of the Zhejiang provincial government. In 1993 the school's name became China Academy of Art.

42. On December 12, 1963 Mao Zedong wrote criticism about the problems in literature and art in reference to an article in an internal publication issued by the Central Propaganda Department of the CCP. Mao's criticism was sent as an instruction to Peng Zhen and Liu Ren, leaders of the Beijing Municipal Party Committee of the CCP.
毛澤東在一九六三年十二月十二日對中央宣傳部的一個內部刊物上刊登的一篇文章作出批示, 批評文藝工作方面存在的問題, 並把這個批示給了中共北京市委負責人彭真、劉仁。

43. The full name should be the Colleges of Beijing Red Guard Third Headquarters. The Cultural Revolution Small Group started backing this Red Guard alliance near the end of 1966.

44. The three seized CCP leaders were Peng Zhen, mayor of Beijing; Lu Dingyi, a CCP leader in charge of cultural and propaganda fields; and Luo Ruiqing, general and chief of staff of the People's Liberation Army. Liu Shikun and other rebel heads also planned to seize Yang Shangkun, director of the General Office of the Central Committee, but Yang could not be found.

45. Premier Zhou's remark was recorded in Liao Jingwen's notes.

46. Wang Li and Guan Feng were the other two arrested members of the Cultural Revolution Small Group.

47. Jiang Qing, Lin Biao tongzhi weituo Jiang Qing tongzhi zhaokai de budui wenyi gongzuo zuotanhui jiyao (Summary of the Forum on Literature and Art in the Armed Forces with Which Comrade Lin Biao Entrusted Comrade Jiang Qing), Central Committee of the Chinese Communist Party document, Beijing: April 10, 1966.
江青:《林彪同志委託江青同志召開的部隊文藝工作座談會紀要》, 北京: 中共中央批發, 1966年4月10日。

48. Xu Beihong, "Beihong zishu" (Beihong Telling His Own Stories), in *Liangyou* (*The Young Companion*), nos. 46, 47, Shanghai: April 1930, 122.
徐悲鴻:《悲鴻自述》, 載《良友》第46、47期, 上海: 1930年4月, 122页。

49. Huang Xiaohe, "Guanyu 'wubiaoti yinyue' dapipan de qianqianhouhou" (About Criticizing "Absolute Music"), in *Remin Yinyue* (People's Music), no. 5, Beijing: Zhongguo yinyuejia xiehui zazhishe, May 2006.
黄曉和:《關於"無標題音樂"大批判的前前後後》, 載《人民音樂》第5期, 北京: 中國音樂家協會雜誌社, 2006年5月。

50. Fu Ningjun, *Beihong shengming—Xu Beihong de shengqian sihou* (Beihong's Life—Xu Beihong's Life and Afterwards), second ed., Beijing: Renmin wenxue chubanshe, 2013, 301.
傅寧軍:《悲鴻生命—徐悲鴻的生前死後》, 北京: 人民文學出版社, 2013年第2版, 301頁。

51. Ibid.

52. According to Xu Beihong Memorial Museum's records, the exhibition catalogues published by some foreign art museums, and the author's attendance at some of the exhibitions, the Xu Beihong Memorial Museum held exhibitions of Xu Beihong's works outside of mainland China, including in India in 1985, the Art Gallery of Greater Victoria and the Royal Ontario Museum in Canada in 1987, Hong Kong and Japan in 1988, Moscow and Romania in 1991, Malaysia in 1993, Taiwan in 1994, Czechoslovakia in 1995, Macao in 2000, Singapore in 1990 and 2008, and in the Denver Art Museum in the U.S. from October 2011 to January 2012.

53. Huang Xiaohe, "Guanyu 'wubiaoti yinyue' dapipan de qianqianhouhou" (About Criticizing "Absolute Music"), in *Remin Yinyue* (People's Music), no. 5, Beijing: Zhongguo yinyuejia xiehui zazhishe, May 2006.
黄曉和:《關於"無標題音樂"大批判的前前後後》, 載《人民音樂》第5期, 北京: 中國音樂家協會雜誌社, 2006年5月。

54. Ibid.

55. Ibid.

56. Ibid.

57. Ibid.

58. Ibid.

59. Ibid.

60. Ibid.

61. Ibid.

62. Li Hu (李斛) (1919-1975), well-known Chinese painter and a faculty member of CAFA.

63. Zhang Anzhi, "Xu er," *Danqing 500 nian—xinzhongguo meishu mingjia—Li Hu* (Introduction II to Chinese Painting 500 Years Series Show—Famous Painting Artists of New China—Li Hu), Shanghai: Shanghai jinxiu wenzhang chubenshe, 2010, 10.
張安治:《序二》,《丹青500年—新中國美術名家—李斛》, 上海:上海錦繡文章出版社, 2010, 10頁。

64. *Xu Beihong: Pioneer of Modern Chinese Painting* held in Denver from October 2011 to January 2012 was Xu Beihong's first comprehensive solo exhibition in the United States. Sixty-one of his best Chinese brush paintings, oil paintings, drawings, pastels, and calligraphy were displayed, including his major historical oil painting *Tian Heng and His Five Hundred Warriors* and major Chinese brush painting *The Foolish Old Man Who Removed the Mountains.* Neither had been exhibited outside of Asia. This exhibition was organized by the Denver Art Museum in collaboration with the Xu Beihong Memorial Museum in Beijing and with generous support from Mr. John Sie, whose father, Sié Chéou-Kang, was one of Xu Beihong's best friends.

INDEX

Note: Page numbers in *italics* refer to illustrations.

18186216R00179

Printed in Poland
by Amazon Fulfillment
Poland Sp. z o.o., Wrocław